American Bar Association
Real Property, Trust and Estate Law Section

AF898523

HISTORIC PRESERVATION LAW

Kevin R. Eberle, Dylan Oliver Malagrinò, Brian R. Turner

Cover design by Andrew Alcala

Printed in the United States of America.

30 29 28 27 26 5 4 3 2 1

Library of Congress Cataloging-in-Publication Data

Names: Eberle, Kevin author | Malagrinò, Dylan Oliver author | Turner, B. R. (Brian R.) author
Title: Historic preservation law / Kevin R. Eberle, Dylan Oliver Malagrinò, Brian R. Turner.
Description: Chicago : American Bar Association, 2026. | Includes bibliographical references and index. | Summary: "Historic preservation law is an evolving and understudied field. It is our hope that the information herein will be a valuable tool for practitioners in accordance with its objective to increase public understanding of and respect for the rule of law and the legal process"—Provided by publisher.
Identifiers: LCCN 2026019750 (print) | LCCN 2026019751 (ebook) | ISBN 9781639058143 paperback | ISBN 9781639058150 epub
Subjects: LCSH: Historic buildings—Conservation and restoration—Law and legislation—United States | Cultural property—Protection—Law and legislation—United States | City planning—Law and legislation —United States
Classification: LCC KF4310 .E24 2026 (print) | LCC KF4310 (ebook)
LC record available at https://lccn.loc.gov/2026019750
LC ebook record available at https://lccn.loc.gov/2026019751

Discounts are available for books ordered in bulk. Special consideration is given to state bars, CLE programs, and other bar-related organizations. Inquire at Book Publishing, ABA Publishing, American Bar Association, 321 N. Clark Street, Chicago, Illinois 60654-7598.

www.shopABA.org

Contents

11. Historic Preservation Laws and Tax Incentives 253

About the Authors

Kevin R. Eberle is the Director of Clinics at the Charleston School of Law in Charleston, South Carolina, where he teaches first-year Legal Research & Writing as well as Appellate Practice. After graduating from the University of South Carolina in 1995, he joined Rosen, Rosen & Hagood, LLC, where his practice included a wide range of topics. He is licensed in the state courts of South Carolina and all levels of the federal bar from the District of South Carolina to the Fourth Circuit and the U.S. Supreme Court. His scholarship includes a five-year series of annual Supreme Court updates and many articles for South Carolina practitioners.

Since moving to Charleston after law school, he has been heavily involved with the cause of historic preservation in Charleston. He served six years on the Preservation Society of Charleston's board of directors and organized the famous Fall House Tours for three of them. Not only has he restored his own 1914 house, but he recently restored a house built in 1873 by a former slave to save it from demolition by its former owner. His work has led to a Carolopolis Award from the Preservation Society and two Whitelaw Founders Awards from the Historic Charleston Foundation. A fixture at meetings of the Board of Architectural Review, he freely assists with research for the city staff and homeowners.

Dylan Oliver Malagrinò is the Associate Dean for Faculty Research & Development and Professor of Law at Charleston School of Law in Charleston, South Carolina. He joined the faculty of Charleston Law in 2017 after ten years of full-time law teaching at ABA-accredited law schools across the country. Professor Malagrinò teaches Property I and II, Land Use, and Wills, Trusts, and Estates, among other courses. Professor Malagrinò is a law graduate of the University of San Diego School of Law and of the London School of Economics and Political Science.

Prior to academia, Professor Malagrinò spent six years in private practice as an attorney in San Diego, practicing complex civil litigation including securities fraud and antitrust class actions. And, more recently, he was a senior attorney at a Texas-based energy resources law firm, where he provided counsel for the firm's real property and corporate law groups. He is licensed to practice law in the state courts of California and in the U.S. District Courts for the Southern and Central Districts of California.

Professor Malagrinò researches and writes in the areas of property law, comparative property law, land use, and legal anthropology. He has published three books and more than 20 law review articles. His casebook, *Land Use and Zoning Law: Planning for Accessible Communities 2e* (Carolina Academic Press 2022) (with Robin Paul Malloy) comprehensively integrates the Americans with Disabilities Act with land-use and zoning laws, addressing the complexities of aging in place and of disability in the context of local land regulation.

Brian Roberts Turner is a licensed attorney with over 20 years' experience working as an advocate for historic preservation. From 2008 to 2020 he served as counsel for the National Trust for Historic Preservation in its San Francisco office, engaging in grassroots campaigns to save historic places throughout the American West. In this role he gained wide exposure to the intersections of federal, state, and local preservation law and policy.

Turner currently serves as President & CEO of the Preservation Society of Charleston (PSC) in Charleston, South Carolina, a non-profit organization founded in 1920. The PSC advocates on behalf of its over 4000 members for the preservation of the region's distinct character, quality of life, and diverse neighborhoods. It educates the public on the art and science of preservation practice and works to ensure that land-use plans and major projects are designed to be consistent with Charleston's reputation as a world-class history city.

Turner obtained his B.A. in history at Grinnell College and J.D. from Vermont Law School and serves as a lecturer in preservation law for the Clemson University School of Architecture. During law school he interned with the National Trust's Law Department in Washington, D.C.; served as a Fellow at the European Academy in Bolzano, Italy; and completed a semester of study at the University of Trento.

Preface

Historic preservation ranges across multiple disciplines of legal practice. Because specialists are scarce, lawyers often engage in the field in an ad hoc manner, say, when they come across a client with a historic building "problem."

As the authors of this first edition practice guide can attest, confusion in the layperson is excusable. The field is replete with unique and almost proprietary terminology that can trip up even the most well practiced.

Yet at its heart, the reason historic preservation laws exist is quite basic. Regulatory tools and economic incentives are justified because the physical places that showcase the nation's heritage are irreplaceable. This volume explores the federal, state, and local framework of laws that encourage public and private actors to take the long view and not sacrifice the places that tell our story for short-term gain.

Our volume begins with an introduction from Professor Dylan Malagrinò that will benefit the novice to the field. How our laws have evolved is a critical component in understanding the variety of approaches and types of places protected.

In Chapter 2, Professor Kevin Eberle explores the contested area when otherwise private property is designated as "historic," which can occur with or without the owners' consent. It bears mentioning that an old place, for the purposes of the law, is not necessarily a "historic" one. The latter is a designation type grounded in documentation that is often (though not always) a key trigger for regulatory protections.

Chapters 3, 4, and 5 focus on signature laws at the federal level that form the core of federal agency responsibility as they make decisions about the funding and permitting of projects. In Chapter 3 on the National Historic Preservation Act (NHPA), Professor Malagrinò evaluates the signature law in the United States from which much of the field's terminology and precepts are derived.

Although the NHPA is key to understanding how the federal preservation program is structured, federal agencies have independent responsibility for compliance with these additional congressional directives. In Chapter 4, Brian Turner describes how the federal and state environmental policy acts function to protect historic resources. The primary focus of this chapter is on the requirements of the National Environmental Policy Act (NEPA). Federal agency practice under NEPA is currently undergoing a shift with the recent recession of longstanding regulations, though Congress's core requirement that agencies evaluate alternatives to action harmful to the "human environment" still undergirds federal funding and permitting decisions.

Federal transportation agencies are uniquely responsible for compliance with Section 4(f) of the Department of Transportation Act. In Chapter 5, Brian Turner explains the core tenets of the law that add a substantive requirement to adopt feasible alternatives to harmful action. Section 4(f) is thus differentiated from the NHPA and NEPA, which courts have described as procedural in nature.

Chapters 6 and 7 shift direction from the federal to the municipal level, focusing on local regulation and constraints imposed by constitutional laws protecting private property owners. In Chapter 6, Brian Turner provides a broad overview of how municipal regulations are structured and their considerable variation. A background in the NHPA intentionally precedes this chapter as many local government policies, following state enabling legislation, use principles and concepts that inform designation procedures, assessments of impact, and best practices for adapting properties for new uses sensitive to the historic attributes of a property. In Chapter 7, Professor Eberle describes the full suite of constitutional constraints on local and state action that local governments must be aware of in implementing these local rules.

In Chapter 8, Brian Turner focuses on the protection of the often-unseen cultural environment. The laws protecting archaeological sites, traditional cultural places, and burial sites deserve independent treatment from other laws protecting the built environment largely because they have historically integrated more scientific practice into the field of preservation.

In Chapter 9, Professor Eberle describes how primarily private conservation restrictions like easements function to confer additional protections to historic properties. These agreements can be particularly essential in areas and for properties where local governmental protection is more limited. In Chapter 10, Professor Malagrinò describes unique challenges confronting the future of historic preservation efforts and modern development.

Finally, in Chapter 11, Professor Malagrinò explores how federal tax policy has served the interest of historic preservation. Although merely a survey of some relevant tax incentives, two key tools are relevant for discussion: the federal historic tax credit and the enabling of private preservation restrictions in the form of easements.

As this volume reveals, historic preservation law is an evolving and understudied field. It is our hope that the information herein will be a valuable tool for practitioners in accordance with its objective to increase public understanding of and respect for the rule of law and the legal process.

An Introduction to Historic Preservation Laws: Safeguarding the Past for the Future

1

Historic preservation laws play a crucial role in maintaining and protecting the architectural, cultural, and historical integrity of sites and structures across the United States and around the world.[1] These laws are designed to safeguard heritage resources from neglect, demolition, or inappropriate alteration.[2] By ensuring that future generations can access

1. *See* D.O. Malagrinò, *Constitutional Perspectives on Historic Preservation Law: Mediating the Balance Between Private Owners and Their Historic Properties*, 91 MISS. L.J. 389 (2023) ("Historic preservation zoning laws limit property owner sovereignty to protect cultural and heritage resources."); *see also* 54 U.S.C.A. § 300101 (West, Westlaw through Pub. L. No. 119-59) (defining the promotion of "harmony" between "modern society and our history property" as a "policy of the Federal Government" designed to safeguard the "social, economic, and other requirements of past and future generations").

2. 54 U.S.C.A. § 300101 (West, Westlaw through Pub. L. No. 119-59) ("It is the policy of the Federal Government . . . to use measures, including financial and technical assistance, to foster conditions under which our modern society and our historic property can exist in productive harmony and fulfill the social, economic, and other requirements of present and future generations[.]").

and learn from these remnants of the past, historic preservation laws also support cultural identity, education, tourism, and economic development.[3] Though many important sites have become derelict, historic preservation laws work to keep our heritage resources alive.

The urgency surrounding historic preservation has intensified in recent decades as development pressures, climate change, and shifting demographic patterns threaten significant cultural resources. Each year, communities across the nation lose irreplaceable architectural landmarks and historically significant sites to the wrecking ball, often because adequate legal protections were not in place or were insufficiently enforced. Countless historic structures are demolished annually, erasing tangible connections to our collective past before comprehensive documentation and other preservation efforts can even be completed. This loss represents not merely the destruction of old buildings, but the severing of cultural continuity that binds communities to their heritage and provides context for understanding contemporary society.

Moreover, historic preservation serves functions that extend well beyond nostalgic reverence for antiquity. Modern preservation practice recognizes that historic buildings often embody sustainable design principles that predate contemporary green building movements, featuring superior craftsmanship, durable materials, and climate-responsive architectural elements that reduce energy consumption and environmental impact. The adaptive reuse of historic structures frequently proves more environmentally sound than new construction, as it avoids the substantial carbon emissions associated with demolition and new building materials. Economic analyses consistently demonstrate that preservation-led revitalization generates substantial returns on investment, stimulating local economies through heritage tourism, supporting traditional crafts and trades, and catalyzing neighborhood renewal that benefits existing residents rather than displacing them through wholesale redevelopment. As a former president of the American Institute of Architects once said, "The greenest building is one that already exists."[4]

---

3. *See* Alexander Kazam, *From Independence Hall to the Strip Mall: Applying Cost-Benefit Analysis to Historic Preservation*, 47 Envtl. L. 429, 432–33 (2017) (describing historic preservation laws as "enabl[ing] communities to safeguard their cultural heritage, preserve beautiful architecture, foster civic pride, [and] attract tourism").

4. "The greenest building is the one that already exists" is a saying coined in 2007 by architect Carl Elefante, FAIA, to highlight that preserving and reusing existing buildings is often more environmentally sustainable than tearing them down to build new ones. Carl Elefante, Carl Elefante, *The Greenest Building Is . . . One That Is Already Built.*, https://carlelefante.com/insights/the-greenest-building-is/ (last visited Feb. 14, 2026).

The legal framework governing historic preservation reflects a complex interplay between property rights, public interest, and governmental authority that continues to generate vigorous debate. Property owners often view preservation regulations as unwarranted intrusions on their rights to modify or demolish structures they own, arguing that such restrictions diminish property values and constrain economic opportunities. Conversely, preservation advocates contend that historically significant properties carry obligations that transcend individual ownership, as these structures constitute irreplaceable cultural assets whose loss would impoverish society as a whole. Courts have generally upheld the constitutionality of preservation laws under the police power doctrine, recognizing that governments possess legitimate authority to regulate property use when doing so serves valid public purposes, though the precise boundaries of permissible regulation remain contested terrain.

A. ORIGINS AND DEVELOPMENT OF HISTORIC PRESERVATION LAWS

The roots of historic preservation legislation in the United States can be traced back to the early 20th century.[5] One of the earliest and most significant efforts was the Antiquities Act of 1906.[6] This federal law empowered the president to designate national monuments on federal land to protect significant natural, cultural, or scientific features, laying the foundation for future preservation efforts.[7]

The passage of the Antiquities Act emerged from growing public concern over the systematic looting of archaeological sites, particularly indigenous ruins in the American Southwest. During the late 19th century, private collectors and commercial interests routinely plundered Native American archaeological sites, removing artifacts for sale to museums and private

5. H.R. Rep. No. 96-1457, at 18 (1980), *as reprinted in* 1980 U.S.C.C.A.N. 6378, 6381 ("The first Federal Preservation project was in the late 19th century[.]").

6. *See* Francis P. McManamon, *Cultural Resources and Protection Under United States Law*, 16 Conn. J. Int'l L. 247, 256–57 (2001) ("[The effort] to protect places and objects of antiquity culminated in the Antiquities Act. On June 8, 1906, President Theodore Roosevelt signs the Antiquities Act into law.").

7. *Id.* at 257 ("The Antiquities Act . . . has been used by presidents throughout the twentieth century to establish National Monuments[.]").

buyers while destroying irreplaceable contextual information in the process. The lack of federal authority to prevent such depredations on public lands galvanized preservationists, archaeologists, and concerned citizens to advocate for protective legislation. The Antiquities Act represented a watershed moment in American conservation policy, establishing the principle that certain cultural and natural resources possess value transcending private economic interests and warrant protection through governmental action.

The Antiquities Act's implementation, however, revealed tensions that would characterize preservation efforts throughout the 20th century. Presidents have exercised their designation authority in widely varying ways, sometimes protecting vast landscapes encompassing millions of acres and other times focusing on more modest sites of specific historical or scientific importance. This flexibility, while enabling responsive preservation of threatened resources, has also generated controversy when designations conflict with extractive industries, recreational uses, or local development plans. Western states, in particular, have periodically challenged presidential monument designations as federal overreach, arguing that such actions improperly lock up lands that should remain available for economic exploitation or state management.[8]

Another pivotal moment in the development of preservation laws was the Historic Sites Act of 1935, which declared it a national policy to preserve historic sites, buildings, and objects for public use.[9] This law authorized the National Park Service to survey, document, and acquire historically significant properties.[10] The Historic Sites Act emerged during the New Deal era, when the federal government expanded its role in numerous policy domains previously left to states and private actors. The Act reflected Progressive Era convictions that government bore responsibility for safeguarding cultural

---

8. *See* Dan Newhouse, Congressional Western Caucus, *It's Time to End Abuse of the Antiquities Act*, https://westerncaucus.house.gov/news/documentsingle.aspx?DocumentID=5788 (last visited Feb. 14, 2026); *see also* Adam G. Griffin, The Federalist Society, *Litigation Update: Sagebrush Rebels and Western States Challenge Presidential Monument Designations*, https://fedsoc.org/events/litigation-update-sagebrush-rebels-and-western-states-presidential-monument-designations (last visited Feb. 14, 2026).

9. H.R. Rep. No. 96-1457, at 18 (1980), *as reprinted in* 1980 U.S.C.C.A.N. 6378, 6381 ("The Historic Sites Act of 1935 Declared for the first time a national policy of historic preservation and authorized the Secretary of the Interior to initiate a number of preservation programs . . . with the goal of identifying and evaluating nationally significant properties.").

10. *Id.*

heritage as a public trust, coupled with New Deal pragmatism that saw historic preservation as a vehicle for providing employment through survey work, architectural documentation, and restoration projects.

The Historic Sites Act's most enduring contribution was establishing systematic processes for identifying and evaluating heritage resources. Prior to 1935, preservation efforts in America largely proceeded on an ad hoc basis, driven by patriotic associations' campaigns to save structures associated with prominent historical figures or events. The Mount Vernon Ladies' Association's successful effort to preserve George Washington's estate exemplified this pattern, as did campaigns to protect other homes of Founding Fathers and Revolutionary War sites. While laudable, such efforts created a preservation landscape heavily weighted toward properties associated with elite White men and military history, while neglecting other cultural architecture, sites significant to women's history, African American heritage, immigrant communities, and indigenous peoples.

However, it was not until the passage of the National Historic Preservation Act (NHPA) of 1966 that a comprehensive preservation framework was established.[11] The NHPA created the National Register of Historic Places, established the Advisory Council on Historic Preservation, and mandated the designation of state historic preservation officers (SHPOs) to coordinate efforts at the state level.[12] The 1966 Act represented Congress's response to accelerating post–World War II development that was rapidly transforming American cities and landscapes, often with devastating consequences for historic resources.

The urban renewal programs of the 1950s and early 1960s, despite worthy intentions to address urban blight and substandard housing, frequently resulted in wholesale demolition of historic neighborhoods, particularly those inhabited by minority and low-income populations. Highway construction projects carved through established communities, destroying countless historic structures in the process. Suburban sprawl consumed agricultural landscapes and scattered historic rural resources. Growing public

---

11. *Id.* ("The 1966 Act was a major step forward in preservation law. For the first time, it recognized the importance of preserving properties of state and local, as well as national, significance.").

12. *Id.* ("The 1966 Act directed the Secretary of the Interior to maintain an expanded listing of buildings, sites, districts, structures, and objects significant in American History, architecture, archeology, and culture—the national register of historic places. It also . . . created the advisory council on historic preservation.").

alarm at this destruction, combined with influential preservationist voices and the nascent environmental movement, created political momentum for comprehensive federal preservation legislation.

The NHPA's genius lay in creating a flexible federal framework that respected state and local prerogatives while establishing national standards and processes. Rather than imposing rigid federal mandates, the Act encouraged states to develop their own preservation programs meeting federal guidelines, thereby accommodating regional variations while ensuring minimum protective standards. The Section 106 review process, requiring federal agencies to consider effects on historic properties before proceeding with undertakings, represented a paradigm shift: federal actions could no longer proceed without at least considering impacts on heritage resources, even if such consideration did not guarantee preservation outcomes.

B. KEY COMPONENTS OF U.S. HISTORIC PRESERVATION LAWS

1. National Register of Historic Places

This official list includes districts, sites, buildings, structures, and objects deemed worthy of preservation.[13] Listing provides recognition, limited protection, and access to federal preservation grants and tax incentives.[14]

The National Register operates according to specific criteria that evaluate properties' historical significance and integrity.[15] Properties may qualify for listing if they are associated with significant events or persons, embody distinctive architectural characteristics, or possess potential to yield important historical information. The National Register distinguishes between significance and integrity: a property might be historically important but lack sufficient integrity if alterations have compromised its ability to convey that significance. This distinction acknowledges that not all old buildings merit preservation—only those retaining sufficient original character to effectively communicate their historical associations or architectural values warrant Register listing.

---

13. *See* National Park Service, *National Register of Historic Places*, www.nps.gov/subjects/nationalregister/index.htm (last visited June 10, 2025).

14. 54 U.S.C.A. § 302103(2) (West, Westlaw through Pub. L. No. 119-59); *see* National Park Service, *What Is the National Register of Historic Places?*, www.nps.gov/subjects/nationalregister/what-is-the-national-register.htm (last visited June 10, 2025).

15. *See infra* Chapter 2.

National Register listing confers primarily honorific recognition rather than absolute protection. Properties listed in the Register gain no automatic immunity from demolition or alteration by private owners, though they do receive procedural protections under Section 106 when federal undertakings might affect them. This limited protective scope reflects the drafters' deliberate choice to avoid creating federal property rights restrictions that might face constitutional challenges or generate political opposition. Nevertheless, Register listing provides important benefits: eligibility for rehabilitation tax credits, qualification for certain grants, and enhanced consideration in local planning processes. Moreover, many states and localities have enacted laws providing additional protections to Register-listed properties, supplementing federal baseline protections with more robust safeguards.

2. Section 106 Review Process

One of the NHPA's most important provisions, Section 106 requires federal agencies to consider the effects of their undertakings on historic properties.[16] This review process involves consultation with SHPOs, tribal historic preservation officers (THPOs), and other stakeholders.[17]

The Section 106 process unfolds through a series of prescribed steps designed to identify historic properties, assess effects, and resolve adverse effects through consultation. Federal agencies must first determine whether their undertaking constitutes the type of action requiring Section 106 review—generally any project involving federal funding, permits, or licenses or occurring on federal land. Agencies then identify the geographic area of potential effects and inventory historic properties within that area, consulting with SHPOs or THPOs to determine which properties are listed ineligible

---

16. U.S. General Services Administration, *Section 106: National Historic Preservation Act of 1966*, www.gsa.gov/real-estate/historic-preservation/historic-preservation-policy-tools/legislation-policy-and-reports/section-106-of-the-national-historic-preservation-act (last visited Feb. 14, 2026) ("Section 106 of the NHPA requires that each federal agency identify and assess the effects its actions may have on historic buildings.").

17. *Id.* ("Consultation is between the federal agency, the State Historic Preservation Officer (SHPO) or Tribal Historic Preservation Officer, and other consulting parties[.]"); *see also* 54 U.S.C.A. § 306108 (West, Westlaw through Pub. L. No. 119-59) ("The head of any Federal agency having direct or indirect jurisdiction over a proposed Federal or federally assisted undertaking in any State and the head of any Federal department or independent agency having authority to license any undertaking, prior to the approval of the expenditure of any Federal funds on the undertaking or prior to the issuance of any license, shall take into account the effect of the undertaking on any historic property.").

or eligible for the National Register. Following identification, agencies assess whether the undertaking would affect historic properties and whether any such effects would be adverse.

When adverse effects are identified, the Section 106 process requires agencies to consult with relevant parties to seek ways to avoid, minimize, or mitigate those effects. This consultation must include SHPOs or THPOs, but frequently expands to encompass additional consulting parties: local governments, preservation organizations, property owners, and any parties with demonstrated interest in the undertaking's effects on historic properties. The Advisory Council on Historic Preservation may participate in consultations involving particularly complex or controversial undertakings. Successful consultation typically culminates in a memorandum of agreement documenting how adverse effects will be addressed, though agencies may proceed even without agreement if they follow prescribed procedures and document their considerations.

Critics have argued that Section 106 review too often becomes a mere paper exercise, with agencies going through required motions without genuinely considering preservation alternatives. The process requires consideration but not preservation—agencies may proceed with projects that will destroy historic properties so long as they have followed consultation procedures and considered mitigation measures. Preservationists sometimes characterize Section 106 as providing historic properties their "day in court" but not guaranteeing favorable verdicts. Nevertheless, the process has prevented or modified numerous projects that would have harmed significant historic resources, and even when preservation outcomes are not achieved, Section 106 review generates documentation of lost resources that serves important archival and scholarly purposes.

3. Certified Local Governments

The NHPA encourages establishing certified local governments (CLGs), which are municipal governments that have made a commitment to historic preservation.[18] These governments are eligible for grants and play an integral role in the review process.[19]

---

18. Advisory Council on Historic Preservation, *Streamlined Process for Certified Local Governments*, www.achp.gov/preserve-america/streamlined-process (last visited Feb. 14, 2026) ("Each participating local community works through a certification process to become recognized as a [CLG]. CLGs then become active partners in the National Historic Preservation Program with certain benefits and responsibilities.").

19. Eligibility and responsibility of certified local government, 54 U.S.C.A. § 302505(1) (West, Westlaw through Pub. L. No. 119-59) ("Any local government that is certified under this chapter shall be eligible for funds under [the Historic Preservation Fund].").

The CLG program, established through 1980 amendments to the NHPA, recognizes that effective preservation requires robust local participation. To achieve CLG certification, municipalities must enforce appropriate legislation for designating and protecting historic properties, establish an adequate and qualified historic preservation review commission, maintain a system for surveying and inventorying historic properties, and provide for adequate public participation in the preservation program. Some certified communities may qualify to receive a percentage of their state's annual federal preservation grant allocation and assume certain responsibilities in the National Register nomination process, reviewing nominations for properties within their jurisdictions before forwarding them to SHPOs.

The CLG program reflects preservation's essentially local character. While federal and state frameworks provide important structure and resources, preservation decisions ultimately affect specific communities and properties, making local involvement indispensable. Successful CLG programs demonstrate how municipal governments can integrate preservation into comprehensive planning, zoning, and economic development strategies. However, CLG participation remains voluntary, and many communities lack the resources or political will to pursue certification, resulting in uneven preservation capacity across the nation. Rural and economically disadvantaged communities, in particular, often struggle to maintain the staffing and expertise necessary for effective CLG programs, potentially leaving significant heritage resources in these areas vulnerable to neglect or loss.

4. Tax Incentives

The federal government provides tax credits for the rehabilitation of income producing historic buildings.[20] This incentive encourages private investment in preservation projects.[21]

The federal rehabilitation tax credit program, currently providing a 20% credit for qualified rehabilitation expenditures on income-producing historic buildings, represents preservation policy's most successful economic incentive. Since its inception in 1976, the program has leveraged billions of dollars in private investment for historic preservation, rehabilitating tens

20. *See* 26 U.S.C.A. § 47 (West, Westlaw through Pub. L. No. 119-59).

21. Carolyn Ells Cheverine, *Rehabilitation Tax Credit: Does It Still Provide Incentives?* 10 VA. TAX REV. 167, 169 ("In 1976, Congress decided that in order to preserve our nation's historic structures, tax incentives and disincentives were needed to encourage developers and owners not to raze their buildings.").

of thousands of historic buildings that might otherwise have been demolished or left to deteriorate. The program requires that rehabilitations meet the Secretary of the Interior's Standards for Rehabilitation, ensuring that tax-subsidized projects respect historic character while permitting contemporary uses and necessary modifications.

Tax credit projects have transformed countless urban cores, converting vacant or underutilized historic buildings into productive uses including housing, offices, restaurants, and cultural venues. The program demonstrates that preservation and economic vitality need not conflict—indeed, historic buildings rehabilitated through tax credits often command premium rents and contribute substantially to neighborhood revitalization. Nevertheless, the program faces ongoing challenges: periodic legislative proposals to reduce or eliminate the credit, complexity in applying for and receiving credits, and limitations that exclude owner-occupied residential properties from eligibility. Some critics contend that tax credits disproportionately benefit wealthy developers and investors while providing limited housing affordability benefits, though defenders argue that without such incentives, many historic buildings would face demolition.

5. Preservation Easements

Property owners can enter into legal agreements that place restrictions on the alteration or development of a property.[22] These easements are typically held by nonprofit organizations or government agencies and are enforceable in perpetuity.[23] Preservation easements function similarly to conservation easements protecting natural landscapes, allowing property owners to voluntarily restrict future alterations to their properties in exchange for tax benefits. The easement holder—often a preservation organization or governmental entity—monitors the property to ensure compliance with easement terms and can take legal action if violations occur. Easements typically prohibit demolition and regulate exterior alterations, interior modifications to significant spaces, and sometimes site changes. Well-drafted easements balance preservation goals with reasonable property use, permitting maintenance and modifications that do not compromise historic character while preventing destructive changes.

---

22. *See* 26 U.S.C.A. § 170(h) (West, Westlaw through Pub. L. No. 119-59).

23. *Id.*

For property owners, donating preservation easements can generate substantial tax benefits through charitable contribution deductions based on the easement's value—essentially the difference between the property's fair market value before and after easement encumbrance. This tax treatment reflects public policy recognizing that voluntary preservation restrictions serve public purposes by protecting heritage resources. However, preservation easements remain relatively uncommon compared to conservation easements, partly because property owners may be reluctant to accept permanent restrictions on historically significant properties that might be their primary residences or businesses. Moreover, the Internal Revenue Service has subjected conservation and preservation easement deductions to increased scrutiny in recent years, investigating potentially abusive tax shelters and proposing regulations that could discourage legitimate easement donations.

C. STATE AND LOCAL PRESERVATION LAWS

Although federal laws provide an overarching framework, states and municipalities often enact their own preservation laws and ordinances.[24] These laws can be more stringent than federal regulations and may include the following.

1. Local Historic Districts

Designation of historic districts often comes with design review requirements to ensure that changes to buildings within the district are in keeping with the historic character.[25]

---

24. *See, e.g.*, S.C. Code Ann. § 60-12-10 to -90 (Westlaw through 2025 Act No. 94); California Pub. Res. Code §§ 5001–5877 (Westlaw through Ch. 790 of 2025 Reg. Sess. and Governor's Reorganization Plan No. 1 of 2025); New York State Historic Preservation Act of 1980, N.Y. Parks Rec. & Hist. Preserv. §§ 1.01–43.19 (McKinney, Westlaw through L. 2025 chapters 1–713); Fla. Stat. Ann. § 267.011–.22 (West, Westlaw from the 2025 Special Session C and through July 1, 2025, of the 2025 first regular session).

25. *See* Fla. Stat. Ann. § 267.0612(1)(a)(1) (West, Westlaw from the 2025 Special Session C and through July 1, 2025, of the 2025 first regular session) (requiring a "professional architectural historian" and a "licensed architect who has experience in historic preservation and architectural history" on the Commission charged with historic property designations); DC.gov, *Permits & Design Review*, https://planning.dc.gov/es/page/permits-design-review ("The

Local historic districts represent preservation law's most direct and potentially powerful tool for protecting historic resources. Unlike National Register listing, which confers primarily procedural protections triggered by federal involvement, local historic district designation typically empowers review commissions to approve or deny proposed alterations to contributing properties within district boundaries. This regulatory authority derives from municipal police powers to protect public health, safety, and welfare, with courts consistently recognizing aesthetic and historic preservation as legitimate welfare concerns justifying reasonable land-use regulations.

Design review processes vary considerably across jurisdictions but typically require property owners to obtain certificates of appropriateness before undertaking visible alterations to contributing structures within historic districts. Review boards evaluate proposed changes against established design guidelines assessing compatibility with the district's historic character. Well-designed review processes focus on preserving significant character-defining features while permitting appropriate changes, additions, and contemporary interventions that respect historic context without engaging in false historicism. However, design review can generate friction when property owners view commission decisions as arbitrary or overly restrictive, particularly when guidelines are vague or commissioners lack clear standards.

The designation of local historic districts often proves politically contentious. Property owners within proposed districts sometimes organize in opposition, fearing that design review will diminish property values, restrict renovation options, or impose expensive maintenance obligations. Economic analyses examining this question have reached mixed conclusions, with some studies finding preservation restrictions either increase or have neutral effects on property values, while others identify potential negative impacts. The reality likely varies depending on local real estate markets, the rigor of design review, and the character of particular districts. Moreover, property value impacts represent only one consideration in assessing historic district desirability—broader community benefits including enhanced

---

District of Columbia's historic preservation law is intended to ensure that work done on historic properties is compatible with their historic character. This is accomplished through design review of building plans, permits, and subdivision applications.") (last visited Feb. 16, 2026).

neighborhood character, tourism potential, and cultural heritage preservation may justify modest economic trade-offs.

2. Demolition Delay Ordinances

These ordinances temporarily prevent the demolition of historic structures, providing time to explore preservation alternatives.[26]

Demolition delay ordinances offer a middle-ground preservation approach suitable for communities lacking comprehensive historic district regulations or wishing to extend protection to individual landmarks outside designated districts. These ordinances typically require property owners seeking demolition permits for buildings meeting specified age or significance criteria to wait for a designated period—commonly 30 to 90 days, though some jurisdictions impose longer delays—before demolition may proceed. During the delay period, preservation commissions work to identify alternatives: potential purchasers willing to preserve the building, relocation options, or negotiated modifications to development plans that might permit retention.

Demolition delay ordinances rest on the premise that many historically significant buildings are demolished not because preservation is impossible but because insufficient time exists to organize preservation responses before demolition occurs. By imposing a waiting period, these ordinances create opportunities for preservationists to mobilize, though they provide no guarantee of preservation outcomes if no viable alternative emerges. Critics argue that demolition delays merely postpone inevitable losses while imposing costs on property owners, while supporters contend that even temporary delays save significant structures that would otherwise be hastily demolished. The effectiveness of demolition delay ordinances depends substantially on community preservation capacity—jurisdictions with active preservation organizations, revolving funds, and skilled advocacy are far more likely to convert delays into preservation outcomes than communities lacking such resources.

---

26. *See* Julie H. Miller, *Protecting Landmarks Through Demolition Review*, www.denvergov.org/content/dam/denvergov/Portals/646/documents/landmark/Ordinance_task_force/Protecting_Potential_Landmark_Demolition_Review.pdf (including a list of demolition delay ordinances).

3. Landmark Designation

State and local governments can designate individual landmarks that warrant special protection due to their historical or architectural significance.[27]

Individual landmark designation extends preservation protections to properties outside historic districts, recognizing that significant structures may exist in areas where comprehensive district regulation would be inappropriate or infeasible. Landmark designation procedures typically resemble historic district designation but apply to single properties, evaluating whether structures meet specified significance and integrity criteria. Designated landmarks commonly receive protection against demolition and must undergo design review for proposed alterations, similar to properties within historic districts.

Landmark designation can prove particularly valuable for protecting isolated significant structures in otherwise non-historic areas—a notable example of cultural architecture in a modern suburb, an important historical industrial building in a commercial zone, or an architecturally distinguished building standing amid less significant neighbors. However, landmark designation targeting individual properties can generate more intense political opposition than district designation, as affected property owners may feel singled out for restrictions not imposed on neighboring properties. Courts have consistently upheld landmark designation against constitutional challenges, but jurisdictions must follow prescribed procedures and demonstrate that regulations bear reasonable relationships to legitimate preservation objectives.

D. INTERNATIONAL PERSPECTIVES ON HISTORIC PRESERVATION LAWS

Historic preservation is not a uniquely American effort. Globally, historic preservation is guided by international treaties and the laws of individual countries.[28] The most significant international agreement is the UNESCO

27. *See* Fla. Stat. Ann. § 267.11 (West, Westlaw from the 2025 Special Session C and through July 1, 2025, of the 2025 first regular session) ("The division may publicly designate an archaeological site of significance to the scientific study or public representation of the state's historical, prehistoric, or aboriginal past as a 'state archaeological landmark.'").

28. Historic England, *International Treaties and Obligations*, https://historicengland.org.uk/about/what-we-do/international/treaties-obligations/ (last visited Feb. 14, 2026) (describing

World Heritage Convention of 1972.[29] This treaty promotes the identification, protection, and preservation of cultural and natural heritage around the world.[30]

The World Heritage Convention emerged from recognition that certain heritage resources possess "outstanding universal value" transcending national boundaries and constituting patrimony of all humanity. Properties inscribed on the World Heritage List receive international recognition and, theoretically, enhanced protection through signatory nations' treaty obligations. The Convention establishes processes for nominating properties, evaluating their significance, and monitoring their conservation status. While the treaty itself provides no direct enforcement mechanisms—World Heritage inscription creates moral rather than legal obligations—listing can increase international attention, tourism, and pressure on national governments to protect inscribed properties.

World Heritage designation has evolved considerably since 1972, with the World Heritage Committee working to address persistent criticisms regarding geographic imbalance and narrow definitions of significance. Early World Heritage lists heavily favored European monuments and monumental architecture, reflecting selection processes dominated by Western nations and traditional conceptions of heritage emphasizing grand architectural achievements. Recent decades have witnessed efforts to expand representation of non-Western heritage, cultural architecture, industrial sites, 20th-century properties, intangible property, and landscapes.

Many countries have established governmental bodies to manage heritage resources, such as English Heritage in the United Kingdom or the National Heritage Board in Singapore.[31] These organizations oversee

---

"conventions" as a term describing legal treaties often used in the historic preservation context).

29. UNESCO, The World Heritage Convention, https://whc.unesco.org/en/convention/#:~:text=Facebook%20Youtube%20Twitter-,The%20World%20Heritage%20Convention,the%20preservation%20of%20cultural%20properties (last visited Feb. 14, 2026) ("The most significant feature of the 1972 World Heritage Convention is that it links together in a single document the concepts of nature conservation and the preservation of cultural properties.").

30. *Id.*

31. Historic England, *About Us*, https://historicengland.org.uk/about/ ("We work together with people and organisations across England, to discover, protect, and bring new life to our shared historic environment.") (last visited Feb. 14, 2026); National Heritage Board,

national registers, provide guidance on preservation practices, and often manage public heritage sites.[32]

National heritage systems vary substantially in their structures, authorities, and effectiveness. Some nations vest considerable regulatory authority in heritage agencies, empowering them to prevent demolitions or alterations to protected properties. Others rely primarily on financial incentives and voluntary cooperation. European nations generally maintain more centralized, robust heritage protection systems than exist in the United States, reflecting different constitutional traditions regarding property rights and governmental authority. Countries like France and Italy have long-established national inventory and protection systems predating American preservation laws by decades, while emerging economies frequently struggle to balance development pressures against heritage preservation objectives.

E. CHALLENGES AND CRITICISMS

Despite their importance, historic preservation laws are not without challenges and criticisms.[33] Common issues include the following.

1. Balancing Preservation with Development

Urban growth and infrastructure projects often clash with preservation goals.[34] Critics argue that strict preservation laws can stifle economic development or infringe on property rights.[35]

About Us, www.nhb.gov.sg/who-we-are/about-us ("The National Heritage Board (NHB) is the custodian of Singapore's heritage.") (last visited Feb. 14, 2026).

32. National Heritage Board, *What We Do*, www.nhb.gov.sg/what-we-do/our-work (last visited Feb. 14, 2026).

33. *See* Melissa E. Honsermyer, *The Fate of Historical Preservation Laws in Pennsylvania*, 97 Dick. L. Rev. 719 (1993) (outlining challenges to Pennsylvania historic preservation law ranging through an examination of case law and other constitutional challenges); David A. Lewis, *Identifying and Avoiding Conflicts Between Historic Preservation and the Development of Renewable Energy*, 22 N.Y.U. Envtl. L.J. 274 (2015) (examining the juxtaposition of historic preservation law with renewable energy initiatives while highlighting the tiered development process that investors push to avoid historic preservation review).

34. *See* Lewis, *supra* note 33 (defining the obstacles to laying electrical transmission lines over large distances due to historic preservation laws).

35. *Id.* at 362 ("Preservation often competes with other influences, including demand for new and greater amounts of housing and commercial space, investment in real estate for pecuniary gain, the exploitation of natural resources, and the development of new infrastructure, among many others."). Harvard University economist Professor Edward Glaeser has argued that

The tension between preservation and development persists as perhaps preservation law's most fundamental challenge. Rapidly growing cities face enormous pressure to accommodate new residents, employment centers, and infrastructure, often viewing historic buildings as obstacles to necessary change rather than assets worthy of retention. Developers and property rights advocates argue that preservation regulations improperly elevate aesthetic preferences above economic efficiency, constraining market forces and property owners' fundamental rights to use their land as they choose. Some economists contend that preservation restrictions reduce housing supply in desirable urban areas, exacerbating affordability crises and potentially harming lower-income residents whom preservation purportedly serves.

Preservation regulation does constrain property rights and can complicate development, though whether such restrictions truly harm economic growth or housing affordability remains hotly debated. Preservation advocates counter that heritage conservation frequently enhances rather than hindering economic development, citing evidence that preservation-led revitalization outperforms wholesale redevelopment in generating sustainable economic benefits. Moreover, the property rights argument, while politically potent, oversimplifies complex legal realities: American property law has never recognized absolute dominion untampered by public welfare considerations, and courts consistently uphold reasonable regulations serving legitimate public purposes against property rights challenges.

2. Funding and Resources

Preservation efforts often depend on limited funding.[36] Many historic properties suffer from neglect due to a lack of maintenance and restoration funds.[37]

---

strict historic preservation laws often stifle economic development, reduce housing affordability, and violate property rights by acting as an "anti-growth" mechanism that restricts building in productive urban areas. Edward L. Glaeser, City Journal, *Preservation Follies*, www.city-journal.org/article/preservation-follies#:~:text=It's%20hard%20to%20fault%20the,Tobio%20for%20heroic%20research%20assistance (last visited Feb. 14, 2026).

36. American Alliance of Museums, *Issue: Historic Preservation*, www.aam-us.org/programs/advocacy/policy-issues/issue-historic-preservation/ (advocating for congressional support to vote against decreased historic preservation funding) (last visited Feb. 14, 2026); *see also* National Trust for Historic Preservation, *Speak Up for Federal Historic Preservation Investment*, https://savingplaces.org/action-center/updates/speak-up-for-federal-historic-preservation-investment (highlighting issues facing historic preservation funding as a result of the current [2025] executive administration) (May 9, 2025) (last visited Feb. 14, 2026).

37. National Trust for Historic Preservation, *51 Projects for Preservation: The Historic Preservation Fund Across the United States*, https://savingplaces.org/stories/

Chronic underfunding plagues preservation efforts at all governmental levels. Federal appropriations for preservation programs constitute tiny fractions of overall federal budgets, and preservation consistently loses out when competing against seemingly more urgent priorities in budget negotiations. State preservation offices operate with skeletal staffs inadequate to handle their responsibilities for Section 106 review, National Register nominations, grant administration, and technical assistance. Local preservation commissions frequently function with volunteer members receiving minimal staff support, limiting their capacity to conduct sophisticated analyses or provide property owners with detailed guidance.

Beyond governmental funding limitations, many historic properties require substantial private investment for maintenance and rehabilitation. Older buildings inevitably need more maintenance than new construction, and owners sometimes defer necessary work due to cost constraints, initiating deterioration cycles where neglect generates additional damage requiring ever more expensive interventions. Properties in economically distressed areas face particular challenges: depressed local markets may not support rehabilitation costs, creating situations where preservation is theoretically desirable but economically infeasible. The loss of traditional building crafts compounds these challenges—skilled masons, plasterers, and other craftspeople capable of proper historic building maintenance have become increasingly rare and expensive, raising preservation costs beyond many property owners' means.

3. Inclusivity and Representation

Early preservation efforts often prioritized grand architecture and sites associated with prominent historical figures.[38] Modern efforts aim to address this imbalance by recognizing sites of significance to marginalized communities.[39]

The historic bias toward elite, predominantly White, male-associated heritage represents perhaps preservation's most serious credibility

---

projects-of-the-historic-preservation-fund (May 12, 2025) (outlining 51 different historic preservation projects across the entirety of the United States in need of historic preservation funding) (last visited Feb. 14, 2026).

38. *See* Jess R. Phelps, *Preserving National Historic Landmarks?*, 24 N.Y.U. Envtl. L.J. 137, 143 (2016) ("American historic preservation begins with the purchase and subsequent operation of [the nation's first president, George Washington,] Mount Vernon[,] as a house museum by the Mount Vernon Ladies Association.").

39. *See* Fla. Stat. Ann. § 267.0625 (through 2025 Special Session C and through July 1, 2025, of the 2025 first regular session) ("The Legislature finds that certain place names for geographic sites are offensive or derogatory to the state's people, history, and heritage.").

challenge. Traditional preservation practice emphasized the homes of Founding Fathers, grand civic monuments, and architecturally pretentious mansions while systematically overlooking sites documenting working-class life, African American history, women's achievements, indigenous heritage, and immigrant communities. This selectivity reflected not merely oversight but active value judgments about which histories merited preservation and whose stories deserved telling. The consequences persist: underrepresentation of diverse heritage in preservation programs perpetuates historical erasure and undermines preservation's claims to serve broad public interests rather than narrow elite preferences.

Contemporary preservation increasingly recognizes these failings and works toward more inclusive heritage identification. Recent decades have witnessed growing attention to African American heritage sites including slave quarters, churches, schools, and Civil Rights landmarks; industrial and labor history sites; vernacular architecture documenting everyday life; and landscapes significant to indigenous peoples. The National Park Service has undertaken thematic studies examining underrepresented histories and encouraged nominations of properties documenting diverse heritage. State and local preservation programs increasingly prioritize diverse heritage identification and develop community partnerships to identify significant sites that might escape notice through traditional survey methods.

Nevertheless, achieving genuinely inclusive preservation requires more than adding underrepresented sites to existing lists. It demands fundamental reconsideration of how significance is defined and assessed, who participates in preservation decision-making, and whose narratives shape heritage interpretation. Communities whose heritage has been marginalized sometimes view preservation programs with suspicion, perceiving them as instruments of gentrification or cultural appropriation rather than authentic heritage stewardship. Building trust requires sustained engagement, resource commitments, and willingness to cede authority to communities in determining how their heritage should be preserved and interpreted.

Historic preservation laws are essential tools for protecting our cultural heritage.[40] They reflect a collective recognition that the past has value not only as a record of human achievement but also as a foundation for future growth

---

40. *See* 54 U.S.C.A. § 302101 (West, Westlaw through Pub. L. No. 119-59) ("The Secretary may expand and maintain a National Register of Historic Places composed of districts, sites, buildings, structures, and *objects significant in American history, architecture, archeology, engineering, and culture*.") (emphasis added).

and identity.[41] As these laws evolve, it is crucial to ensure they are inclusive, adequately funded, and adaptable to contemporary challenges.[42] Through thoughtful preservation, society can honor its past while enriching its future.[43]

Looking forward, preservation law faces both unprecedented challenges and remarkable opportunities. Climate change threatens heritage resources through increased flooding, wildfires, and extreme weather events, requiring preservationists to develop adaptation strategies balancing protection with resilience. Technological advances offer new tools for documenting, monitoring, and maintaining historic properties, from laser scanning that captures precise architectural details to artificial intelligence applications that might streamline identification of endangered resources. Demographic shifts, including urbanization and changing cultural preferences, will reshape which resources are valued and how preservation integrates into broader social objectives.

Perhaps most fundamentally, preservation must continue evolving from protecting isolated "great buildings" toward comprehensive heritage stewardship recognizing the interconnectedness of built environments, landscapes, and communities. This expanded vision embraces preservation not as backward-looking nostalgia but as forward-thinking sustainability, recognizing that reusing existing resources, maintaining community character, and honoring diverse heritage serve pragmatic contemporary needs while respecting the past. Success will require preservation advocates, property owners, developers, and communities to engage in constructive dialogue, seeking common ground while acknowledging legitimate disagreements about how best to balance competing values in an era of rapid change.

---

41. *See* Zachary Bray, *We Are All Growing Old Together: Making Sense of America's Monument-Protection Laws*, 61 Wm. & Mary L. Rev. 1259, 1266 (2020) ("Many [monuments] are sources of community pride or distinction, touchstones of collective memory, or merely part of the visual and mental backdrop of their neighbors' daily lives."). As Bray points out, these same monuments have in recent years become catalysts for popular protests demonstrating the utility of historic sites as vehicles capable of pushing progressive societal changes. *Id.*

42. *See* Fla. Stat. Ann. § 267.0625 (through 2025 Special Session C and through July 1, 2025, of the 2025 first regular session) ("The Legislature finds that certain place names for geographic sites are offensive or derogatory to the state's people, history, and heritage.").

43. H.R. Rep. No. 96-1457, at 18 (1980), *as reprinted in* 1980 U.S.C.C.A.N. 6378, 6384 ("Historic preservation, as it is practiced today, incorporates many important national priorities—the need to conserve energy resources, to fight inflation, to revitalize our cities and to provide more opportunities for local employment. Recent studies have shown that historic preservation contributes to greater housing supply, increased tax revenues, new business starts, growth in retail sales, expanded tourism and convention activity, and increased public and private investments.").

Designations 2

Unlike beauty, antiquity is not its own excuse for being.[1] Not every building that survives a century is necessarily worth preserving for the next century. For many buildings, the condition or quality of a building might be torpedoed by the cost of saving it. Deciding that a building is worth saving is known as *designating* it.

Just being *designated* does not mean that a building cannot be altered or even demolished. Being designated is simply a status that, depending on what sort of designation has been appended, opens the door to other preservation issues. On the other hand, *not* being designated at all by any jurisdiction is not necessarily the end of the line in a preservation battle. An opponent to demolition might still assert other issues having nothing in particular to do with preservation to slow or even stop some demolition or alteration. For example, if Ned Neighbor wants Owen Owner to save an old warehouse next to Ned's house, then even

---

1. Ralph Waldo Emerson, *The Rhodora*, in The Selected Writings of Ralph Waldo Emerson 765, 765 (1950).

with no designation in place from anyone on the warehouse, Ned could still raise issues about asbestos mitigation—which might add enormous costs to demolition—to dissuade Owen Owner from tearing down the warehouse.

Different jurisdictions have widely different processes for designating properties for preservation. Differences include the mechanics and paperwork for pursuing a designation, the types of properties for which designations are even available, the identity of decision-makers in the process, the standards used for judging applications, and the resulting protections. Those aspects and others all differ from jurisdiction to jurisdiction and from program to program. Each one must be reviewed on its own terms.

The easiest division to draw is the difference between federal and state[2] designations.

A. FEDERAL DESIGNATIONS

At the federal level, the most famous designation is inclusion on the National Register of Historic Places. Many museum houses, battlefields, and other tourist sites are built around National Register properties. National Register properties can be individual sites or contributors to a district. In many neighborhoods on the National Register, realtors use the National Register as a selling point as a shorthand for good quality, old, and well-appreciated houses. And countless owners of individually listed buildings go to great time and expense to secure a National Register listing for the tax consequences and for simple bragging rights.

What might surprise most preservation advocates is just how little protection a federal designation offers. A designation is primarily honorific and does not limit an owner absent a local ordinance or federal agency action. In the latter case, the federal government must "take into account" the effects of its actions with respect to National Register–listed properties as well as those determined eligible for listing.[3] The directive limits the conduct only of federal agencies.[4] National Park Service regulations explain: "Listing of

2. For the sake of brevity, this book will often refer to states, although the message very well could involve a county or town or a Native American tribe.

3. 54 U.S.C.A. § 306108 (West, Westlaw through Pub. L. No. 119-59); *see id.* § 300308 (West, Westlaw through Pub. L. No. 119-59); *see supra* Chapter 3.

4. Kaufmann v. Fed. Aviation Admin., 722 F. App'x 438, 442 (6th Cir. 2018).

private property on the National Register does not prohibit under Federal law or regulation any actions which may otherwise be taken by the property owner with respect to the property."[5] Therefore, the listing of private property on the National Register does not normally restrict an owner's use of his or her property.

The National Historic Landmarks program was conceived of prior to the passage of the NHPA in 1960 and is reserved for properties of truly national importance and not just those of importance to a state or locality.[6] While there are over 90,000 listings on the National Register,[7] only about 2600 historic properties have been designated landmarks under the National Historic Landmarks program.[8] A potential landmark must meet all the same requirements for the National Register of Historic Places but then must also be "judged by the Secretary [of the Interior] to possess national significance."[9] Inclusion on the NHL list automatically means that the property is on the National Register of Historic Places, but the opposite is not true.

Landmarks receive enhanced protections beyond those given to National Register listings; for instance, a federal agency must "tak[e] into account" the effect of agency actions on National Register listings, but the agency must "minimize harm" to landmark-status properties.[10] While the statute would seem to command a literal minimization of harm, the extra burden has been interpreted as a merely procedural requirement, not a substantive one. In *Presidio Historical Association v. Presidio Trust*,[11] the court had to review changes to the Presidio—sometimes described as the

---

5. 36 C.F.R. § 60.2 (2025).

6. National Park Service, *Roots of the National Historic Landmarks Program*, www.nps.gov/articles/roots-of-the-national-historic-landmarks-program.htm (last visited Feb. 14, 2026).

7. State Historic Preservation Office, *National Register: Facts & Figures*, www.hpo.nc.gov/survey-and-national-register/national-register-historic-places/national-register-facts-figures#:~:text=There%20are%20more%20than%2090%2C000,United%20States%20and%20its%20territories (last visited Feb. 14, 2026).

8. National Park Service, *National Historic Landmarks Program*, www.nps.gov/orgs/1582/index.htm#:~:text=The%20over%202%2C600%20NHLs%20found,of%20American%20history%20and%20culture (last visited Feb. 14, 2026).

9. 36 C.F.R. § 65.3 (2025).

10. *Compare* 54 U.S.C.A. § 306107 (West, Westlaw through Pub. L. No. 119-59) *with* 54 U.S.C.A. § 306108 (West, Westlaw through Pub. L. No. 119-59).

11. 811 F.3d 1154, 1157 (9th Cir. 2016).

birthplace of San Francisco. The Presidio was made a National Historic Landmark in 1962 as the property shifted from being a traditional military base to a recreational preserve. The Presidio Trust was created by Congress to manage the Presidio with dual—somewhat conflicting—goals of preserving its history and also making it self-funding.

The Presidio Trust announced long-considered plans to add a series of buildings to part of the Presidio, and an assortment of preservation organizations challenged the plans. The groups asserted that the Presidio Trust had failed to apply heightened preservation standards applicable to National Historic Landmark properties. Projects affecting government-owned sites and National Historic Landmarks trigger extra requirements under Section 110. Section 110 sought to "clarif[y] and codif[y] the minimum responsibilities expected of federal agencies in carrying out the purposes of the [NHPA]."[12] For instance, agencies must develop a preservation program for federally owned properties. National Historic Landmarks are subject to the specific requirements of Section 110(f): "Prior to the approval of any Federal undertaking that may directly and adversely affect any National Historic Landmark, the head of the responsible Federal agency shall to *the maximum extent possible* undertake such planning and actions as may be necessary to *minimize harm* to the landmark."[13]

On appeal, the Ninth Circuit ruled that the Presidio Trust had done enough to satisfy the heightened standards by at least thoughtfully considering the options, even if other plans might have better preserved the site. The court threaded the needle and noted that, while literal compliance was not a requirement, the statute was not adding nothing to the process:

> In holding that Section 110(f) does not impose a substantive obligation, we do not mean that Congress failed to heighten the procedural hurdles an agency must satisfy with respect to projects affecting National Historic Landmarks. The Trust cannot rest on the fact that, by all indications, it complied with the letter of Section 106. Something more was required under Section 110(f). The best indication of what else was required can be found in the legislative history, which says that the agency should at least "consider prudent and feasible alternatives" to avoid adverse

12. H.R. Rep. No. 96-1457, at 36 (1980).

13. 54 U.S.C.A. § 306107 (West, Westlaw through Pub. L. No. 119-59) (emphasis added).

> effects. This obligation stands on top of the more general duty in the Section 106 consultation process to "seek ways to avoid, minimize or mitigate . . . adverse effects." In short, the Trust was required to thoroughly consider—rather than simply identify and catalog—prudent and feasible alternatives to its proposed lodge design and in its planning process.[14]

Designation opens the doors to federal, state, and local tax credits, and there are researchers and historians who build cottage industries around researching and writing nominations for the National Register. Only in limited cases does inclusion on the National Register limit development.

The National Landmark Program traces its origins back to the Historic Sites Act of 1935, when properties were examined for possible purchase by the federal government to become part of the national parks system, and Congress sought an inventory of nationally significant sites. Later, the National Park Service started cataloging properties without an eye toward buying them and published the first listing in 1960. In 1966, Congress passed the National Historic Preservation Act, which established the National Register. The Secretary of the Interior was to "maintain and expand a National Register of Historic Places composed of districts, sites, buildings, structures, and objects significant in American history, architecture, archeology, engineering, and culture."[15] The Secretary was vested with broad discretion to develop standards for inclusion and the designation process. The National Park Service was tasked with carrying out those jobs. The actual grunt work of designation is performed at a state level with the State Historic Preservation Officer (SHPO) having the responsibility to identify possible properties for National Register inclusion and administer the process.[16] To assist the public and the SHPOs, the National Park Service has adopted regulations refining its standards[17] as well as publishing more user-friendly bulletins to explain the standards and processes in closer to lay language.[18]

---

14. *Presidio Hist. Ass'n*, 811 F.3d at 1170 (citations omitted).

15. 54 U.S.C.A. § 302101 (West, Westlaw through Pub. L. No. 119-59).

16. Each Indian tribe was granted the same power in a 1992 amendment to the National Historic Preservation Act.

17. 36 C.F.R. pt. 60 (2025).

18. National Park Service, *Publications of the National Register of Historic Places*, www.nps.gov/subjects/nationalregister/publications.htm (last visited Feb. 14, 2026).

The NHPA identifies five types of property that can be included on the National Register: structures, buildings, objects, sites, and districts. The categories can overlap, but each has a specific meaning. A *structure* is the broadest category and includes all human construction with a definite pattern of organization.[19] For example, a silo, cobblestone street, or garden wall are all forms of structures. A *building* is a subset of structures where the structure is meant to provide shelter for human activity.[20] Houses, barns, and churches are all forms of structures that are, more specifically, also buildings. An *object* is a "material thing" that relates to a particular place and that is of "functional, aesthetic, cultural, historical or scientific value";[21] even when the object is movable, it should be related to a location. For example, in 2001, a bronze statue, *Liberty Arming the Patriot*, was added to the National Register as an example of an important manufacturer's work, an example of sculptures of the period, and as an example of the movement of honoring Civil War service.[22] A *site* is a location where something of historical significance happened even though no structures remain from that activity. For example, a battlefield with no physical evidence of its use could still qualify as a site.[23] Finally, a *district* is a collection of the former types of property that has significance, even if no single part of the district would otherwise qualify itself; the collection has a greater value than the sum of its parts.[24] For example, the Hampton Park Terrace National Register District in Charleston, South Carolina, was designated for its especially intact collection of dwellings built during a very small build-out period in the early 20th century even though none of the houses would likely be eligible for listing individually.

Of course, not all things within one of the five categories are worthy of preservation. Once a category of property has been identified, it still must have both *significance* and *integrity* to qualify for inclusion on the National Register. *Significant* properties are those that are associated with

---

19. 36 C.F.R. § 60.3(p) (2025).

20. 36 C.F.R. § 60.3(a) (2025).

21. 36 C.F.R. § 60.3(j) (2025).

22. Library of Congress, *Liberty Arming the Patriot, Sometimes Called Freedom Arming the Patriot, a Bronze Sculpture Designed by William Granville Hastings in Pawtucket, Rhode Island, That Commemorates City Citizens' Participation in the American Civil War of the 1860s*, www.loc.gov/item/2018700648/ (last visited Feb. 14, 2026).

23. 36 C.F.R. § 60.3(l) (2025).

24. 36 C.F.R. § 60.3(d) (2025).

significant historical events or people, that reflect distinctive styles or methods of construction, or that might yield important historical information in the future.[25] Integrity is the ability of the property to communicate its significance. For example: When a Queen Anne house has been renovated in such a way that it has lost its shingled siding, stained glass windows, and eave brackets, does it really convey what it means to be a Queen Anne house in the first place? Does a covered bridge that has been relocated to a grassy field in a public park still convey its bridge-ness?

Lastly, many of the rules and regulations about properties guide when a property can be included on the National Register. On the other hand, the regulations also give some guidance as to property that should *not* be included.[26] Each guideline has an exception, but for the most part, the following are not eligible:

> Ordinarily cemeteries, birthplaces, or graves of historical figures, properties owned by religious institutions or used for religious purposes, structures that have been moved from their original locations, reconstructed historic buildings, properties primarily commemorative in nature, and properties that have achieved significance within the past 50 years shall not be considered eligible for the National Register.[27]

Assuming that a property can make out a possible case for inclusion on the National Register, the Department of the Interior's regulations also explain the process for having that designation granted. Nominations come from federal agencies, the states' Historic Preservation Officers, or Tribal Historic Preservation Officers (THPOs). Individuals do not list their own properties. A federal agent titled the Keeper of the National Register ultimately stamps applications approved or not.

1. National Register Listings for Federal Properties

Section 110 of the NHPA requires that federal agencies maintain a historic preservation program with an aim to "provide a process for the identification

25. 36 C.F.R. § 60.4 (2025).

26. *Id.*

27. National Register of Historic Places, *Frequently Asked Questions*, https://nationalregisterofhistoricplaces.com/faq.html (last visited Feb. 14, 2026).

and evaluation of historic property for listing on the National Register."[28] For federally owned or controlled properties, the designation process starts with a proposal from a federal agency, the Federal Preservation Officer, to first solicit input from state, tribal, and local officials.[29] The official considers that input and may then submit the application to the Keeper of the National Register along with that feedback. The nomination is listed in the *Federal Register* so that the wider public may support or oppose it. Lastly, the Keeper must consider all the input from the process and make the decision.

2. National Register Listings for State and Local Properties

Far more common are nominations begun at the state, local, or tribal level. In every state, there is an established State Historic Preservation Plan, so all nominations must flow through the SHPO. In the case of properties on tribal land, the THPO serves that role.[30] Again, individuals may not submit their own nominations directly to the Keeper for approval; the SHPO serves as a gatekeeper in the flowchart.

Generally, one seeking a designation first prepares a well-researched argument for a building's worth. Nothing compels an applicant to hire a professional researcher and nomination writer to do the paperwork, but many owners will outsource that work. Even if the owner is fluent in a building's history, a professional nomination writer can repackage the owner's content using familiar jargon to grease the skids. Prior to formal nominations being submitted, the SHPO may advise the preparer to first submit a Preliminary Information Form and receive initial feedback prior to investing in a complete nomination.

Once a nomination is received, the SHPO passes it on to the State Review Board, which is made up of representatives of relevant fields including architecture, history, and archeology.[31] In most cases, the SRB and the SHPO will arrive at an agreement about whether the nomination is worthy of being forwarded up the ladder to the Keeper. If they do not agree, the SHPO may nevertheless send the nomination along based on his or her own

28. 54 U.S.C.A. § 306102(b)(5)(B) (West, Westlaw through Pub. L. No. 119-59).

29. 36 C.F.R. § 60.9(c) (2025).

30. 54 U.S.C.A. § 302702 (West, Westlaw through Pub. L. No. 119-59).

31. 36 C.F.R. § 60.3(o) (2025).

support (but include the dissenting view or the SRB) and must do so if the SRB is the party supporting the nomination. Likewise, the chief elected official of the local government can trump the decisions of the others and force a nomination on to the Keeper.[32]

Notice is an important feature of the relevant regulations. The local government must be notified of the intent to submit a nomination for a property within its jurisdiction to the Keeper and must have the chance to comment.[33] The local official does not have the power to veto nominations, but when the chief elected official (often the mayor of a city) and the local preservation review commission concur in their opposition, the SHPO should not advance the nomination unless someone appeals.[34] The public too has to right to notice (albeit only through the publication of the *Federal Register*) and a chance to weigh in on the nomination.[35]

Before submitting a nomination, the SHPO must also notify the affected property owners that their property is being considered for inclusion in the National Register.[36] That way, the property owners have a "reasonable period of time" to "concur in, or object to, the nomination of the[ir] property."[37] That opportunity is essential to objecting property owners because if "a majority of the owners of privately owned properties" within the proposed district object to the listing, the district "shall not" be listed in the National Register "until the objection is withdrawn."[38]

The notice requirements for owners of affected property are especially specific. Objecting owners have the right to not have their property listed and instead simply be designated as eligible for listing.[39] Notice to owners is ordinarily required to be in writing. But, for nominations concerning more than 50 property owners, the SHPO is not required to individually notify the owners in writing of its intent to nominate their properties.[40] It may,

32. 36 C.F.R. § 60.6(l) (2025).

33. 54 U.S.C.A. § 302504 (West, Westlaw through Pub. L. No. 119-59).

34. *Id.*

35. 36 C.F.R. § 60.6(t).

36. 54 U.S.C.A. §§ 302103(2)(F), 302105(a) (West, Westlaw through Pub. L. No. 119-59).

37. *Id.* § 302105(a).

38. *Id.* § 302105(b).

39. 54 U.S.C.A. § 302105 (West, Westlaw through Pub. L. No. 119-59).

40. 36 C.F.R. § 60.6(c)–(d).

instead, publish a notice in local newspapers at least 30 days prior to the State Review Board meeting.[41] The notice must provide property owners with the opportunity to submit written comments and object to the nomination in writing.[42] For counting purposes, "[e]ach owner of private property in a district has one vote regardless of how many properties or what part of one property that party owns."[43] The SHPO is responsible for counting objections.[44] But even if a majority of owners do object, the SHPO nevertheless submits the nomination to the Keeper to determine whether the property is eligible for listing.[45]

After a property is listed in the National Register, a property owner may petition for its removal.[46] The procedure obstacles are extremely high. Pursuant to 36 C.F.R. § 60.15(c), "[a]ny person or organization may petition in writing for removal of a property from the National Register by setting forth the reasons the property should be removed on the grounds established in paragraph (a) of this section." Importantly, paragraph (a) provides that properties may be removed from the National Register for "[p]rejudicial error in the nomination or listing process."[47]

In one case, the unhappy owners contested the number of objections. "If the owner or owners of any privately owned property, or a majority of the owners of such properties within the district in the case of [a] historic district, object to such inclusion or designation, such property shall not be included on the National Register or designated as a National Historic Landmark until such objection is withdrawn."[48] When the dust settled from the objection process, the Keeper was convinced that errors had led to an undercount of objections and that delisting the property was called for. At first, the federal district court had ruled in favor of the Keeper, but the circuit court reversed and instructed the district court to reexamine the matter in further proceedings.

---

41. *Id.*

42. *Id.* § 60.6(d).

43. *Id.* § 60.6(g).

44. *Id.*

45. *Id.* § 60.6(n); 54 U.S.C. § 302105(c).

46. 54 U.S.C. § 302104(d); 36 C.F.R. § 60.15(c).

47. *Id.* § 60.15(a)(4).

48. 16 U.S.C. § 470a(a)(1)(A), *repealed by* Pub. L. No. 113-287, § 7, Dec. 19, 2014, 128 Stat. 3272.

What resulted was an exhaustive decision, not of the merits of vote counting, but of the standard of review. The Keeper's decision could not be affirmed if it had been arbitrary or capricious. "Although there is no formula for what constitutes reasoned decision making, this Circuit has identified principles to guide this inquiry. This Court categorizes these principles as follows: deliberation, transparency, rationality, and evidentiary propriety. Regarding deliberation, the agency must 'engage the arguments raised before it.'"[49]

In Kentucky, the SHPO sought to have the "Upper Reaches of Boone Creek Historic District"—a rural and agriculturally significant district of properties spanning approximately 10,000 acres—listed on the National Register. As the process played out in administrative hearings, public meetings, and different level of state courts, the facts shifted. Owners changed their minds on being included or not, so the exact amount of opposition was slippery. And, just how to object and the rules governing objections were unclear and unclearly conveyed. The total number of objections were pegged at 84, 88, 90, 91, 103, and 129, and even the number of properties within the boundaries changed.[50] And making matters worse, the objecting owners claimed that the SHPO was simply set on submitting the designation no matter what the owners said.

In the end, the SHPO submitted the nomination, along with the objections, and asserted that precisely 90 objections were properly filed from the 182—exactly one objection below becoming a majority. The listing was approved by the Keeper, and the next round of litigation began.

As to the owners' claim that the SHPO wrongfully denied their request to be delisted, the Sixth Circuit ruled that simply being listed on the National Register is not the sort of "injury" that supports standing. To have an "injury" for standing, the injury must be particular (i.e., not one shared by everyone else in a general sense) and not "speculative" (i.e., it has to be concrete). Although physical and monetary damages are common forms of injuries, the invasion of one's rights can itself qualify too. The question is whether a recognized sort of injury exists, not whether the size of the injury is large enough; even an "'indentifiable trifle'" is enough.[51]

---

49. Sierra Club v. Salazar, 177 F. Supp. 3d 512, 532 (D.D.C. 2016) (citing Del. Dep't of Nat. Res. & Envtl. Control v. EPA, 785 F.3d 1, 11 (D.C. Cir. 2015)).

50. Norton v. Beasley, No. 21-6053, 2022 WL 17348385, at *7 (6th Cir. Dec. 1, 2022).

51. *Id.* (quoting United States v. Students Challenging Regul. Agency Procs., 412 U.S. 669, 689 n.14 (1973)).

When the parties have standing, a challenge to a decision by the Keeper will be reviewed using an arbitrary and capricious standard. And while that is an extremely deferential standard, it is not insurmountable. For example, in *Sierra Club v. Salazar*,[52] the court ruled that a delisting had been arbitrary. After much effort by preservation and environmental groups, the Keeper of the National Register of Historic Places had added Blair Mountain to the National Register as the site of an important fight (a literal one involving homemade bombs and machine guns) between miners and strikebreakers.[53] Later, the Keeper reversed course and delisted the property at the urging of coal companies who wanted to pursue coal excavation on the land.

The ensuing litigation led to a ruling that the Keeper's delisting had been arbitrary and capricious. The long and very detailed opinion focused not on anyone's view of the property as worthy of preservation or not, but instead on the highly technical way the Keeper had counted property owners for purposes of tabulating objections to the designation. Most of the opinion reads like a primer on standards of review with the court collecting dozens of snippets from precedent fleshing out what makes a decision arbitrary and capricious. In summary, the court described the standard this way: "Although there is no formula for what constitutes reasoned decisionmaking, [the D.C.] Circuit has identified principles to guide this inquiry. This Court categorizes these principles as follows: deliberation, transparency, rationality, and evidentiary propriety."[54] The court then ticked through each of those guideposts and concluded that the Keeper had failed each of them.

A designation does *incentivize* owners to preserve their properties through beneficial tax treatment, but the NHPA does not *require* owners to preserve their properties. A congressional "carrot" is different from a "stick."[55] In fact, those who assert that their properties were wrongfully included on the National Register have been bounced from court for lacking an injury necessary for standing.[56] All the Sixth Circuit could find in

---

52. 177 F. Supp. 3d 512 (D.D.C. 2016).

53. *Id.* at 515.

54. *Id.* at 532.

55. *See* F.P. Dev., LLC v. Charter Twp. of Canton, 16 F.4th 198, 201 (6th Cir. 2021) (distinguishing "carrot" measures from "stick" ones).

56. *Norton*, 2022 WL 17348385 at *7 ("Because the NHPA places an obligation only on federal agencies, and not on the owners of listed properties, the listing of the district does not in itself injure the owners."); *see also* Moody Hill Farms Ltd. P'ship v. U.S. Dep't of Interior,

the record was evidence that the owners did not want to be included. The owners did not—despite the inclusion of their properties 13 years earlier—produce any evidence of *how* they had been injured.

The district court had relied on the *potential* impact of a National Register designation to justify standing. For example, if an owner ever wanted to apply for a coal-mining permit from the federal government, the federal government would be obligated to consider the impact of its permit on the National Register properties. While such a thing might conceivably happen in the future, the Sixth Circuit was unmoved: "[U]nsupported shoulda-coulda-woulda allegations are not enough." The owners had to have an injury that was "'certainly impending.'"[57]

It might have been possible for the unhappy owners to assert a different type of standing in connection with their due process claim. In such a case, the injury is the one to their constitutional rights in having the designation forced on them, not the resulting status as a designated property. However, the circuit court was wholly unimpressed by their argument. The owners used a single conclusory sentence that referred to an unexplained statement in dicta from a state action that there had been due process issues. The owners' argument was so underdeveloped that the court deemed it waived.

In every jurisdiction, laws might *inadvertently* promote protection of historic and architectural resources as a consequence of workaday zoning and safety laws. For example, the City of Franklin might adopt a law prohibiting buildings more than 50 feet tall or mandating the use of brick. However, in far more cases, the amount of protection a building gets depends on its zoning category or on where it is located.

Designating a building for protection can be challenged on several theories, most commonly as a violation of the equal protection clause.

---

205 F.3d 554, 562 (2d Cir. 1999) (finding that a listing on the National Register "on its own does not impose any burdens on plaintiffs' use of their property"); Arizona v. Biden, 40 F.4th 375, 383 (6th Cir. 2022) (finding a high likelihood of no injury because the challenged action did "not regulate the [plaintiffs] by telling them what they can or cannot do in their jurisdictions"); Huff v. Telecheck Servs., Inc., 923 F.3d 458, 463 (6th Cir. 2019) (finding no injury where the challenged conduct "did not 'have any effect on [the plaintiff] whatsoever'"); California v. Texas, 141 S. Ct. 2104, 2121 (2021) (Thomas, J., concurring) (agreeing with the majority's finding that the plaintiffs lacked standing because their "only [alleged] harm [was] caused by the bare existence of an unlawful statute that d[id] not impose any obligations or consequences" on them).

57. *Norton*, 2022 WL 17348385 at *8 (quoting Clapper v. Amnesty Int'l USA, 568 U.S. 398, 409 (2013)).

The equal protection clause provides: "[N]or [shall any State] deny to any person within its jurisdiction the equal protection of the laws."[58] In equal protection challenges to designation decisions, the owner's argument is basically that the owner's property does not deserve to have been placed in a protective designation on its merits (i.e., the zoning was overinclusive); that the subject property was unfairly placed in the zone while other comparable parcels were not (i.e., the zoning was underinclusive); or that the parcel was included for personal reasons unrelated to the protective zoning (i.e., the designation was a "vindictive action"). Often a property owner will lodge more than one of the challenges in the same suit.

If the SHPO either does not forward the nomination to the Keeper or simply finds that the nomination does not merit inclusion on the National Register, any person or the local government may appeal to the Keeper.[59] Failing to appeal means that the party has failed to exhaust the administrative remedies and is therefore barred from further judicial review.

Once all the preliminary steps have been finished, the nomination can finally advance to the Keeper of the National Register. The official has the power to make a decision on the nomination whether the state board believed the nomination was worthy[60] or that it was not.[61] Moreover, an appeal of a decision by the Keeper faces extremely long odds since the standard of review is mere reasonableness of the Keeper's choice. The APA provides a "narrow" standard of review, and the Keeper's decision will be upheld unless the court finds the decision to have been "arbitrary, capricious, an abuse of discretion, or otherwise not in accordance with law."[62]

B. STATE AND LOCAL DESIGNATIONS

A local historic district is one designated by a locality that is within the jurisdiction of a local historic preservation review commission. Of course, many local laws govern all manner of property rights such as use. Local

---

58. U.S. Const. amend XIV, § 1.

59. 36 C.F.R. § 60.12 (2025).

60. *Moody Hill Farms*, 205 F.3d at 558.

61. Stop H-3 Ass'n v. Coleman, 533 F.2d 434, 441 (9th Cir. 1976).

62. 5 U.S.C.A. § 706(2)(A) (West, Westlaw through Pub. L. No. 119-59); FCC v. Fox Television Stations, Inc., 556 U.S. 502, 513 (2009) (quotation omitted).

historic districts do not replace the underlying laws but rather add to them or modify them. A local historic district ordinarily does not exempt subject properties from other limits. For example, when a historic district is created, a set of zoning laws are overlaid on the included parcels, often restricting changes in the properties' appearances. A parcel within a historic district does not suddenly acquire the ability to host short-term rentals if the underlying zoning otherwise prohibits it.

There are two basic approaches to designating a building for special protection: contiguous and scattershot.

First, in contiguous zoning, a city might draw lines around neighborhoods on a map to define those areas deserving special examination, looping in all properties inside the line. For example, the fictional city of Franklin might draw a line around its historic, 19th-century wool-making center and limit changes to all those buildings within the district. Doing so risks leaving important, thematically related buildings outside the coverage of the new district because they happen to have been built a block or two too far while picking up buildings with no connection, historical or thematic, to the district based on nothing more than having been built within the lines chosen by planners.

Second, using the scattershot method, a city might include specific parcels on a case-by-case basis. For example, if the city of Franklin had used the scattershot method, a historic wool mill might have been included even if built outside the center of the city a century ago and slowly swallowed up by suburban sprawl. Without reference to its environs, the city of Franklin might want to protect the mill by granting it "landmark" status even though it is not contiguous to any other historic properties and even though nothing else within a mile is worthy of architectural protection.

One more method is sometimes seen that combines the first two. A city can designate scattershot properties that nevertheless have a common characteristic. For example, in Charleston, South Carolina, the city council adopted a Landmark Overlay Zone, which expressly applied to the then-existing, individually listed National Register properties that were not already within the coverage of the Board of Architectural Review. As with the "group basis," a collection of buildings is covered, but like in the "case-by-case basis," properties are either protected or not based on their specific circumstances. In the years since, as new properties have been individually listed on the National Register, they have not fallen within Charleston's Landmark Overlay Zone.

Adding to the complexity is *when* the decisions are made and *by whom*. A city ordinance might specifically protect certain buildings and freeze those protections. Or, a city could create a layer of zoning that is vested in a zoning board to apply on a rolling basis.

C. DESIGNATION CHALLENGES

In either scenario, owners of supposedly protection-worthy buildings might chafe at the restrictions. A locality might provide a statutory avenue for avoiding a designation or even removing one already in place. For example, in Oregon, a state law allows a property owner—but only one who owned the property at the time of the designation and not a subsequent owner—to have a designation removed.[63] In the overwhelming number of cases, no such avenue exists, and owners are left to traditional legal challenges that typically raise the same constitutional issue: Was the inclusion of a property justifiable?

Whether a building deserves to be protected at all as historic is an administrative task, not a judicial one. Unless the decision is arbitrary or irrational, it will not be changed. For example, in one case arising in New York City, the relevant body—the New York City Landmarks Preservation Commission—decided to expand an existing historical district over the objection of property owners within the newly designated block.[64] When a block of New York City was designated for protection, some of the owners challenged the designation. The court began by explaining that landmark designations are administrative, not judicial, and that public hearings are not adversarial or adjudicative but for information gathering.[65]

However, when there is no fundamental right or suspect classification alleged behind the choice of what to include, there is no equal protection violation unless there is no "rational relationship between the disparate treatment and a legitimate government objective."[66] All the government must do is establish some explanation that is "rationally related" to a "legitimate state interest" and is not arbitrary, unreasonable, or irrational. If all that has happened is that some property owners were more successful at pulling the

63. Lake Oswego Pres. Soc'y v. City of Lake Oswego Hanson, 379 P.3d 462 (Or. 2016).

64. Gilbert v. Bd. of Estimate of City of N.Y., 177 A.D.2d 252, 252 (N.Y. 1991).

65. *Id.*

66. Van Horn v. Town of Castine, 167 F. Supp. 2d 103, 107 (D. Me. 2001).

political levers to avoid a designation they did not want, the unhappy (and rezoned) owner has no claim.[67] One court has even noted that the process of drawing zoning boundaries is a legislative process that is, by its very nature, "more or less arbitrary."[68]

In *Northwestern University v. City of Evanston*,[69] Northwestern University challenged a historic district on equal protection grounds. The university is located in Evanston, Illinois, and has, for nearly 200 years, enjoyed freedom from municipal taxation because of its state charter.[70] Starting in 1997, an advocacy group began a push for a historic district that would include parts of the campus. The school strongly objected to including any of its buildings lest it lose development potential. According to the school, the historic designation was being considered only as a payback for the school's refusal to volunteer payments to Evanston to compensate the city for the services it had to provide. Eventually, a district was created over the objection of three members of city council and over the veto by the mayor.[71]

In the resulting lawsuit, Northwestern University alleged *both* forms of equal protection violations:

> In Count I, Northwestern alleges the City violated its right to equal protection by vindictively including University property in the Final Local District in retaliation for the University's refusal to make financial contributions to the City. In Count II, Northwestern maintains the City violated its right to equal protection by including University property but excluding property of similarly-situated parties in a manner that was not rationally related to any legitimate government interest.[72]

An equal protection claim is basically a "reverse" spot-zoning challenge. In a traditional spot-zoning case, a property owner is singled out to receive *beneficial* zoning treatment that is not bestowed upon supposedly similar

---

67. *Id.* at 108 ("A local government's responsiveness to political pressure is neither arbitrary, nor unreasonable, nor irrational.").

68. Fairfax County v. Williams, 216 S.E.2d 33, 41 (Va. 1975).

69. No. 00 C 7309, 2002 WL 31027981, at *3 (N.D. Ill. Sept. 11, 2002).

70. *Id.*, 2002 WL 31027981, at *1.

71. *Id.* at *2.

72. *Id.* at *3.

properties. A "reverse" spot zoning is the same idea except that the zoning allegedly *burdens* the oddball property while not burdening like properties.[73]

In the case against Evanston, the university alleged that *traditional* equal protection protections had been violated when Evanston drew maps that included its properties while also excluding other properties that were at least equally as important to the supposed zoning goals. In other words, the university alleged a sort of preservation gerrymander. To win, the university had to prove that (1) it was being treated differently than similar properties and that (2) no rational basis existed for the different treatment.[74] The "deferential rational basis test" begins with a presumption that a rational basis for the city's line drawing exists,[75] and the challenger bears the burden of overcoming that presumption.[76]

Northwestern pointed to a decision during the drafting of the historic boundaries to exclude 13 properties after the owners of all the buildings in a small area said they were opposed to the designation.[77] Even though the buildings would have been contributing to the district's theme, the court ruled that the exclusion of them had been rational. The court explained, "'The opinion of area residents concerning neighborhood preservation is an appropriate factor for consideration in zoning decisions.'"[78] Plausibility is a very low threshold to overcome, and "zoning is inescapably a political function."[79] Judge Posner once remarked that

> nothing is more common in zoning disputes than selfish opposition to zoning changes. The Constitution does not forbid government to yield to such opposition; it does not outlaw the characteristic operations of democratic . . . government, operations which are permeated by pressure from special interests.[80]

---

73. Peck Slip Assocs., L.L.C. v. City Council of City of N.Y., 789 N.Y.S.2d 806 (Sup. Ct. 2004), *aff'd sub nom.* Peck Slip Assocs. LLC v. City Council of City of N.Y., 809 N.Y.S.2d 56 (2006).

74. Nw. Univ. v. City of Evanston, No. 00 C 7309, 2002 WL 31027981, at *4 (N.D. Ill. Sept. 11, 2002).

75. Hager v. City of West Peoria, 84 F.3d 865, 872 (7th Cir. 1996).

76. Heller v. Doe, 509 U.S. 312, 320 (1993).

77. *Nw. Univ.*, 2002 WL 31027981 at *5.

78. *Id.* (quoting Nelson v. City of Selma, 881 F.2d 836, 840 (9th Cir. 1989)).

79. Sylvia Dev. Corp. v. Calvert Cnty., 48 F.3d 810, 828 (4th Cir. 1995).

80. Coniston Corp. v. Vill. of Hoffman Ests., 844 F.2d 461, 467 (7th Cir. 1988).

The university nevertheless argued that it was being treated differently, not just on the merits of the buildings but on the fact that, if the 13 properties could be excluded based only on their owners' objection, then the school too should have its properties excluded based on nothing more than its objection. In response to that argument, the court explained that there was a different fear about redevelopment and density on the university's parcels that was not as present in the 13 excluded properties; protecting against noise, traffic, encroachment of dissimilar uses, and overcrowding are all rational justifications for the lines used.[81]

Next, the university argued that the supposed justifications for different treatment of the properties were mere pretext and that the school was itself being purposely singled out in retribution for unrelated financial issues. The court, however, rejected that argument and explained that the *real* reason for rational action is not important in most cases—at least in traditional equal protection cases.[82] Rather, what matters is that such an explanation *could* explain the distinction. Legislatures may be motivated by one particular actor and the dangers that that actor might cause as long as the resulting legislation is generally applicable and rationally related to the problem.[83]

Subjective motivation for a designation can, however, be considered in a *non-traditional* equal protection case. To establish a "vindictive action" equal protection claim, a challenger must show that it is, in all relevant respects, identical to others and that the cause of the different treatment is, in reality, a "totally illegitimate animus toward the plaintiff by the defendant."[84] Only that sort of equal protection claim delves into the legislature's actual subjective motivation.

The unresolved issue in vindictive action suits is how widespread the animus must be to taint the resulting law. Since historic designations will almost always be decided by zoning boards or commissions or perhaps by city councils, does the motivation of one or two members satisfy the burden

81. *Nw. Univ.*, 2002 WL 31027981 at *5.

82. When the alleged real reason is one that would trigger heightened scrutiny, the analysis shifts to discrimination where motivation is a concern. *Id.* at *6 n.14.

83. *Id.* at *6. When a law expressly applies to only one actor or has no realistic application other than to one actor, the enactment itself might be challenged as a bill of attainder. *Id.* at *6 n.13.

84. Albiero v. City of Kankakee, 246 F.3d 927, 932 (7th Cir. 2001) (quoting Olech v. Vill. of Willowbrook, 160 F.3d 386, 388 (7th Cir. 1998) (internal citations omitted).

of proving that the body itself shared those motives? Some courts have ruled that proof of a "significant bloc" of the body is enough, while others have held that a majority of the votes must have been infected by improper purposes.[85] Both views can be justified:

> The precedent in this area is uncertain, and persuasive arguments can be made on both sides. On the one hand, because a municipal ordinance can become law only by a majority vote of the city council, there is a certain incongruity in allowing fewer than a majority of the council members to subject the city to liability under section 1983. On the other hand, because discriminatory animus is insidious and a clever pretext can be hard to unmask, the law sometimes constructs procedural devices to ease a victim's burden of proof.[86]

Not only do challenges to designations face a difficult test, but their position grows harder on further appeal where the standard of review is abuse of discretion.[87]

---

85. *Compare* United States v. City of Yonkers, 856 F.2d 444, 457–58 (2d Cir. 1988) *and* Church v. City of Huntsville, 30 F.3d 1332, 1343–44 (11th Cir. 1994)) *with* United States v. City of Birmingham, 538 F. Supp. 819, 828 (E.D. Mich. 1982), *aff'd*, 727 F.2d 560 (6th Cir. 1984) *and* United States v. Yonkers Bd. of Educ., 837 F.2d 1181, 1221–23 (2d Cir. 1987).

86. Scott-Harris v. City of Fall River, 134 F.3d 427, 438 (1st Cir. 1997), *rev'd sub nom.* Bogan v. Scott-Harris, 523 U.S. 44 (1998) (citations omitted).

87. Osuchowski v. City of Syracuse, 56 A.D.3d 1189, 1189 (N.Y. App. Div. 2008).

The National Historic Preservation Act

3

The National Historic Preservation Act (NHPA) of 1966 stands as one of the most significant U.S. legislative actions aimed at protecting and preserving the nation's historical and cultural resources.[1] Enacted in response to widespread concern over the loss of historic sites amid rapid urban development and infrastructure expansion, the NHPA laid the foundation for a comprehensive preservation policy.[2] It established structures, processes, and funding mechanisms

1. Pub. L. No. 89-665, Oct. 15, 1966, 80 Stat. 915; *see* National Park Service, *National Historic Preservation Act of 1966*, www.nps.gov/subjects/archeology/national-historic-preservation-act.htm (last visited Feb. 14, 2026); *see* 54 U.S.C.A. §§ 300101–320303 (Westlaw through Pub. L. No. 119-59).

2. Section 1 of the National Historic Preservation Act (Pub. L. No. 89-665, as amended by Pub. L. No. 96-515); *see* 54 U.S.C.A. § 300101 (Westlaw through Pub. L. No. 119-59); National Park Service, *National Historic Preservation Act of 1966*, *supra* n.131 ("By the mid-1960s, federally-funded infrastructure and urban renewal projects had resulted in the rapid destruction of places significant in the nation's history . . . [the Act] was enacted in recognition that historic places were being lost or altered, and that preservation was in the public's interest.").

to identify, evaluate, and protect historic properties, reflecting a growing recognition of the value of America's cultural heritage.[3] This chapter examines the NHPA's framework for historic preservation, with particular focus on the Section 106 review process, the National Register of Historic Places, and the roles of federal, state, and local actors in preservation planning. Understanding the NHPA is essential for attorneys advising clients on development projects, government agencies undertaking federal actions, and property owners seeking to list or protect historic resources.

A. ORIGINS AND CONTEXT

The mid-20th century in the United States was marked by dramatic changes in urban landscapes fueled by economic growth, suburbanization, and federal infrastructure projects like the Interstate Highway System.[4] These developments often came at the expense of older buildings and neighborhoods, prompting concerns from historians, architects, and the public about the irreversible loss of America's historic fabric.[5] The 1963 demolition of New York's Pennsylvania Station, a Beaux-Arts architectural masterpiece, became a rallying point for preservation advocates.[6]

In this context, Congress passed the NHPA in 1966, influenced by the recommendations of the 1966 report "With Heritage So Rich," which emphasized the irreplaceable nature of historic sites and called for a national

---

3. *See* 54 U.S.C.A. §§ 300101–320303 (Westlaw through Pub. L. No. 119-59) (formerly 16 U.S.C. § 470 (repealed 2014)); National Park Service, *National Historic Preservation Act of 1966*, *supra* n.131.

4. *See* Jess R. Phelps, *The National Historic Preservation Act at Fifty: Surveying the Forest Service Experience*, 47 Envtl. L. 471, 478 (2017) (describing "large-scale urban renewal projects during the post-World War II build-out" as a key inspiration for the NHPA).

5. *See* Advisory Council on Historic Preservation, *The National Historic Preservation Program at 50: Priorities and Recommendations for the Future*, 2 (Mar. 2017), www.achp.gov/digital-library-section-106-landing/national-historic-preservation-program-50-priorities-and ("Neighborhoods were destroyed, historic buildings razed, and archaeological sites ravaged.") (last visited Feb. 14, 2026).

6. Eric J. Plosky, *The Fall and Rise of Pennsylvania Station: Changing Attitudes Toward Historic Preservation in New York City* (Mass. Inst. of Tech. 2000), https://dspace.mit.edu/bitstream/handle/1721.1/69419/45617506-MIT.pdf?sequence=2&isAllowed=y; Michael Kimmelman, *When the Old Penn Station Was Demolished, New York Lost Its Faith*, N.Y. Times (Apr. 24, 2019), www.nytimes.com/2019/04/24/nyregion/old-penn-station-pictures-new-york.html.

preservation policy.[7] The Act was signed into law by President Lyndon B. Johnson on October 15, 1966.[8]

B. OBJECTIVES OF THE NHPA

The NHPA was designed with several key objectives. First, at the highest level, the NHPA works to establish clear national and legislative policy for the preservation of historic properties.[9] Moreover, by creating administrative frameworks that both identify and protect these historic properties, the NHPA provides the foundation for historic preservation policy federally, and inspires similar efforts locally.[10] The NHPA also encourages federal, state, local, and private efforts in historic preservation.[11]

In addition to providing the foundations for historic preservation while simultaneously demonstrating the need for coordinated efforts among federal, state, and municipal governments, the NHPA provides for greater future historic preservation efforts by forcing the integration of these concerns in ongoing development planning.[12] The NHPA also promotes public awareness and appreciation of the nation's historical and cultural heritage.[13]

C. KEY PROVISIONS OF THE NHPA

The NHPA introduced several landmark provisions that have had a lasting impact on historic preservation in the United States.

---

7. U.S. Conf. of Mayors Special Comm. on Hist. Pres., *With Heritage So Rich* (Helen D. Bullock & Joseph Watterson eds., 1966), www.slideshare.net/PreservationNation/with-heritage-so-rich-compressed?utm_source=chatgpt.com; *see* ADVISORY COUNCIL ON HISTORIC PRESERVATION, *supra* note 5, at 2 ("The report influenced Congress to enact a strong, new statute establishing a nationwide preservation policy[.]").

8. ADVISORY COUNCIL ON HISTORIC PRESERVATION, *supra* n.135, at 2.

9. 54 U.S.C.A. § 300101 (Westlaw through Pub. L. No. 119-59).

10. 54 U.S.C.A. §§ 302101–302108 (Westlaw through Pub. L. No. 113-287).

11. *Id.*; 54 U.S.C.A. § 300101(5)–(6).

12. 54 U.S.C.A. §§ 306101–306112 (Westlaw through Pub. L. No. 113-287); 54 U.S.C.A. § 300101(3).

13. 54 U.S.C.A. §§ 300101(5), 305101–305505; Pub. L. No. 89-665, as amended by Pub. L. No. 96-515 (emphasizing the positive impact of "increased knowledge of our historic resources" on "growth and development").

1. National Register of Historic Places (NRHP)

The Act established the NRHP as an official list of districts, sites, buildings, structures, and objects deemed worthy of preservation.[14] Properties listed in the Register can qualify for federal preservation grants and tax incentives.[15] The criteria for listing properties on the National Register are outlined in 36 C.F.R. § 60.4,[16] which requires that properties possess integrity of location, design, setting, materials, workmanship, feeling, and association and meet at least one of four criteria related to historical significance.[17]

The significance of National Register listing was examined in *National Trust for Historic Preservation v. Blanck*,[18] where the court considered whether listing a property on the National Register created enforceable rights against federal agencies.[19] The court held that while listing provides certain procedural protections under Section 106, it does not create a substantive right to prevent all adverse effects on the property.[20] This distinction between procedural and substantive protections has become a cornerstone of NHPA jurisprudence.

The four criteria for National Register eligibility reflect different dimensions of historical significance. Criterion A encompasses properties associated with events that have made significant contributions to the broad patterns of American history. This criterion has proven particularly flexible, covering everything from Civil War battlefields to sites associated with the Civil Rights Movement to properties reflecting industrial or agricultural history. Courts have generally deferred to the National Park Service's expertise in determining what constitutes a significant contribution to broad historical patterns, though they have required agencies to articulate a reasoned basis for such determinations.

Criterion B addresses properties associated with the lives of persons significant in our past. This criterion has sometimes generated controversy regarding how "significant" a person must be to justify listing. The National

14. 54 U.S.C.A. §§ 302101–302108; Advisory Council on Historic Preservation, *supra* note 5, at 2.

15. 54 U.S.C.A. §§ 302901–302910; 26 U.S.C.A. § 47(a)–(b), (c)(3) (Westlaw through Pub. L. No. 119-12).

16. 36 C.F.R. § 60.4 (2025).

17. *Id.* at § 60.4(a)–(g).

18. 938 F. Supp. 908 (D.D.C. 1996).

19. *Id.* at 916–24.

20. 54 U.S.C.A. §§ 302303 (Westlaw through Pub. L. No. 113-287).

Park Service has developed guidance indicating that mere local prominence is generally insufficient; the person must have made demonstrable contributions of national or statewide importance. Additionally, the property must be associated with the person's productive life, not merely their residence at some point. The question of which properties associated with living persons can be listed has also been addressed through regulations limiting such listings to exceptional circumstances.

Criterion C focuses on properties that embody distinctive characteristics of a type, period, or method of construction; represent the work of a master, or possess high artistic values; or represent a significant and distinguishable entity whose components may lack individual distinction. This criterion has enabled the listing of architectural resources ranging from individual buildings of exceptional design to vernacular structures that exemplify regional building traditions. The concept of a "master" has been interpreted broadly to include not only famous architects but also skilled craftspeople and builders whose work demonstrates exceptional achievement.

Criterion D addresses properties that have yielded, or may be likely to yield, information important in prehistory or history. While originally conceived primarily for archaeological sites, this criterion has proven applicable to a broader range of resources, including historic structures that may contain information about construction techniques or material culture. The "may be likely to yield" language makes clear that actual excavation or investigation is not required for eligibility; potential information value suffices.

Beyond meeting one of these four criteria, properties must possess integrity—the ability to convey their significance through retention of physical characteristics. The seven aspects of integrity identified in the regulations (location, design, setting, materials, workmanship, feeling, and association) need not all be present; the particular aspects critical for a property depend on its significance. A property significant for its association with an event (Criterion A) might retain integrity even with alterations to its design, while a property significant for architectural merit (Criterion C) would typically require greater retention of original design features. This flexible approach to integrity has allowed the National Register to accommodate properties that have evolved over time while still conveying their historic character.

2. State Historic Preservation Offices (SHPOs)

The NHPA required each state to establish a SHPO to manage preservation activities, maintain an inventory of historic properties, and oversee the nomination of sites to the NRHP.[21] SHPOs serve as the primary state-level liaisons in the Section 106 consultation process and play a crucial role in identifying and evaluating historic properties within their jurisdictions.

The role and authority of SHPOs were clarified in *Muckleshoot Indian Tribe v. U.S. Forest Service*,[22] where the court emphasized that while SHPOs have significant expertise and authority in the Section 106 process, their determinations are not binding on federal agencies.[23] However, agencies must give substantial weight to SHPO recommendations and provide reasoned explanations for any departures from SHPO guidance.[24]

SHPOs have evolved into sophisticated agencies with broad responsibilities extending well beyond Section 106 consultation. Each SHPO maintains a comprehensive inventory of historic properties within its state, conducts survey and identification programs, administers federal and state grants, provides technical assistance to property owners and local governments, and implements public education programs. The organizational placement of SHPOs varies among states—some are housed within state park agencies, others within departments of economic development or culture, and still others operate as independent agencies. SHPOs are appointed by the "chief elected official of the State" per 54 U.S.C. § 302301(1).

The staffing and expertise within SHPOs reflect the multidisciplinary nature of historic preservation. Most SHPOs employ architectural historians, archaeologists, historians, and preservation planners, along with administrative staff to manage grant programs and process National Register nominations. The federal government, through the National Park Service, provides funding to support SHPO operations, though this funding typically covers only a portion of costs. States supplement federal funding

---

21. 54 U.S.C.A. §§ 302301–302303 (Westlaw through Pub. L. No. 113-287); National Park Service, *State Historic Preservation Offices*, www.nps.gov/subjects/historicpreservation/national-historic-preservation-act.htm (last visited Feb. 14, 2026); Advisory Council on Historic Preservation, *supra* note 5, at 2.

22. 177 F.3d 800 (9th Cir. 1999).

23. *Id.* at 806 ("The Forest Service initially concluded that the Huckleberry Divide Trail ('Divide Trail') was ineligible for listing. After the SHPO suggested otherwise, the Forest Service reconsidered and found it eligible for listing but nonetheless included it in the lands exchanged to Weyerhaeuser.").

24. *See id.* The Section 106 regulations provide that disputes regarding eligibility are ultimately resolved by the Advisory Council on Historic Preservation. *See* 36 C.F.R. § 800.4(d)(1)(ii) (2025).

with varying levels of state appropriations, creating significant disparities in SHPO capacity across different states.

One critical SHPO function involves maintaining and updating statewide historic preservation plans. These plans identify preservation priorities, assess threats to historic resources, and establish strategies for addressing preservation challenges. The quality and comprehensiveness of these plans vary considerably, with some states developing detailed, data-driven analyses while others produce more perfunctory documents. These plans can play an important role in Section 106 consultations by providing context for how the SHPO evaluates the significance of particular properties and the relative severity of different adverse effects.

SHPOs also serve as the primary point of contact between federal agencies and state and local preservation constituencies during the Section 106 process. This intermediary role requires SHPOs to balance multiple interests—responding to federal agency schedules and needs, representing state preservation priorities, and incorporating input from local governments, tribal governments, and the public. The effectiveness with which individual SHPOs manage these competing demands significantly affects the overall functioning of the Section 106 process within their jurisdictions.

3. Section 106 Review Process

Section 106 of the NHPA requires federal agencies to consider the impact of their "undertakings" on historic properties and to provide the Advisory Council on Historic Preservation (ACHP) an opportunity to comment. More than a simple veto, Section 106 does not require agencies to choose the least harmful alternative or to avoid all impacts on historic properties. Rather, it mandates a procedural review: agencies must identify historic properties, assess effects, resolve effects that are adverse, and consult with stakeholders at each stage before making final decisions.[25]

The procedural nature of Section 106 has been extensively litigated. In the landmark case *Preservation Coalition, Inc. v. Pierce*,[26] the Ninth Circuit established that Section 106 imposes procedural requirements but does

25. 54 U.S.C.A. § 306108 (Westlaw through Pub. L. No. 119-59) (requiring the head of both those with jurisdiction and authority over an undertaking to "take into account the effect of the undertaking on any historic property" and to "afford the Council a reasonable opportunity to comment with regard to the undertaking").

26. 667 F.2d 851–60 (9th Cir. 1982).

not mandate any particular substantive outcome.[27] The court held that once an agency has complied with the consultation process and considered the ACHP's comments, it may proceed with an undertaking even if it will result in adverse effects to historic properties.[28] This interpretation has been consistently followed by courts across the country.

The scope of what constitutes an "undertaking" subject to Section 106 review was addressed in *Morris County Trust for Historic Preservation v. Pierce*.[29] The court held that federal approval of funding for a project constitutes an undertaking, triggering Section 106 obligations.[30] The court emphasized that the review must occur early enough in the planning process to allow genuine consideration of alternatives and mitigation measures.[31]

In *Te-Moak Tribe of Western Shoshone of Nevada v. U.S. Department of Interior*,[32] the Ninth Circuit examined the temporal scope of Section 106 compliance, holding that agencies cannot segment their review to avoid considering cumulative effects on historic properties.[33] The court held that the Bureau of Land Management had violated Section 106 by failing to consider the aggregate impact of multiple related actions related to a gold mine expansion.[34]

The definition of "adverse effect" under Section 106 was explored in *National Trust for Historic Pres. v. U.S. Army Corps of Engineers*.[35] The

---

27. *Id.* at 859 ("On balance, the careful manner in which the BRA considered historic information and the thoroughness of its statement explaining its decision not to require an EIS convinces us that the BRA's finding of no significant impact on the historic environment was reasonable.").

28. *See id.*

29. 714 F.2d 271 (3d Cir. 1983).

30. *Id.* at 279 ("Moreover, if the statute intended to establish a cut-off once an agency gave preliminary approval to expenditures, one might expect it to read 'prior to the approval of the undertaking,' rather than prior to the approval of the expenditure of any Federal funds on the undertaking.").

31. *Id.* ("Thus, the first sentence of § 106 states that a federal agency having jurisdiction over a 'proposed Federal or federally-assisted undertaking' shall consider its effect on listed properties.").

32. 608 F.3d 592 (9th Cir. 2010).

33. *Id.* at 603 ("In a cumulative impact analysis, an agency must take a 'hard look' at all actions. An EA's analysis of cumulative impacts 'must give a sufficiently detailed catalogue of past, present, and future projects, and provide adequate analysis about how these projects, and differences between the projects, are thought to have impacted the environment.'").

34. *Id.*

35. 552 F. Supp. 784 (S.D. Ohio 1982).

court held that adverse effects include not only direct physical damage but also indirect effects such as changes to a property's setting, context, or the patterns of use that contribute to its historic significance.[36] This broad interpretation ensures comprehensive consideration of impacts on historic properties, which has been reinforced by the definition of "adverse effect" provided in the Section 106 regulations. The interpretation in this case was reinforced by the specific definition of adverse effects in the Section 106 regulations in 2000.[37]

4. Advisory Council on Historic Preservation (ACHP)

The Act created the ACHP as an independent federal agency to advise the president and Congress on preservation policy and to oversee the Section 106 review process.[38] The ACHP has promulgated regulations at 36 C.F.R. pt. 800 that provide detailed procedures for Section 106 compliance.[39]

The authority and role of the ACHP were examined in *Vieux Carre Property Owners v. Brown*,[40] where the court considered whether the ACHP's comments were binding on federal agencies.[41] The court held that while agencies must afford the ACHP a reasonable opportunity to comment, the ACHP's recommendations are advisory rather than mandatory.[42] However, agencies must consider the ACHP's comments in good faith and provide reasoned explanations for decisions that diverge from ACHP guidance.[43]

---

36. *Id.* at 788 ("The Advisory Council's Criteria of Adverse Effect Section 800.3(b)(1) are applicable because the proposed barge facility could diminish the historical integrity of the Anderson Ferry through visual impact.").

37. *See* 36 C.F.R. § 800.5(1) (2025).

38. 54 U.S.C.A. § 304101 (Westlaw through Pub. L. No. 119-59) ("There is established as an independent agency of the United States an Advisory Council on Historic Preservation[.]").

39. 36 C.F.R. pt. 800 (2025).

40. 948 F.2d 1436 (5th Cir. 1991).

41. *Id.* at 1445.

42. *Id.* at 1447 ("As the Corps points out, the Advisory Council's comments are advisory only and do not bind the Corps to a particular course of action.").

43. *Id.* at 1445 ("The district court also found that to require historic review of the park project after its 'virtual completion' would unduly penalize private developers who acted in good faith reliance on the Corps's representations that the project could proceed as proposed."); *see also* Friends of Atglen-Susquehanna Trail v. Surface Transp. Bd., 252 F.3d 246 (3d Cir. 2001) (ruling that the STB did not afford the Council a reasonable opportunity to comment when it

The ACHP occupies a unique position in the federal preservation infrastructure. As an independent agency, it maintains a degree of separation from both the regulatory agencies it advises and the advocacy organizations that promote preservation. The Council's membership reflects this intermediary status, consisting of representatives from federal agencies, state and local governments, tribal governments, and the private sector, along with expert members appointed by the president. This diverse composition enables the ACHP to consider multiple perspectives when developing policy guidance and commenting on specific undertakings.

Over its nearly 60-year history, the ACHP's role has evolved significantly. Initially focused primarily on reviewing individual Section 106 cases and issuing formal comments, the Council has increasingly emphasized policy development, technical guidance, and training. The ACHP's regulations at 36 C.F.R. pt. 800 have been revised multiple times to streamline procedures, clarify agency obligations, and address new preservation challenges. These regulations function as the primary implementation mechanism for Section 106, translating the statute's general requirement to "take into account" effects on historic properties into specific procedural steps.

The Council has also developed numerous program alternatives and guidance documents that provide flexibility in Section 106 compliance. These include provisions for programmatic agreements covering categories of undertakings, exemptions for undertakings with minimal potential to affect historic properties, and procedures for resolving disputes among consulting parties. This emphasis on flexibility reflects a pragmatic recognition that rigid, one-size-fits-all procedures would prove unworkable given the enormous variety of federal undertakings subject to Section 106 review. In 2016, Congress created a full-time role for an ACHP chair.[44]

5. Certified Local Governments (CLGs)

The NHPA encouraged the establishment of CLGs, which are local governments that meet federal standards for preservation and are eligible for grants and technical assistance.[45] The CLG program, established through

"terminated" consultation, which is the definition of the process that allows them to proceed with an objectionable ACHP comment).

44. *See* Advisory Council on Historic Preservation, *Congress Authorizes ACHP Full-Time Chairman and Reauthorizes Historic Preservation Fund*, www.achp.gov/news/congress-authorizes-achp-full-time-chairman-and-reauthorizes-historic-preservation-fund (Dec. 19, 2026) (last visited Feb. 14, 2026).

45. 54 U.S.C.A. §§ 302501–302505 (Westlaw through Pub. L. No. 119-59).

the 1980 amendments to the NHPA, creates a partnership between federal, state, and local governments in preservation efforts.[46]

The CLG program represents an important extension of the federal preservation framework to the municipal level. To achieve CLG certification, a local government must meet several requirements: enforce appropriate legislation for the designation and protection of historic properties, establish an adequate and qualified historic preservation review commission, maintain a system for the survey and inventory of historic properties, and provide for adequate public participation in the local preservation program. These requirements ensure that CLG designation reflects genuine local preservation capacity rather than merely nominal compliance.

CLG certification provides several benefits beyond eligibility for federal grant funding. Certified local governments gain a formal role in the Section 106 consultation process for undertakings affecting properties within their jurisdictions. They also receive certain preferences in National Register nominations and enhanced access to technical assistance from their SHPOs. Perhaps most importantly, CLG status signals to property owners, developers, and the general public that the locality takes preservation seriously and has established professional standards for preservation decision-making.

The distribution of CLGs across the United States remains uneven. Some states have robust CLG programs with dozens of certified communities, while others have only a handful. This variation reflects differences in state commitment to the program, the strength of local preservation constituencies, and the resources available to support local preservation activities. Urban communities have been more likely to pursue CLG certification than rural ones, partly because they typically possess greater administrative capacity and face more acute development pressures threatening historic resources.

D. THE SECTION 106 CERTIFICATION PROCESS

The Section 106 process consists of several distinct steps, each with specific requirements and potential for legal challenges. At every stage in the process, the regulations stress consultation with the effected parties. Understanding these steps is essential for practitioners navigating preservation law.

46. *See* Hualapai Indian Tribe v. Haaland, 755 F. Supp. 3d 1165 (D. Ariz. 2024); 54 U.S.C.A. § 300101 (Westlaw through Pub. L. No. 119-59).

1. Initiation and Identification

The process begins when a federal agency determines it has an undertaking that may affect historic properties. The agency must first establish the undertaking's area of potential effects (APE), which is the geographic area within which the undertaking may directly or indirectly cause alterations in the character or use of historic properties. Once the APE is established, the agency identifies eligible historic properties within the APE. *National Mining Association v. Slater*[47] upheld the ACHP regulations that allowed for protections of all listed and eligible NRHP properties in Section 106 consultation. And so, each consultation requires the agency to ensure it is accounting for the most updated information. Identification of efforts is governed by a standard of reasonableness based on the nature of the undertaking.[48]

In *Communities Against Runway Expansion, Inc. v. FAA*,[49] the court held that the Federal Aviation Administration's determination of the APE was arbitrary and capricious because it failed to consider noise impacts that extended beyond the physical footprint of runway construction.[50] This case illustrates that the APE must encompass all areas where effects may occur, not just areas of direct physical impact.

Determining the appropriate APE represents one of the most consequential early decisions in the Section 106 process. An APE drawn too narrowly may exclude historic properties that will actually be affected by the undertaking, potentially resulting in inadequate review and legal vulnerability. An APE drawn too broadly may impose unnecessary consultation burdens and delay project timelines. Federal agencies must balance these competing concerns while ensuring compliance with regulatory requirements.

The regulatory definition of APE focuses on where the undertaking "may directly or indirectly cause alterations in the character or use of historic properties." This language requires agencies to consider not only physical impacts but also visual, auditory, and other sensory effects that might diminish a property's integrity. For linear projects like highways or pipelines, the APE typically extends outward from the physical footprint

47. 167 F. Supp. 2d 265, 285 (D.D.C. 2001).

48. Pueblo of Sandia v. United States, 50 F.3d 856 (10th Cir. 1995).

49. 355 F.3d 678, 681 (D.C. Cir. 2004) (citing Robertson v. Methow Valley Citizens Council, 490 U.S. 332, 349 (1989)).

50. *Id.*

to encompass areas visible from the undertaking or from which the undertaking will be visible. The specific distance varies depending on topography, vegetation, and the scale of the undertaking.

Particularly complex APE determinations arise for undertakings with multiple types of effects. A dam project, for example, might have direct physical effects within the reservoir area, visual effects extending to viewsheds from the dam structure, noise effects in adjacent areas, and induced development effects in surrounding communities that gain improved access to water or power. Similarly, telecommunications towers may have limited physical footprints but significant visual effects extending for considerable distances. Agencies must consider all reasonably foreseeable effects when delineating the APE.

Consultation with the SHPO typically occurs during APE development, and SHPO concurrence with the APE determination is generally sought before proceeding with identification efforts. This early consultation helps ensure that the APE reflects appropriate consideration of all potential effects and incorporates relevant expertise. However, the APE is not immutable; if new information emerges during the Section 106 process indicating that effects will extend beyond the initially defined APE, the agency must revise the APE accordingly.

2. Assessment of Effects

Once historic properties within the APE are identified, the agency must assess whether the undertaking will have an effect on these properties. Under 36 C.F.R. § 800.5,[51] an undertaking has an adverse effect when it may diminish the integrity of a property's location, design, setting, materials, workmanship, feeling, or association.[52]

The standards for assessing effects were examined in *Druid Hills Civic Association v. Federal Highway Administration*.[53] The court held that the Federal Highway Administration had failed to adequately consider visual and auditory impacts of a highway project on a historic district.[54] The

51. 36 C.F.R. § 800.5 (2025).

52. *Id.*

53. 772 F.2d 700 (11th Cir. 1985).

54. *Id.* at 716–17 ("From this it is evident that the administrative record must contain adequate information to enable the Secretary to weigh the relative damage to protected properties which would result from building each of these roads.").

decision emphasized that effects assessment must consider all aspects of a property's historic character, including intangible elements like setting and feeling.

The Section 106 regulations establish three possible findings regarding effects: no historic properties affected, no adverse effect, or adverse effect. Each finding has different procedural implications. A finding of no historic properties affected terminates the Section 106 process, though it requires documentation demonstrating either that no historic properties exist within the APE or that the undertaking is designed to avoid any effects on such properties. This finding must be supported by adequate identification efforts—an agency cannot claim no historic properties are affected simply because it failed to look for them.

A finding of no adverse effect acknowledges that the undertaking will affect historic properties but concludes that these effects do not rise to the level of diminishing integrity. Examples might include routine maintenance activities that preserve a property's character, installation of equipment in a manner that respects historic fabric, alterations that are consistent with a property's historic use and character or otherwise consistent with the Secretary of the Interior's Standards. The regulations specify that an undertaking has no adverse effect when it does not diminish the characteristics that qualify the property for inclusion in the National Register. This standard requires careful analysis of which characteristics qualify a particular property and how the undertaking will affect those specific characteristics.

An adverse effect finding triggers the most extensive consultation requirements under Section 106. The regulations provide examples of adverse effects, including physical destruction or damage, alteration inconsistent with the Secretary of the Interior's Standards, removal from or alteration of the property's setting, introduction of visual or audible elements out of character with the property, and neglect leading to deterioration. These examples are illustrative rather than exhaustive—any action that diminishes integrity constitutes an adverse effect.

One area of ongoing debate involves cumulative effects—situations where an individual undertaking might have only minimal effects but contributes to a pattern of incrementally harmful actions. The regulations require consideration of cumulative effects, but applying this requirement in practice poses challenges. When does the accumulation of minor effects become an adverse effect? How far back in time should past actions be considered when assessing cumulative effects? How should reasonably foreseeable future actions be incorporated into the analysis? Courts have generally required agencies to address cumulative effects but have not imposed rigid methodologies for such analyses.

3. Consultation and Resolution

If an undertaking will have an adverse effect, the agency must consult with the SHPO, ACHP, and other consulting parties to seek ways to avoid, minimize, or mitigate the adverse effects. The goal of consultation is "to identify historic properties potentially affected by the undertaking, assess its effects and seek ways to avoid, minimize or mitigate any adverse effects on historic properties" and that it be done in the early stages of project planning.[55] This consultation typically results in a memorandum of agreement (MOA) that stipulates agreed-upon mitigation measures.

The adequacy of consultation was challenged in *Te-Moak Tribe of Western Shoshone v. U.S. Department of Interior*.[56] The court held that the Bureau of Land Management had failed to engage in meaningful consultation with Native American tribes regarding a mining project's effects on sacred sites.[57] The decision emphasized that consultation must be genuine and occur early enough in the planning process to allow for substantive input.[58]

In *National Trust for Historic Preservation in the U.S. v. Federal Deposit Insurance Corp.*,[59] the court held that while MOAs represent binding commitments by federal agencies, private parties generally lack standing to enforce MOAs unless they can demonstrate that Congress intended to create private rights of action. This limitation on private enforcement has significant implications for preservation advocates seeking to hold agencies accountable.

MOAs represent negotiated solutions to adverse effects on historic properties. The content of MOAs varies tremendously depending on the

55. 36 C.F.R. § 800.1 (2025).

56. 608 F.3d 592 (9th Cir. 2010).

57. *Id.* at 603 ("In a cumulative impact analysis, an agency must take a 'hard look' at all actions. An EA's analysis of cumulative impacts 'must give a sufficiently detailed catalogue of past, present, and future projects, and provide adequate analysis about how these projects, and differences between the projects, are thought to have impacted the environment.'").

58. *Id.*

59. 995 F.2d 238 (D.C. Cir. 1993).

nature of the undertaking, the significance of affected properties, and the interests of consulting parties. Some MOAs are brief documents stipulating straightforward mitigation measures like documentation or salvage. Others are lengthy, complex agreements addressing multiple properties and implementing phased mitigation programs extending over many years.

Effective MOAs typically follow a structure that includes stipulations (the specific commitments the agency agrees to undertake), procedures for implementing the stipulations, provisions for dispute resolution, conditions for amendment or termination, and identification of the signatories. The stipulations themselves might address measures to avoid adverse effects, minimize such effects, or mitigate unavoidable effects. Common mitigation measures include documentation through drawings, photographs, or written histories; archaeological data recovery; interpretive programs; rehabilitation of related historic properties; and restrictions on future alterations.

The question of what constitutes adequate mitigation has generated considerable discussion but relatively little case law. Unlike environmental mitigation under NEPA, where courts have developed doctrines regarding the relationship between impact severity and mitigation extent, Section 106 mitigation operates within a more discretionary framework. The regulations require only that consulting parties seek agreement on measures to avoid, minimize, or mitigate adverse effects. They do not establish quantitative standards for determining when mitigation is sufficient. This flexibility allows tailored solutions but can also result in inconsistency across different consultations.

E. STANDING AND PROCEDURAL REQUIREMENTS

Courts have consistently held that Section 106 creates procedural rather than substantive rights. This distinction affects both the scope of judicial review and the types of remedies available to challengers.

In *Presidio Golf Club v. National Park Service*,[60] the court held that plaintiffs challenging Section 106 compliance must demonstrate that the agency failed to follow required procedures, not merely that it made an incorrect substantive decision.[61] The court emphasized that once an agency

---

60. 155 F.3d 1153 (9th Cir. 1998).

61. *Id.* at 1161 ("The Park Service also considered the option of leasing the Club but rejected that option because the cost of retrofitting would be prohibitive, and because the covenants,

has complied with consultation requirements and considered preservation concerns, courts will not second-guess the agency's ultimate decision regarding the undertaking.[62]

The question of who has standing to challenge Section 106 compliance was addressed in *Pit River Tribe v. U.S. Forest Service*.[63] The court held that tribes have standing to challenge inadequate consultation under Section 106 when they can demonstrate that the affected properties have religious or cultural significance to the tribe.[64] The decision recognized that procedural rights under Section 106 create cognizable injuries sufficient to establish standing.[65]

F. TRIBAL CONSULTATION AND SACRED SITES

The relationship between Section 106 and tribal rights has been an area of significant development. Although Section 106 requires consultation with tribes regarding undertakings that may affect historic properties of religious and cultural significance to them, courts have struggled with balancing preservation obligations against other federal interests.

In *Pueblo of Sandia v. United States*,[66] the court considered whether the Forest Service had adequately consulted with a pueblo regarding a ski area expansion that would affect a mountain considered sacred by the tribe.[67]

---

conditions, and restrictions in the Club's deed require the Club to remain private. Under the circumstances, the Park Service considered sufficient alternatives to permit a reasoned choice.").

62. *See id.*

63. 469 F.3d 768 (9th Cir. 2006).

64. *Id.* at 779 ("The first sentence of the 1996 draft ethnographic report commissioned by the agencies reads: 'Previous research has indicated that the Medicine Lake Highland and Timber Mountain areas have long been recognized by non-tribal scholars as traditional cultural properties of . . . the Pit River Nation. . . .' Pit River states that it has used the lands in question for cultural and religious ceremonies 'for countless generations.' Pit River has adequately demonstrated an injury in fact for standing purposes.").

65. *See* Pye v. United States, 269 F.3d 459 (4th Cir. 2001) (ruling an adjacent landowner had rights to challenge a highway expansion in South Carolina); *see also* Neighborhood Ass'n of the Back Bay v. Fed. Transit Admin., 463 F.3d 50 (1st Cir. 2006) (ruling a consulting party request should be made in writing to afford the complaining parties the right of objection later in the process).

66. 50 F.3d 856 (10th Cir. 1995).

67. *Id.* at 858.

The court held that although Section 106 requires meaningful consultation, it does not grant tribes veto power over federal undertakings.[68] However, agencies must demonstrate that they have made a good faith effort to accommodate tribal concerns.

The scope of tribal consultation obligations was further refined in *Quechan Tribe of Fort Yuma Indian Reservation v. U.S. Department of Interior*.[69] The court held that the Bureau of Land Management had violated Section 106 by failing to adequately consult with tribes regarding the cumulative effects of multiple solar energy projects on a traditional cultural landscape.[70] The decision emphasized that consultation must address landscape-level effects, not just impacts on individual sites.[71]

Traditional cultural properties (TCPs) present distinctive challenges within the Section 106 framework. Unlike conventional historic properties that derive significance from architectural merit or association with documented historical events, TCPs are significant because of their association with cultural practices and beliefs of living communities. The National Park Service's Bulletin 38 provides guidance on evaluating and documenting TCPs, but applying conventional preservation approaches to these properties remains problematic.

Many TCPs are landscapes rather than discrete sites or structures. A mountain range, river corridor, or expansive desert area might constitute a single TCP from a tribal perspective, while containing numerous individual sites that could be separately listed. The question of how to address effects on such landscape-scale properties has proven difficult. Is an undertaking that affects one portion of a vast TCP an adverse effect on the entire property, or should effects be assessed in relation to the specific portion affected? Different consulting parties and federal agencies have approached this question differently.

---

68. *Id.*

69. 755 F. Supp. 2d 1104 (S.D. Cal. 2010).

70. *Id.* at 1119 ("The court therefore determines the Tribe is likely to prevail at least on its claim that was not adequately consulted [by the Bureau of Land Management] under NHPA before the project was approved.").

71. *Id.* at 1120 ("The evidence shows, and the parties do not dispute, that the planned project is extensive. The size and number of suncatchers, not to mention roads, buildings, and other supporting infrastructure, ensures this will be a massive project. The undisputed evidence also shows the 459 historic properties extend from one end of the area to the other, so some type of impact on the properties is likely.").

Confidentiality poses another challenge for TCPs. Tribal communities may be reluctant to disclose specific information about sacred sites, practices, or beliefs, particularly when such disclosure might lead to vandalism, unauthorized visitation, or appropriation of cultural knowledge. The Section 106 regulations acknowledge this concern and provide mechanisms for withholding sensitive information from public disclosure.[72] However, federal agencies still require sufficient information to assess eligibility, identify effects, and develop appropriate treatment measures. Balancing the need for information against legitimate confidentiality concerns requires careful negotiation and trust between agencies and tribes.

The timing of tribal consultation has emerged as a critical factor in successful Section 106 compliance. Consultation that begins only after an agency has made fundamental decisions about an undertaking's design and location often proves ineffective. Tribes may identify concerns that would have been easily addressed through design modifications but become intractable once designs are finalized and budgets established. Recent guidance from the ACHP and National Park Service has emphasized the importance of early tribal consultation, ideally beginning at the planning stage before major project commitments are made.

G. INTEGRATION WITH NEPA

The Section 106 process often runs parallel to compliance with the National Environmental Policy Act (NEPA), and courts have addressed the relationship between these two procedural statutes. In *North Idaho Community Action Network v. U.S. Department of Transportation*,[73] the court held that while Section 106 and NEPA serve different purposes, agencies may integrate their compliance with both statutes.[74] However, NEPA compliance

72. Section 304 of the NHPA, 54 U.S.C. § 307103, authorizes federal agencies, in consultation with the Secretary of the Interior, to withhold from public disclosure information regarding the location, character, or ownership of historic properties. This confidentiality is mandatory if disclosure could risk harm to the property, cause a significant invasion of privacy, or impede the use of a traditional religious site by practitioners.

73. 545 F.3d 1147 (9th Cir. 2008).

74. *Id.* at 1158 ("All federally funded highway projects must comply with not only federal environmental protection laws, such as NEPA, but also with historic preservation laws, including Section 106 of the National Historic Preservation Act.").

does not automatically satisfy Section 106 obligations, as the latter requires specific consultation procedures and substantive consideration of preservation values.[75]

The integration of Section 106 and NEPA was further explored in *Coliseum Square Association, Inc. v. Jackson*.[76] The court held that while an Environmental Impact Statement may discuss historic preservation issues, it does not substitute for the formal consultation process required under Section 106.[77] The decision emphasized that Section 106 imposes specific procedural requirements that must be satisfied independently of NEPA review.[78]

Despite serving different statutory purposes, Section 106 and NEPA share sufficient procedural similarities that integrated compliance makes practical sense. Both require identification of potentially affected resources, assessment of effects or impacts, consideration of alternatives, and opportunities for public involvement. The timing requirements also overlap—both processes should begin early in project planning and conclude before final agency decisions. The Section 106 regulations explicitly contemplate integration with NEPA and provide procedures for agencies choosing this approach.

Successful integration requires careful attention to the distinct requirements of each statute. NEPA focuses on environmental effects and requires agencies to consider a range of alternatives with meaningful differences. Section 106 focuses specifically on historic properties and requires consultation with identified parties. NEPA requires disclosure and analysis sufficient to inform decision-making and public review. Section 106 requires consultation leading to agreement on treatment of adverse effects. An agency cannot simply include historic properties as one impact category in a NEPA document and consider Section 106 satisfied.

The most effective integration strategies involve using NEPA documents as vehicles for presenting Section 106 information while conducting separate Section 106 consultation processes. For example, an Environmental

---

75. *See id.* (stating that "'all federally funded highway projects' must adhere to processes outlined in the NEPA, Section 106 of the NHPA, and Section 4(f) of the DTA before outlining the precise sequence for proper compliance with each of them").

76. 465 F.3d 215, 241–42 (5th Cir. 2006).

77. *See id.* (mentioning that findings of "no adverse effect [on historic property]" arising from agency statements, like the NEPA, "triggers a consulting party review" under Section 106).

78. *Id.*

Impact Statement might include a chapter discussing historic properties, identification efforts, effects assessment, and proposed mitigation. This provides transparency and enables the public to understand historic preservation issues alongside other environmental concerns. However, the Section 106 consultation process, including meetings with consulting parties, development of memoranda of agreement, and provision of opportunities for comment by the ACHP and SHPO, occurs separately though in parallel with NEPA review.

Timing challenges sometimes arise when integrating Section 106 and NEPA. NEPA documents often follow a fixed schedule driven by planning deadlines and public engagement opportunities. Section 106 consultation can prove more difficult to schedule, particularly when multiple consulting parties are involved or when identification of historic properties requires extensive field survey. Agencies must build sufficient flexibility into their planning schedules to accommodate unanticipated delays in Section 106 consultation without compromising compliance with either statute.

H. PRIVATE PROPERTY AND THE NHPA

A key aspect of the NHPA is its relationship to private property rights. Unlike many environmental statutes, the NHPA does not directly regulate private property owners. Rather, it applies only to federal undertakings—actions carried out by, funded by, or requiring approval from federal agencies.

This limitation was made clear in *Business & Residents Alliance of East Harlem v. Jackson*,[79] where the court held that Section 106 does not apply to state or local actions undertaken without federal funding or approval, even if the actions affect properties listed on the National Register.[80] The court emphasized that listing on the National Register does not restrict private owners' use of their property in the absence of federal involvement.[81]

---

79. 430 F.3d 584, 593 (2d Cir. 2005) ("Section 106 itself still applies only to two types of entities: first, any Federal agency 'having direct or indirect jurisdiction over a proposed Federal or federally assisted undertaking,' and second, 'any Federal department or independent agency having authority to license any undertaking.'").

80. *Id.*

81. *Id.* at 592 ("Thus, unless either of the federal agency defendants—HUD and HHS—can be said to have jurisdiction or licensing authority over the East River Plaza project, Section 106 is inapplicable to the project.").

However, when federal permits or licenses are required, Section 106 is triggered. In *Walsh v. U.S. Army Corps of Engineers*,[82] the court held that the Corps' issuance of a permit under Section 404 of the Clean Water Act constituted an undertaking subject to Section 106 review, even though the applicant was the City of San Antonio, a non-federal entity.[83] This case illustrates how Section 106 can indirectly affect private development through the permitting process.

I. FEDERAL NEXUS AND THE LIMITS OF SECTION 106 JURISDICTION

The requirement of federal involvement for Section 106 applicability creates important boundaries around the statute's reach. Purely private development projects, even those affecting properties listed on the National Register, fall outside Section 106 unless they require some form of federal approval, funding, or licensing. This limitation reflects the constitutional structure of American federalism—the federal government generally lacks authority to regulate land use absent some connection to federal activities or interstate commerce.

Determining whether sufficient federal involvement exists to trigger Section 106 can prove complex. Federal funding represents the clearest form of federal involvement, but even here questions arise. If federal funds constitute only a small percentage of total project costs, does Section 106 apply to the entire project or only to the federally funded portions? The courts and ACHP have generally held that even minimal federal funding triggers Section 106 review of the entire undertaking, reasoning that the federal government bears responsibility for the consequences of its financial support.

Federal permits and licenses present more nuanced jurisdictional questions. Many federal permitting schemes involve limited review of circumscribed aspects of projects. A permit under Section 404 of the Clean Water Act, for instance, addresses only impacts on waters of the United States. Nevertheless, courts have held that issuance of such permits constitutes an

---

82. 757 F. Supp. 781, 786 (W.D. Tex. 1990) (finding that Section 106 was implicated where a § 404 permit was issued by the ACOE).

83. *Id.* (noting that the issuance of a § 404 permit by the ACOE did not violate Section 106's review process).

undertaking subject to Section 106, requiring the permitting agency to consider effects on historic properties even when those effects have no connection to water quality or wetlands protection. This interpretation gives Section 106 broader reach than might be expected from the narrow scope of many federal permits.

The question of when federal approval constitutes an undertaking has generated litigation. Agencies sometimes argue that certain approvals are ministerial rather than discretionary and therefore do not constitute undertakings. Courts have generally rejected this position, holding that any federal decision that enables a project to proceed constitutes an undertaking if the agency has discretion to disapprove the application or impose conditions. Even routine permits involving limited discretion trigger Section 106, though agencies may develop programmatic agreements to streamline review of such permits.

J. REMEDIES AND JUDICIAL REVIEW

When agencies fail to comply with Section 106, courts have broad authority to fashion appropriate remedies. In *Stop H-3 Association v. Coleman*,[84] the court enjoined construction of a highway that would affect historic and archaeological sites until the Federal Highway Administration completed proper Section 106 consultation.[85] The court held that irreparable harm to historic properties justified preliminary injunctive relief.[86]

The standard for judicial review of agency Section 106 compliance is governed by the Administrative Procedure Act's arbitrary and capricious standard. In *City of Grapevine v. Department of Transportation*,[87] the court held that an agency's Section 106 determination would be upheld if it considered relevant factors and made no clear error of judgment. However, the

---

84. 533 F.2d 434 (9th Cir. 1976).

85. *Id.* at 445–46 (holding that a highway project that "used" land on historic sites was enough to justify reversing the dissolution of an injunction stopping highway construction absent evidence of "no feasible and prudent" alternative to "the alleged desecration of the [historic property]").

86. *Id.*

87. 17 F.3d 1502, 1509 (D.C. Cir. 1994) ("In sum, because the FAA's approval of the West Runway was expressly conditioned upon completion of the § 106 process, we find here no violation of the NHPA.").

agency must provide a reasoned explanation for its conclusions regarding historic properties and effects.

Courts have also addressed the question of remedies when Section 106 violations are discovered after a project is completed. In *Reno-Sparks Indian Colony v. Haaland*,[88] the court held that courts have discretion to fashion appropriate remedies even when compliance violations are discovered post-completion, recognizing that some violations may be remedied through documentation, mitigation, or other measures short of project reversal.[89]

The arbitrary and capricious standard of review provides agencies with substantial discretion in implementing Section 106. Courts defer to agency expertise in matters of historic preservation and will not substitute their judgment for that of the agency provided the agency has considered relevant factors, articulated a rational connection between facts and decision, and not committed clear error. This deferential standard reflects both the technical expertise required for preservation decisions and the policy judgment inherent in balancing preservation values against other national interests.

Those challenging agency Section 106 compliance must demonstrate that the agency failed to follow required procedures or that its substantive determinations lack rational basis. Courts distinguish between disagreements over judgment and actual procedural failures. An agency's decision to proceed with an undertaking despite adverse effects on historic properties will survive judicial review so long as the agency engaged in genuine consultation, considered alternatives and mitigation, and provided ACHP an opportunity to comment. The fact that plaintiffs preferred a different outcome does not establish arbitrary and capricious agency action.

The exhaustion of administrative remedies doctrine applies to Section 106 litigation. Plaintiffs generally must raise issues during the consultation process before seeking judicial review. A party that fails to participate in consultation or object to procedural deficiencies may find itself barred from later challenging those deficiencies in court.[90] This requirement encourages parties to engage constructively in the Section 106 process rather than lying in wait to ambush completed projects with litigation.

---

88. 663 F. Supp. 3d 1188 (D. Nev. 2023).

89. *Id.*

90. *See* Neighborhood Ass'n of the Back Bay v. Fed. Transit Admin., 463 F.3d 50 (1st Cir. 2006).

Notably, there is a split in the circuits on whether NHPA confers a private right of action or whether lawsuits must be brought under the Administrative Procedure Act.[91] Also, NHPA allows for attorneys' fees when agencies fail to comply.[92]

K. IMPLEMENTATION AND IMPACT

Since its enactment, the NHPA has significantly transformed the landscape of historic preservation in the United States.[93] The NRHP now includes more than 95,000 listings, representing over 1.8 million contributing resources.[94] The Section 106 process has become a powerful tool in mitigating adverse effects of federal projects on historic properties.[95]

States and local governments, through SHPOs and CLGs, play an active role in preservation planning, education, and outreach.[96] Federal agencies, under the guidance of the ACHP, have integrated preservation into their decision-making processes, balancing development with conservation.[97]

The Act has also catalyzed economic development through heritage tourism and revitalization of historic districts, contributing to community identity and pride.[98] Preservation tax incentives have spurred private

---

91. *See* Boarhead Corp. v. Erickson, 923 F.2d 1011 (3d Cir. 1991); *see also* San Carlos Apache Tribe v. United States, 417 F.3d 1091 (9th Cir. 2005).

92. *See* Pres. Coal. of Erie Cnty. v. Fed. Transit Admin., 356 F.3d 444 (2d Cir. 2004).

93. Advisory Council on Historic Preservation, *supra* note 5, at 4.

94. *Id.* ("More than 91,000 places have been listed on the National Register of Historic Places, including many rural districts and older neighborhoods, representing more than 1.8 million contributing historic resources.").

95. *See* Advisory Council on Historic Preservation, *Section 106 Review Process Success Stories*, www.achp.gov/success-stories (last visited Feb. 14, 2026); *see* Advisory Council on Historic Preservation, *supra* note 5, at 4 (describing the "impressive record of accomplishment carried out under the law").

96. *See* Phelps, *supra* note 4.

97. *See* Advisory Council on Historic Preservation, *Federal Historic Property Stewardship*, www.achp.gov/OFAP/Section%203?utm_source=chatgpt.com (last visited Feb. 14, 2026).

98. Carol M. Rose, *Preservation and Community: New Directions in the Law of Historic Preservation*, 33 Stan. L. Rev. 473, 480–81 (1981) (highlighting how the themes of the National Register of Historic Places "support the inspirational view, promoting tourism fits comfortably with the protection of representative or meritorious structures, and the interest

investment in the rehabilitation of historic buildings, generating jobs and economic activity.[99]

The economic benefits of historic preservation were recognized in *Penn Central Transportation Co. v. City of New York*,[100] though this case involved local landmark designation rather than the NHPA itself.[101] The Supreme Court upheld New York City's landmarks preservation law against a takings challenge, noting that preservation serves important public purposes and that the economic burdens of preservation are appropriately distributed across society.[102] Although not directly interpreting the NHPA, this case established important principles regarding the constitutional validity of preservation regulation.

L. MODERN APPLICATIONS AND EMERGING ISSUES

Recent cases have addressed the application of Section 106 to emerging types of undertakings. In *Protect Our Parks, Inc. v. Buttigieg*,[103] the court considered whether federal approvals related to the Obama Presidential Center triggered Section 106 review.[104] The case illustrates how Section 106 applies even to projects with significant public support when federal involvement is present.

---

in revitalizing city areas to render them stable, useful, and prosperous for current and future residents accompanies the maintenance of a community's sense of place").

99. *See* Advisory Council on Historic Preservation, *supra* note 5, at 3 (stating that preservation tax credits "have catalyzed the rehabilitation of more than 41,250 buildings, created 2.3 million jobs, and leveraged more than $117.6 billion in private investment").

100. 438 U.S. 104 (1978).

101. *Id.* at 107 ("The question presented is whether a city may, as part of a comprehensive program to preserve historic landmarks and historic districts, place restrictions on the development of individual historic landmarks. . . .").

102. *Id.* at 134 ("In any event, appellants' repeated suggestions that they are solely burdened and unbenefited is factually inaccurate. This contention overlooks the fact that the New York City law applies to vast numbers of structures in the city in addition to the Terminal—all the structures contained in the 31 historic districts and over 400 individual landmarks, many of which are close to the Terminal[.]").

103. 97 F.4th 1077, 1093–94 (7th Cir. 2024), *cert. denied sub nom.* Protect Our Parks, Inc. v. Duffy, 145 S. Ct. 2787 (2025) (determining that because "Section 106 only applies to federal projects" rather than a project sponsored by the city of Chicago and because Section 106 procedures were followed anyway, no NHPA violation occurred).

104. *Id.*

Climate change presents new challenges for historic preservation, as rising sea levels, increased storm intensity, and other climate impacts threaten historic properties. While no major cases have yet addressed the intersection of Section 106 and climate adaptation, agencies are increasingly considering climate resilience in their preservation planning.[105] The ACHP has issued guidance encouraging agencies to consider climate impacts on historic properties and to incorporate preservation values into climate adaptation strategies.[106]

Digital infrastructure projects have also raised Section 106 issues. Recently, courts have considered whether installing cellular equipment on or near historic properties requires Section 106 review when federal approvals are involved.[107] These cases illustrate the evolving nature of "undertakings" in the digital age.

M. CHALLENGES AND FUTURE DIRECTIONS

Despite its successes, the NHPA faces ongoing challenges.[108] Urban development pressures, climate change, and limited funding continue to threaten historic resources.[109] Because many minority and marginalized communities continue being historically underrepresented, ensuring equitable representation of diverse cultural histories in the NRHP remains a priority.[110]

---

105. *See* Advisory Council on Historic Preservation, *Climate Adaptation & Resilience*, www.achp.gov/initiatives/sustainability-climate-resilience/climate-adaptation-resilience) (last visited Feb. 14, 2026).

106. *Id.*

107. *See United Keetoowah Band of Cherokee Indians in Okla. v. FCC*, 933 F.3d 728 (D.C. Cir. 2019) (considering whether FCC procedures in place designed to coordinate cellular communications construction within tribal historic preservation interests were adhered to properly); *New Cingular Wireless PCS, LLC v. Plan. Bd. of Town of E. Hampton*, No. 20-CV-3555 (JS)(SIL), 2022 WL 18859063 (E.D.N.Y. Dec. 1, 2022), *report and recommendation adopted in part, rejected in part*, No. 20-CV-3555 (JS)(SIL), 2023 WL 5604248 (E.D.N.Y. Aug. 30, 2023). *See generally In re Nationwide Programmatic Agreement Regarding the Section 106 Nat'l Hist. Pres. Act Rev. Process*, 20 F.C.C. Rcd. 1073 (2004) (discussing the interplay of FCC construction undertakings alongside the NHPA).

108. Advisory Council of Historic Preservation, Priorities and Recommendations for the Future 4 (Mar. 2017), available at www.achp.gov/sites/default/files/documents/2018-06/Preservation50FinalReport.pdf (identifying the primary inspirations behind the NHPA as remaining prevalent today "including potential conflicts with . . . urban revitalization, loss of industry, and rural economic shifts").

109. *Id.*

110. Rose, *supra* note 98, at 478 (identifying the "displacement issue" as a historical consideration to preservation law that is emerging as privileged persons take over "spruced-up 'historic' neighborhoods").

The challenge of achieving diverse representation was acknowledged in *Attakai v. United States*,[111] where the court recognized that traditional Native American cultural properties may not fit easily within conventional historic preservation frameworks.[112] The case prompted revisions to National Register criteria to better accommodate traditional cultural properties and landscapes that are significant to indigenous peoples.[113]

The NHPA has evolved over time through amendments and reinterpretations to address these issues.[114] Recent efforts have focused on integrating preservation with sustainability, resilience, and social justice goals.[115] Continued public engagement, technological innovation, and interdisciplinary collaboration will be crucial in adapting the NHPA to meet 21st-century preservation needs.[116]

N. PROGRAMMATIC AGREEMENTS AND ALTERNATIVE PROCEDURES

To streamline Section 106 compliance for routine undertakings, agencies may enter into programmatic agreements (PAs) that establish alternative procedures.[117] The validity and scope of programmatic agreements were examined in *Muckleshoot Indian Tribe v. U.S. Forest Service*, where the court

---

111. 746 F. Supp. 1395 (D. Ariz. 1990).

112. *Id.* at 1406 (discussing the tension between NHPA review of implicated tribal properties that the Defendant's wrongfully determined did not warrant inclusion on the National Register).

113. 16 Patricia L. Parker, *Traditional Cultural Properties, What You Do and How We Think*, Cultural Resource Management Information for Parks, Federal Agencies, Indian Tribes, States, Local Governments, and the Private Sector (1993) (outlining the impact of the 1992 NHPA amendments on the recognition of properties with cultural significance to native tribes in America).

114. *See* Phelps *supra* note 4, at 478 ("As enacted and subsequently amended, the NHPA is the hallmark of the modern preservation movement, shaping its current structure and defining the overall relationship between the federal government and important historic properties more generally.").

115. *See* Advisory Council on Historic Preservation, *supra* note 5, at 4 (describing how issues ranging from population dynamics, diversity, and climate change are impacting preservation law).

116. *See id.* at 5 (outlining the need for engagement and the combination of different preservation considerations as essential to handle modern challenges).

117. 36 C.F.R. § 800.14(b) (2025).

upheld a PA that delegated certain consultation responsibilities to the Forest Service while maintaining meaningful ACHP and SHPO involvement.[118] The decision recognized that programmatic approaches can provide efficiency while still meeting Section 106's consultation requirements.

However, courts have also imposed limits on programmatic agreements. In *Pit River Tribe v. U.S. Forest Service*,[119] the court held that a PA cannot exempt an entire category of undertakings from Section 106 review without adequate justification.[120] The decision emphasized that programmatic approaches must still provide for meaningful consideration of effects on historic properties.

O. ENFORCEMENT AND COMPLIANCE MONITORING

Because there is a split in the circuits on whether NHPA confers a private right of action, enforcement typically occurs through judicial review under the Administrative Procedure Act. In *San Carlos Apache Tribe v. United States*,[121] the court addressed whether private parties could obtain judicial review of alleged Section 106 violations.[122] The court held that while Section 106 does not create a private cause of action, plaintiffs may challenge agency action under the APA if they can demonstrate that the agency failed to comply with Section 106's procedural requirements.[123]

---

118. 177 F.3d 800, 815 (9th Cir. 1999) (noting that "the Forest Service failed to meet the requirements of NHPA and NEPA" while otherwise upholding a property exchange agreement between the Forest Service and a private entity, instead ruling that the property exchange activities were enjoined "until such time as the Forest Service satisfies its NHPA and NEPA obligations").

119. 469 F.3d 768 (9th Cir. 2006).

120. *Id.* at 787 ("The agencies defend the lack of NHPA analysis on the same grounds that they defended their lack of NEPA analysis: that no analysis was required, and, in the alternative, that the later analysis cured the earlier failure. For the reasons discussed above, we hold that the extension of the leases was a federal undertaking requiring review.").

121. 417 F.3d 1091 (9th Cir. 2005).

122. *Id.*

123. *Id.* at 1094 ("We agree [the inclusion of an Attorney's Fees provision] demonstrates Congressional intent that individuals may sue to enforce NHPA. And we agree that the attorney's fees language evinces congressional intent to cover the costs of those who prevail in a suit under the statute. *But it does not follow that Congress intended these individuals to file suit against the United States under NHPA itself, rather than under the well-established procedures set out under the APA.* At best, the absence of any private right of action language

The scope of judicial review was further clarified in *Coliseum Square Ass'n, Inc. v. Jackson*,[124] where the court held that plaintiffs must demonstrate that the agency's Section 106 compliance was arbitrary and capricious, not merely imperfect.[125] The court emphasized that agencies are entitled to deference in their implementation of Section 106, and courts will not impose rigid requirements beyond those specified in the statute and regulations.[126]

P. TECHNOLOGY AND DIGITAL PRESERVATION

Technological advances have transformed both the threats to historic properties and the tools available for preservation. Digital documentation technologies enable unprecedented precision in recording historic properties. Three-dimensional laser scanning captures minute details of historic structures, creating digital records that can inform restoration or serve as archives if properties are lost. Photogrammetry allows creation of detailed models from photographs, making sophisticated documentation more accessible. Geographic information systems enable complex spatial analyses of historic resources and their contexts.

These technologies have particular relevance to Section 106 compliance. Digital documentation can provide comprehensive records of historic properties that will be adversely affected by undertakings, serving as mitigation when physical preservation is not feasible. Remote sensing technologies can assist in identifying archaeological sites within project APEs, potentially reducing the need for extensive ground surveys. Virtual reality applications can help consulting parties visualize proposed undertakings and their effects on historic properties, facilitating more informed consultation.

However, technology also poses challenges. The deployment of digital infrastructure—cellular towers, fiber optic cables, and other telecommunications equipment—frequently triggers Section 106 review. The Federal

---

in § 106 and the presence of the fee provision render the statute ambiguous on the cause of action point. Without explicit language, such an ambiguity can hardly be converted into an implied right of action.") (emphasis added).

124. 465 F.3d 215 (5th Cir. 2006).

125. *Id.* at 241 ("As under NEPA, an agency's actions under the NHPA are procedural, and our review of its decisions is conducted under the Administrative Procedure Act's 'arbitrary and capricious' standard.").

126. *Id.* at 244 (determining that HUD's respect of a Park Service NHPA recommendation was justified and did not force adherence to any further procedure).

Communications Commission has developed streamlined procedures for reviewing telecommunications undertakings, but these procedures remain controversial, with some preservation advocates arguing they provide insufficient protection for historic properties. The rapid pace of technological change creates ongoing tension between the need for infrastructure deployment and the preservation review process.

Q. THE NATIONAL HISTORIC PRESERVATION ACT AND THE FUTURE

The National Historic Preservation Act of 1966 has fundamentally reshaped how America values and protects its cultural heritage.[127] By institutionalizing preservation at all levels of government and fostering collaboration among stakeholders, the NHPA has ensured that historic places are not only remembered but also preserved for future generations. The extensive body of case law interpreting the NHPA demonstrates both the Act's flexibility in addressing diverse preservation challenges and its limitations as a primarily procedural statute. As the cases discussed in this chapter illustrate, Section 106 provides meaningful opportunities for preservation advocates to influence federal decision-making, while respecting the ultimate authority of federal agencies to balance preservation values against other national interests.

Looking forward, the principles enshrined in the NHPA will remain vital in maintaining the link between past, present, and future.[128] The case law interpreting the Act continues to evolve, adapting preservation law to new contexts and challenges while maintaining fidelity to the NHPA's core purpose: ensuring that federal agencies give meaningful consideration to the effects of their actions on America's irreplaceable historic resources. As new types of undertakings emerge and new preservation challenges arise, courts will continue to play a crucial role in defining the scope and application of the nation's landmark historic preservation statute.

---

127. Phelps, *supra* note 4, at 478 ("[The Act] is the hallmark of the modern preservation movement, shaping its current structure and defining the overall relationship between the federal government and important historic properties more generally.").

128. *See generally* Advisory Council on Historic Preservation, *supra* note 5 (examining the history of the NHPA based on its impact on preservation before emphasizing the need to continue on the same path to ensure preservation into the future).

4 Environmental Policy Acts

A. THE NATIONAL ENVIRONMENTAL POLICY ACT OF 1969

The National Environmental Policy Act (NEPA)[1] places responsibilities on federal agencies to disclose and evaluate the environmental harms that might be caused by their actions. The human environment is the object of protection, and it is broadly defined in NEPA to include historic resources as well as natural resources.

1. Overview and Intent

President Richard Nixon signed NEPA into law on January 1, 1970. Its passage was a significant moment in the history of federal land regulation in the United States. It set forward a bold vision that environmentally conscious decision-making is the "continuing responsibility" of the U.S.

1. 42 U.S.C.A. §§ 4321–4370 (West, Westlaw through Pub. L. No. 119-59).

government.[2] Aspirational language for the values to be protected includes the responsibility to "preserve important historic, cultural, and natural aspects of our national heritage."[3]

The congressional findings in NEPA make clear that its scope is broad. The catalytic problems that gave rise to the legislation included "population growth, high-density urbanization, industrial expansion, resource exploitation, and new and expanding technological advances."[4] Environmental quality was a core purpose, important for the "overall welfare and development of man."[5] For these reasons agencies were instructed to use "all practicable means" to "create and maintain conditions under which man and nature can exist in productive harmony, and fulfill the social, economic, and other requirements of present and future generations of Americans."[6]

The law also contains what courts have described as "action-forcing provisions" that executive branch agencies must comply with in advance of taking discretionary action that will cause significant harm.[7] By requiring the study and disclosure of impacts and an analysis of alternatives, the law serves to ensure that environmental impacts will be considered and widely disclosed.[8]

More resource-specific environmental laws at the federal level passed after NEPA focused in greater detail on more defined issues. Those laws are often specific to the practice of particular federal agencies, like the Environmental Protection Agency in the case of air quality, or the Fish and Wildlife Service in the case of imperiled species. In contrast, NEPA requires a far broader analysis than most other major federal environmental legislation.[9]

---

2. 42 U.S.C.A. § 4331(b).

3. 42 U.S.C.A. § 4331(b)(4).

4. 42 U.S.C.A. § 4331(a).

5. *Id.*

6. 42 U.S.C.A. § 4331(a).

7. *See* Kleppe v. Sierra Club, 427 U.S. 390 n.18 (1976) (describing the legislative history of the term "action-forcing").

8. For a thorough background on the legislative history of NEPA, see Lazarus, Richard, *The National Environmental Policy Act in the U.S. Supreme Court: A Reappraisal and a Peek Behind the Curtains*, 100 Geo. L.J. 1507 (2012).

9. The affected environment studied in an EIS, for example, may contain analyses, among other topics, of land use, geology and soils, coastal hydrodynamics, hydrology and hydraulics, water quality, floodplains, wetlands, special status species, aquatic resources, benthic resources, terrestrial wildlife and upland vegetation, cultural resources, recreation, visuals and

The Council on Environmental Quality (CEQ) is an independent federal agency created by NEPA charged with providing guidance to all federal agencies in their implementation of the law.[10] The CEQ promulgated implementing regulations for NEPA in 1978. Because the statute did not provide it that explicit authority, those regulations were rescinded in 2025, an important topic for modern NEPA practice discussed *infra.* Care must be taken in citing NEPA case law that relied on these former regulations.[11]

Federal agency compliance with NEPA is required for "major federal actions," where there is "substantial Federal control and responsibility."[12] In practice, the trigger for action is the funding, permitting, or licensing of projects. The degree of analysis required rests on the reasonable likelihood of the project "significantly" affecting the quality of the human environment.[13]

NEPA emphasizes agency cooperation with other experts in advance of decision-making. This includes other federal agencies with special expertise as well as the comments and views of state and local government.[14] The law also stresses the importance of notifying the public so that the full extent of a project's scope and impacts are disclosed.

At the time of this publication, NEPA practice is in flux. From the late 1970s until 2025, the compliance process was largely standardized across federal agencies through the adoption of a single set of implementing regulations. The rescission of those regulations, together with recent directives to

---

aesthetics, air quality, noise, hazardous materials and wastes, transportation, utilities, safety, environmental justice, and climate change. *See, e.g.*, Notice of Intent to Prepare a Draft Integrated Feasibility Report and Environmental Impact Statement for the Charleston Peninsula Coastal Flood Risk Management Study, Charleston County, South Carolina, 86 Fed. Reg. 15470 (Mar. 22, 2021).

10. 42 U.S.C.A. § 4342 (West, Westlaw through Pub. L. No. 119-59). CEQ's responsibilities are articulated in the statute to serve as an advisory body to the president on environmental matters.

11. As an example, the regulatory definition of "significantly" was an oft-cited regulatory provision requiring a two-part evaluation of context and intensity of any given action to determine what level of environmental review was warranted in former 40 C.F.R. § 1508.27. In the absence of a standardized definition for the term, individual agency regulation or policy and practice manuals may either continue the former practice or adopt an agency-specific threshold.

12. 42 U.S.C.A. § 4336e(10)(a) (West, Westlaw through Pub. L. No. 119-59).

13. 42 U.S.C.A. § 4332(c) (West, Westlaw through Pub. L. No. 119-59).

14. *Id.*

streamline the compliance process from Congress and the executive branch, has resulted in more divergent compliance practices from agency to agency.

Yet Congress's declaration that NEPA is national policy remains.[15] Its core disclosure requirements remain unaltered, including its signature requirement that, when significant effects are anticipated, a "reasonable range of alternatives" be evaluated "that are technically and economically feasible, and meet the purpose and need of the proposal."[16]

Several states have enacted laws modeled on NEPA's requirements that apply when state agencies have decision-making authority over projects. The California Environmental Quality Act, discussed *infra*, is largely modeled on NEPA. Yet, in California, municipalities have the discretion to implement the law. When they elect to have discretion in reviewing permitting decisions, the law can command a substantive outcome by requiring that less harmful ways of accomplishing any given project be adopted, if feasible.

NEPA and its progeny of state laws are typically focused on ensuring that harmful impacts are disclosed to the public, above all. Transparency is a core policy goal. Section 106 consultations under the NHPA, in contrast, may not be made as visible even if done in conjunction with NEPA compliance.

As an example, in 2010 the Department of the Navy published an Environmental Impact Statement, NEPA's core requirement for "major federal actions," for the development of a live-fire training range complex on Guam, a U.S. territory. The EIS did not analyze alternatives to the location selected for the ranges, which would prohibit public access to Pågat Village, the first site in Guam placed on the National Register in 1974. Objections to the plan from local and national groups came primarily in the NEPA process given that Section 106 consultation had resulted in a understood programmatic agreement that merely promised future consultation as opposed to a full reevaluation of the selected site. Through the threat of NEPA litigation, the Navy was persuaded to conduct a supplemental environmental analysis. Ultimately, it elected to relocate the firing range to an alternative site.[17]

High-profile issues aside, the avoided harmful impacts that can be credited to NEPA's passage are incalculable. For a generation, its disclosure requirements have worked to create an implicit advantage for projects

15. 42 U.S.C.A. § 4331 (West, Westlaw through Pub. L. No. 119-59).

16. 42 U.S.C.A. § 4332(c)(iii).

17. See Guam Pres. Tr. v. Gregory, No. CV 10–00677, 2011 WL 13248292 (D. Haw. June 30, 2011).

with lesser environmental impact as expedited review is allowed by virtually every agency for projects likely to cause no harm or less harm. Practitioners counseling private sector applicants when federal agency permitting is required should be aware of agency-specific practices for categorically exempting minor projects as well as the ways impacts can be reduced to levels of less significance.[18]

2. Application of NEPA and Practice within Federal Agencies

NEPA applies to all federal agencies within the executive branch and some federal boards, commissions, independent agencies, and committees' activities. It does not apply to Congress, the president, or the federal courts.

Many large federal agencies maintain an office dedicated to NEPA policy and program oversight. A senior agency official acts as decision-maker and manages the analyses and production of documents, as well as formulating guidance, policy, and procedures. The NEPA.gov website is an essential resource for finding current information about unique issues in implementation of the law, including coordination with the requirements of the National Historic Preservation Act.[19]

In practice, it has become increasingly common for project applicants seeking federal permits to prepare compliance documentation with agency supervision, even if it raises the potential that produced information could reflect the bias of the applicant. The statute allows for this exigency yet obliges agencies to "ensure the professional integrity, including scientific integrity, of the discussion and analysis in an environmental document" and "make use of reliable data and resources."[20] Agencies must take special care

---

18. 42 U.S.C.A. § 4336(a)(2) (West, Westlaw through Pub. L. No. 119-59) gives agencies the authority to adopt such exclusions, and 42 U.S.C.A. § 4336c (West, Westlaw through Pub. L. No. 119-59) offers a procedure for agencies to adopt other agencies' exclusions.

19. The NEPA NHPA Section 106 Handbook (available at https://ceq.doe.gov/publications/nepa-handbooks.html) is particularly relevant in the context of analyzing impacts on historic resources.

20. 42 U.S.C.A. § 4332(D), (E) (West, Westlaw through Pub. L. No. 119-59). The Section 106 regulations also sanction the use of contractors to prepare compliance documents under the NHPA yet emphasize that the agency official "remains legally responsible for all required findings and determinations." 36 C.F.R. § 800.2(a)(3) (2025).

in reviewing draft documentation to ensure that information is presented accurately relative to the true project impacts.

3. Putting Congressional Intent into Practice

While NEPA is applicable to virtually all federal agencies, practitioners often observe a varied culture of NEPA practice from agency to agency. In every case, however, initial findings must be made to determine if an action is a "federal action."

The statute and controlling case law focus on whether or not the agency is required to act, rather than acting pursuant to an authority that grants discretion.[21] If an agency does not have discretion to disapprove of a project, it has been found not to have NEPA compliance responsibilities. The U.S. State Department did not violate NEPA, for instance, by failing to act to prevent the demolition of the Republic of Turkey's chancery building in Washington, D.C., because it lacked such discretion.[22]

The rescinded NEPA regulations encapsulated within the definition of federal action the issuance of agency rules, regulations, plans, and policies as well as projects "entirely or partly financed, assisted, conducted, regulated, or approved by federal agencies."[23] This has traditionally included, for example, community development block grants administered by the Department of Housing and Urban Development (HUD), which provide funding for the redevelopment of blighted neighborhoods.

4. Exemptions

In NEPA, Congress contemplated a specific procedure for how agencies can make threshold determinations that may result in something less than a "detailed statement."[24] Categorical Exclusions are subsets of project types that agencies identify through their own regulations and policies. These may include, for instance, minor repairs to buildings or routine maintenance, which rarely needs to be evaluated further. The statute also details other situations

---

21. 42 U.S.C.A. § 4336(a)(4) (West, Westlaw through Pub. L. No. 119-59) describes such actions as "nondiscretionary."

22. Nat'l Trust for Hist. Pres. v. Dep't of State, 834 F. Supp. 443 (D.D.C. 1993), *aff'd in part, rev'd in part sub nom.*, Sheridan Kalorama Hist. Ass'n v. Christopher, 49 F.3d 750 (D.C. Cir. 1995).

23. The former regulation was codified at 40 C.F.R. § 1508.18(a).

24. These thresholds are detailed in 42 U.S.C. § 4336.

in which no review is required, such as when there is no final action, when there is a fundamental conflict with compliance and another law, or if it is a nondiscretionary action.[25]

5. Major Federal Projects Requiring an EIS

The core instrument Congress devised to carry out NEPA obligations is the Environmental Impact Statement (EIS). This document is the "detailed statement" on "major Federal actions significantly affecting the quality of the human environment" referenced in the NEPA statute.[26] The EIS is further described in 42 U.S.C. § 4336, which contemplates scenarios in which a lesser level of review might be appropriate. The threshold for developing an EIS is whether a significant effect is "reasonably foreseeable."[27]

The contents of the EIS must include:

(i) reasonably foreseeable environmental effects of the proposed agency action;
(ii) any reasonably foreseeable adverse environmental effects which cannot be avoided should the proposal be implemented;
(iii) a reasonable range of alternatives to the proposed agency action, including an analysis of any negative environmental impacts of not implementing the proposed agency action in the case of a no action alternative, that are technically and economically feasible, and meet the purpose and need of the proposal;
(iv) the relationship between local short-term uses of man's environment and the maintenance and enhancement of long-term productivity; and
(v) any irreversible and irretrievable commitments of Federal resources which would be involved in the proposed agency action should it be implemented.[28]

The alternatives analysis required was described by now-rescinded CEQ regulations as the "heart of NEPA."[29] By requiring an examination of

25. 42 U.S.C.A. § 4336(a)(1)–(4) (West, Westlaw through Pub. L. No. 119-59).

26. 42 U.S.C.A. § 4332(2)(C) (West, Westlaw through Pub. L. No. 119-59).

27. 42 U.S.C.A. § 4336(b)(1).

28. 42 U.S.C.A. § 4332(c).

29. The previous citation, referenced in dozens of NEPA cases, was located at 40 C.F.R. § 1502.14.

alternatives, NEPA set up a process by which the public can understand the trade-offs of any given agency objective using federal funds or triggering federal permitting requirements.

A key issue that NEPA did not address in its statutory text is the foreseeability of supplementary analysis. Federal agencies may change the scope of a project after approval. Some degree of expediency is necessary to avoid a complete redo of the analysis. In *Marsh v. Oregon Natural Resources Council*, the Supreme Court upheld an agency's decision not to supplement an EIS despite changes in the project, holding that such decisions are subject to the Administrative Procedure Act's arbitrary and capricious standard.[30]

6. Major Projects without Significant Effects

Compliance vehicles short of an EIS have been developed to satisfy disclosure requirements for projects with effects that are not significant, as that term is interpreted by the agency. The most common is the Environmental Assessment (EA), which will be developed when the agency makes a reasoned judgment that there are no foreseeable significant effects.[31]

Whether impacts are significant can be fact specific, though in the historic preservation context NEPA determinations may be aided by conclusions made in the NHPA process. A common practice for agencies is to impose a set of binding mitigation measures that would reduce impacts to a level of insignificance. This finding is documented in a "mitigated" Finding of No Significant Impact (FONSI).

7. Public Disclosure

An important directive of Congress in NEPA is to ensure public availability of information about potential environmental harm. The statement must also be made available, not just to other relevant agencies and local and

---

30. 490 U.S. 360, 376 (1989). It is expected that agencies will maintain guidance for standards for supplements as they implement specific regulations. See, for example, 90 Fed. Reg. 29465 (Jul. 3, 2025), which proposes "a process for the preparation of supplemental environmental documents if significant changes to the proposed action occur or if new relevant information arises."

31. 42 U.S.C.A. § 4336(b)(2) (West, Westlaw through Pub. L. No. 119-59). Note that the rescinded regulations at 40 C.F.R. § 1508.27 guided an agency's judgment by urging a focus on context and intensity to determine significance.

state governments, but to the public through the *Federal Register*. This remains the most reliable way for the public to understand federal activities that might affect their local environment. *Federal Register* notices are typically published to notify the public that an agency has an intention to prepare environmental analysis, often called "scoping"; the availability of draft and final documents; and the publication of a final Record of Decision, which must be made available for 30 days prior to the issuance of funding or a permit.

Public disclosure requirements are part of NEPA's broader democratic objective. Public commentary can be informed with objective statements that detail the central facts of any project: the resources at issue and the possible resulting harms relative to a stated government objective.

8. NEPA Litigation

NEPA contains no private right of action. Challenges to agency action are filed through and must adhere to the provisions of the Administrative Procedure Act (APA).[32] Because agencies implementing NEPA are exercising discretion granted by a statute, the APA's deferential arbitrary and capricious standard is typically utilized.[33] When challenges to a NEPA decision-making process are successful, it is typically because the agencies failed to follow the correct process. Broad public awareness of the environmental issues involved and a fair evaluation of the impacts are key to certifying compliance with the broad congressional directive.

Challenges to the substance of an agency's ultimate decision are likely to face headwinds in court. The U.S. Supreme Court has recently made clear in no uncertain terms that agency decisions are afforded "substantial judicial deference" provided in the text of NEPA itself, as well as the court's decisions.[34] *Seven County Infrastructure Coal v. Eagle County* concerned a challenge to the U.S. Surface Transportation Board's decision to approve a new rail line to facilitate crude oil production. The permit applicants had sought to connect Utah's Uinta Basin to the national rail network. The court

32. For a comprehensive view on considerations pertaining to NEPA litigation see Kristen Hite, *Judicial Review and the National Environmental Policy Act*, Congressional Research Service, Sep. 19, 2025, *available at* www.congress.gov/crs-product/R48717#fn130.

33. *Seven Cnty. Infrastructure Coal v. Eagle Cnty.*, 605 U.S. 168 (2025).

34. *Id.* at 180.

evaluated the extent of an agency's obligation to consider the full suite of foreseeable effects of its project. In the case of rail construction, the question concerned the downstream impacts that this facilitation would cause including increased oil production.

The Court made clear that agencies have wide latitude in making factual determinations about separate foreseeable projects when preparing an EIS. It was also highly relevant to the court that the agency had no approval authority over the foreseeable projects consistent with its findings in *DOT v. Public Citizen*.[35]

Further, the court clarified in no uncertain terms that NEPA is a "purely procedural statute."[36] Judicial review is focused on whether the environmental consequences and feasible alternatives have been explored. The rationale stated for a final action must only be "reasonably explained."[37]

In rejecting challenges, courts have often noted the role of NEPA to ensure political accountability for harmful actions. In one representative case, the court rejected plaintiff's claim that HUD violated NEPA in providing a $10 million grant to the city of Philadelphia to enable a 350-room hotel and 500-vehicle parking garage in the Penn's Landing section of the Delaware River waterfront. The court concluded "[p]laintiffs have expressed their grievances often, loudly, and clearly to the decisionmakers. The decisionmakers have heard the complaints but have chosen a path different from that urged by plaintiffs. If they are dissatisfied with the decisions made by their elected officials in this case, their redress lies in the political process, at the ballot box, and not with the federal court."[38]

In other words, the public disclosure requirements of the law can have the effect of affording individuals and public interest organizations the opportunity to push for and shape better outcomes and pressure political leaders. Often the political advocacy inspired by NEPA creates mutually beneficial results to improve projects and minimize harm. Considering the many successes NEPA has created, caution is warranted in considering the disputes featured in published case law to extrapolate to how NEPA functions in practice.

35. 541 U.S. 752 (2004).

36. *Id.* at 172.

37. *Id.* at 180.

38. Soc'y Hill Towers Owners' Ass'n v. Rendell, 20 F. Supp. 2d 855, 874 (E.D. Pa. 1998).

9. Coordination with the National Historic Preservation Act

Triggers for NEPA action also typically require compliance with Section 106 of the NHPA. In the case of federal transportation agencies, an independent review process under Section 4(f) of the Department of Transportation Act may also be required. The existence of this considerable authority at the federal level concerned with historic and cultural resources showcases the seriousness of the legislative directive that federal agency approvals be mindful to protect historic places.

The disclosures required under NEPA can serve to make more public the harm that might otherwise be less publicized under the Section 106 process. For this reason, NEPA can often become more of a poster child for the clash of values that can occur between economic growth and the ideals of preservation. Yet when agencies are committed to using the process to improve planning it can lead to mutually agreed upon solutions.

The NHPA regulations provide guidance for how agencies can meet both legal requirements while honoring Congress's goal in creating separate statutory responsibilities. Section 106 review is often a far more limited conversation, oftentimes between the federal agency and state, tribal, and local governments. Other "consulting parties" must have a "demonstrated interest" in the undertaking.[39] In somewhat of an admission of the public's limited role, the Section 106 regulations explicitly allow agencies to rely on NEPA procedures for their public involvement.[40]

In this sense, Section 106 should be considered more consultative with specific parties whereas NEPA aimed at providing broader public awareness and transparency. NEPA's public disclosure of effects through notice in the *Federal Register* is one of the most significant differentials. Any member of the public, regardless of their interest, is entitled to have their views considered.

It also goes without saying that federal agencies frequently seek to use the analysis and conclusions that result from Section 106 review in efforts to comply with NEPA. As an example, the Section 106 regulations sanction the use of information to meet multiple compliance requirements and urge for "early coordination" with the overall planning schedule and NEPA reviews.[41]

---

39. 36 C.F.R. § 800.2(c)(5) (2025).

40. 36 C.F.R. § 800.2(d)(3).

41. 36 C.F.R. § 800.3(b) (2025).

Yet there are limitations. Care must be exercised that agencies do not misinterpret Section 800.8 of the NHPA regulations to ensure that compliance efforts do not run afoul of each legislative mandate. This is because a categorically excluded action under NEPA may still qualify as a Section 106 undertaking, for example.[42] NEPA compliance efforts should also be mindful to correspond with consulting parties engaged as part of the Section 106 process. The NHPA regulations specifically require engagement early in the NEPA process "when the purpose of and need for the proposed action as well as the widest possible range of alternatives are under consideration."[43]

10. Rescission of the CEQ Regulations and Agency Response

There have been several major changes to NEPA in the recent past that have reshaped the landscape for agency compliance. The Fiscal Responsibility Act of 2023 represents the most recent legislative update to NEPA.[44] The amendment added requirements to facilitate timely and unified federal reviews. Additional clarity is offered to agencies on lead, joint lead, and cooperating agency designations.

Congress also imposed certain requirements in that law, for instance, limiting the length of EISs.[45] Such an arbitrary limitation, however, can conflict with a central directive of NEPA to provide adequate analysis. Agencies with complicated projects and severe impact may limit their risk of litigation by ensuring that the record reflects a thorough consideration through development of appendices and other supplementary material.

Judicial review of NEPA compliance has also led to major policy change within the Executive Branch. In late 2024 in *Marin Audubon v. FAA*, the D.C. Circuit, following directives of the U.S. Supreme Court's decision in *Loper Bright Enterprises v. Raimondo*, held that the CEQ lacked the authority to issue implementing NEPA regulations.[46] The CEQ had

---

42. 36 C.F.R. § 800.8(b) (2025).

43. 36 C.F.R. § 800.8(a)(2).

44. Fiscal Responsibility Act of 2023, Pub. L. No. 118-5 (Jun. 3, 2023).

45. Page limits for an EIS, not including appendices, are capped at 150 pages and environmental assessments at 75 pages. 42 U.S.C.A. § 4336(e) (West, Westlaw through Pub. L. No. 119-59).

46. Finding that, as a general matter, when an agency interprets a statute, judicial review of the agency's interpretation is de novo. Loper Bright Enters. v. Raimondo, 603 U.S. 369, 391–92 (2024).

promulgated its original regulations in 1978 following President Carter's Executive Order 11991, *Relating to Protection and Enhancement of Environmental Quality*.[47]

Following the court decision, the rescission was formally effectuated by President Trump's Executive Order 14154, *Unleashing American Energy*.[48] The directive simultaneously required federal agencies to revise their NEPA implementing regulations and procedures. This is because agency-specific rules had been developed merely as supplements to the CEQ's framework for compliance. The broader effect of the reevaluation of CEQ guidance is expected to facilitate expedited and timely reviews.

11. Conclusion

NEPA practice is shifting territory. Federal, state, and local agencies; applicants; environmental service firms; and the general public will need to adjust to new supplementary procedures as they are issued. At the time of this writing, those procedures are expected to be issued in the Code of Federal Regulations agency by agency. That said, the initial procedures developed by larger federal agencies are in development and are likely highly relevant for understanding how smaller agencies are likely to comply.

B. THE COASTAL ZONE MANAGEMENT ACT

The Coastal Zone Management Act (CZMA) is relevant in the context of environmental policy acts as it was designed to ensure states consider potential harms to the broad suite of cultural and natural resources in proximity to the U.S. coastal zone. The CZMA created the National Coastal Zone Management Program, which is managed by the National Oceanic and Atmospheric Administration (NOAA). The Program relies on principles of federalism by giving states the primary role in setting standards for how resources within the coastal zone will be protected.[49]

Each coastal state is required by the CZMA to develop a management plan or program document, and direct a process to ensure that actions

47. 42 Fed. Reg. 26967 (May 24, 1977).

48. 90 Fed. Reg. 8353 (Jan. 29, 2025).

49. 16 U.S.C.A. § 1452 (West, Westlaw through Pub. L. No. 119-59).

permitted by state agencies are "consistent with" its standards.[50] In turn, the federal government assures that states have a policy framework for disclosing and, ideally, avoiding harm to vulnerable properties from major new development.

NOAA maintains regulations that states must follow in development, modification, funding, and review of state coastal management programs.[51] States are required to include an inventory and designation of areas of particular concern. In making this inventory, states are also required to "consider" whether to designate sites of "historical significance, cultural value or scenic importance (including resources on or determined to be eligible for the National Register of Historic Places.)"[52] Thus, typically states rely on their State Historic Preservation Officers (SHPO) to make critical decisions on which sites are eligible for protection under the Act. SHPOs have advisory power and can consider views from the public in making their decisions.

For federally funded or licensed projects, the CZMA requirements often overlap with a Section 106 compliance process. Yet CZMA often reaches farther than Section 106 as state permitting processes that do not involve federal funding can trigger an assessment of harm to historic resources and mitigation to reduce that harm. In these cases, states may follow a process similar to Section 106 that includes consultation with locally affected parties with an interest in the issue.

C. STATE ENVIRONMENTAL POLICY ACTS

NEPA has inspired a litany of state-specific legislation that mirrors its objective to provide public disclosure of environmental impact.[53] The California Environmental Quality Act (CEQA) is one of the most significant with particularly robust protections for historic resources.

---

50. *See* 15 C.F.R. § 930, subpts. A–I (2025).

51. 15 C.F.R. § 923 (2025).

52. 15 C.F.R. § 923.21(b)(1).

53. *E.g.*, CONN. GEN. STAT. §§ 22a-14 to -20 (West, Westlaw through 2025 Regular Session and the 2025 November Special Session); GA. CODE ANN. §§ 12-16-1 to -9 (West, Westlaw through legislation passed at the 2025 Regular Session of the Georgia General Assembly); HAW. REV. STAT. § 343-1 to -8 (West, Westlaw through the 2025 Regular Session); MD. CODE ANN., NAT. RES. §§ 1-301 to -305 (West, Westlaw through all legislation from the 2025

Through local codes, municipalities in California have the authority to approve actions that affect publicly and privately owned historic resources, which trigger the review process of CEQA.[54] CEQA provides legal protections for the "environment" in California, which is specifically defined to include historic resources. Municipalities thereby have discretionary review of permitting decisions that might result in demolition or substantial alteration of eligible sites, which are primarily buildings and archeological sites.

The lead agency in project review is ultimately responsible to comply with the law. A critical objective of CEQA is to ensure informed decision-making by giving the public the opportunity to review and comment on projects that have harmful consequences for the environment. The public disclosure requirements of CEQA hold elected officials accountable for causing such harm, especially if the environmental review process demonstrates that such harm could have been avoided. CEQA's statutory text and its regulatory guidelines offer some of the most far-reaching environmental protections as compared to laws in other U.S. states. CEQA has procedural protections as well as a substantive mandate. Municipalities implementing CEQA are legally barred from approving a project if "there are feasible alternatives or feasible mitigation measures available that would substantially lessen the environmental effects of such projects."[55]

CEQA's implementing regulations (the "Guidelines") provide the public step-by-step guidance on what the law requires during project review.[56] In brief, before approving a project that would impact a tangible historic resource, the agency is responsible for (1) assessing the baseline

---

Regular Session and 2025 1st Special Session of the General Assembly); MASS. GEN. LAWS ANN. ch. 30, §§ 61–62L (West, Westlaw through Chapter 65 of the 2025 1st Annual Session); MINN. STAT. ANN. § 116D.01-.11 (West, Westlaw through legislation from the 2025 Regular and First Special Sessions); MONT. CODE ANN. §§ 75-1-101 to -1101 (West, Westlaw through the end of the 2025 Regular Session of the Montana Legislature, with the exception of Senate Bill 437); NEW YORK ENVTL. CONSERV. LAW §§ 8-0101 to -0117 (West, Westlaw through L. 2026, chapter 2); N.C. GEN. STAT. §§ 113A-1 to -259 (West, Westlaw through S.L. 2025-97 of the 2025 Regular Session of the General Assembly); S.D. CODIFIED LAWS §§ 34a-9-1 to -13 (West, Westlaw through the 2025 First Special Session and Supreme Court Rule 25-16).

54. CAL. PUB. RES. CODE, §§ 21000 to 21006 (West, Westlaw through Ch. 2 of 2026 Reg. Sess.).

55. CAL. PUB. RES. CODE § 21002.

56. CAL. CODE REGS. tit. 14, div. 6, ch. 3, app. N (West, Westlaw through 1/30/26 Register 2026, No. 5).

environmental condition, (2) determining the environmental impacts likely to result if the project is approved, and (3) calculating the degree of significance of those impacts. If impacts cross a threshold of significance, the agency must consider alternatives to lessen the significance of the impacts. If alternatives that would lessen the impacts are infeasible, the agency may decide to proceed by citing other societal benefits that outweigh the unavoidable environmental impacts.

The public may have multiple opportunities to participate during the agencies' consideration of any given project; the specifics depend on the scope of the potential harm. Public participation is an essential part of the CEQA process. If significant impacts are anticipated, advocates may assist the agency in critical ways, such as determining the scope of the review or on the formation of alternatives that may result in less harm.

CEQA makes clear that a project that will cause a "substantial adverse change in the significance of a historical resource is a project that may have a significant effect on the environment."[57] In determining whether a historic resource will be affected by a project, CEQA instructs lead agencies to consider its eligibility for the California Register of Historical Places.[58] The law affords the same protection to places listed on as well as eligible for listing on that Register. As a result, each permit application triggering CEQA review requires an evaluation of the historic character of the property. This process generally occurs in consultation with the permit applicant, who may be required to provide the agency with a historical resources evaluation.

---

57. Cal. Pub. Res. Code § 21084.1.

58. *Id.*

Section 4(f) of the Department of Transportation Act of 1966

5

Federal transportation agencies in the United States are uniquely responsible for complying with environmental laws in the Department of Transportation [DOT] Act of 1966. Section 4(f) of the DOT Act requires these agencies to avoid harm to historic sites, recreation areas, and wildlife or waterfowl refuges when using their discretion to fund or permit projects.[1]

In the context of historic preservation, the law requires the Secretary of Transportation to only "use" historic properties in cases where it has been demonstrated that there is no other feasible alternative to achieve the project goals. The term "use" is generally synonymous with harmful action and is unique to Section 4(f). The law further requires that, if "use" of a historic properties is anticipated, the agency must make efforts to minimize harm.

Compliance with Section 4(f) requires transportation agencies to conduct an analysis of feasible alternatives that

1. 49 U.S.C.A. § 303(c) (West, Westlaw through Pub. L. No. 119-59); 23 U.S.C.A. § 138 (West, Westlaw through Pub. L. No. 119-59).

would avoid harmful impacts. These alternatives are to be fully described and disclosed to the public in a written evaluation that satisfies specific criteria outlined in the law and its regulations. Section 4(f) evaluations typically are developed concurrently with NEPA and NHPA review[2] and track conclusions reached in fulfillment of the agencies' responsibilities under those laws. They are frequently packaged for public review as an appendix to NEPA analyses, such as an Environmental Impact Statement.

Section 4(f) compliance requires close coordination with other agencies and broad public disclosure of effects. By inviting comments on draft analyses in advance of final decisions, the agency can better determine the location of and details about protected sites and consider solutions for minimizing harm.

Section 4(f) is also distinct among federal laws protecting historic resources because it requires substantive action in addition to procedural review. The Supreme Court distinguished the law from NEPA in *Robertson v. Methow Valley Citizens Council*, citing Section 4(f) as an example of a statute that imposes "substantive environmental obligations on federal agencies."[3] NEPA, in contrast, "merely prohibits uninformed—rather than unwise—agency action."[4] Several circuit courts have reinforced the substantive mandate in Section 4(f), making it frequently cited as the most stringent of all federal historic preservation laws for preventing harmful action.[5]

The U.S. Supreme Court stated in the seminal case of *Citizens to Preserve Overton Park, Inc. v. Volpe* that agency responsibilities under the law are "clear and specific directives."[6] The case involved the approval of a six-lane

---

2. See Chapters 3 and 4.

3. 490 U.S. 332, 351 n.14 (1989).

4. *Id.* at 351.

5. In *Stop H-3 Ass'n v. Coleman*, 533 F.2d 434, 438 (9th Cir. 1976), the court stated of Section 4(f), "[t]he requirements are stringent. Congress clearly reflected its intent that there shall no longer be reckless, ill-considered, wanton desecration of natural sites significantly related to our country's heritage." In *Neighborhood Ass'n of the Back Bay, Inc. v. Fed. Transit Admin.*, 463 F.3d 50, 64 (1st Cir. 2006), the court stated, "Section 4(f), unlike sections 106 and 110(f), imposes a substantive mandate." In *Presidio Historical Association v. Presidio*, 811 F.3d 1154 (9th Cir. 2016), the court distinguished Section 4(f) from the NHPA because it has "a very important qualifier not present in the NHPA, namely that historic sites may be approved '*only* if . . . there is no prudent and feasible alternative to using that land[.]'" *Id.* at 1170 (italics in original).

6. 401 U.S. 402, 411 (1971).

highway through downtown Memphis, Tennessee, that would cross through the 342-acre Overton Park. The new highway would have separated the zoo from other public amenities including a municipal golf course, outdoor theater, nature trails, bridle path, art academy, and picnic areas. Writing for the Court, Justice Marshall evaluated the text of the statute and concluded that the statute is a "plain and explicit bar to the use of federal funds for construction of highways through parks—only the most unusual situations are exempted."[7] The court established a standard that avoidance alternatives could be rejected only if they involved "truly unusual factors" or costs or community disruption of "extraordinary magnitudes."[8]

The policy rationale for singling out transportation agencies for these added requirements relates to the relative seriousness of the potential harm at stake. Highways and rail lines are typically growth inducing, and, once established, they are likely to be subject to further expansion.

Section 4(f) was passed to counter the detriment caused by post-war urban renewal programs. Virtually every major city in America exhibits scars from these programs, which often aimed to deliver poverty alleviation and make urban life more efficient. The New York State Supreme Court's rejection of an eminent domain challenge to the Cross Bronx Expressway in 1948 reflected the attitude of the time. In justifying the taking, the court offered that "[w]isdom, vision and courage of the highest order in road planning and building, as well as in civic enterprise are indeed required to meet the challenge of this city's future greatness."[9]

In reality, more often urban renewal programs caused blight, fractured well-established communities, and exacerbated disparities. At the time of the passage of Section 4(f) in 1966 there was a compelling need for imposing a responsibility on federal transportation agencies to plan new road infrastructure mindful of the permanent impacts it can cause. Remarkably, the House of Representatives passed the law in a roll-call vote of 336–42. For the first time, road planners that received federal funding, including state transportation agencies throughout the country, became subject to the legal requirement that they implement the least harmful way to achieve project goals.

---

7. *Id.*

8. *Id.* at 416.

9. *In re* Cross-Bronx Expressway, 82 N.Y.S.2d 55, 61 (Sup. Ct. 1948).

A. AGENCIES RESPONSIBLE

The several agencies within the Department of Transportation with compliance responsibilities under Section 4(f) include the Federal Highway Administration (FHWA), the Federal Aviation Administration, the Federal Transit Administration, and the Maritime Administration. These agencies have responsibilities despite how passive their actions may be with respect to any individual "program" or "projects" that require compliance.

Frequently, a state highway authority or other regional nonfederal entity that is the recipient of federal funding takes initiative in preparing the requisite analysis. Despite the state role, the federal agency must exhibit oversight of the process given it is legally responsible to ensure the findings are defensible if challenged. The Secretary of the U.S. DOT is ultimately responsible to make the formal approval. In doing so, it can invite consultation with the Secretaries of the Interior, Housing and Urban Development, and Agriculture as well as states in making decisions.

B. STATUTORY FRAMEWORK

Under the text of the statute, a federal transportation agency may "only" approve a project that requires the "use" of a protected site if:

(1) there is no prudent and feasible alternative to using that land; and
(2) the program or project includes all possible planning to minimize harm to the park, recreation area, wildlife and waterfowl refuge, or historic site resulting from the use.[10]

When harm is contemplated, a Section 4(f) evaluation is required to be completed prior to the distribution of funding. This written statement must describe the action and the protected resources at stake and identify and evaluate alternatives including harm-mitigation activities. The "all possible planning" requirement ensures that the agency properly quantifies the harm and performs a balancing test of the costs and benefits of each alternative. The evaluation also discloses the coordination the agency has engaged in with relevant parties.

10. 49 U.S.C.A. § 303(c) (West, Westlaw through Pub. L. No. 119-59).

C. SECTION 4(F) REGULATIONS

The Section 4(f) regulations, codified at 23 C.F.R. pt. 774, give certain federal officials unique responsibilities in the process of developing an evaluation. The regulations were last amended in 2008 as a directive from Congress in the Safe, Accountable, Flexible, Efficient Transportation Equity Act: A Legacy for Users.[11] The Section 4(f) Policy Paper issued by the FHWA provides a comprehensive overview of relevant case law.[12]

D. "USES" OF PROTECTED PROPERTIES UNDER SECTION 4(F)

A threshold determination in a Section 4(f) analysis is whether a project proposes to "use" a historic resource or other protected property. The Section 4(f) regulations describe three distinct categories of uses that must be analyzed:[13]

- **Permanent occupation:** actions where a historic site is proposed to be substantially altered or demolished as they are incorporated into the project. Other potential harmful actions include sale out of federal control or conversion into a highway right of way.
- **Temporary occupation:** actions where construction activities have the potential to affect historic sites. These impacts can often be mitigated, but they can also cause permanent harm. The regulations contain five criteria that must be met for reducing impacts to reach a standard called "de minimis," which ensures the public that harm will be largely avoided.[14]
- **Constructive use:** actions that cause "substantial impairment" as defined in 23 C.F.R. § 774.15. Such use can be triggered as a result of excessive noise, visual or aesthetic impacts, or enjoyment of a historic site when it is an important quality of its significance. In general, the analysis will focus on whether or not the integrity of the resource will be reduced or lost.

---

11. Pub. L. No. 109-59 (Aug. 10, 2005), 119 Stat. 1144.

12. Section 4(f) Policy Paper, www.environment.fhwa.dot.gov/legislation/section4f/4fpolicy.pdf (July 20, 2012).

13. 23 C.F.R. § 774.17 (2025).

14. 23 C.F.R. § 774.13(d) (2025).

The Section 4(f) regulations make clear that potential uses shall be evaluated as early as practicable in the review process.[15] This allows for harm avoidance measures to be given greatest consideration.

Agency decisions made concerning whether an action is a use of a protected property have a "presumption of regularity," but that does not preclude a "thorough, probing, in-depth review."[16] Judicial review occurs under the Administrative Procedure Act and will not be overturned unless arbitrary, capricious, an abuse of discretion, or otherwise not in accordance with law.[17]

In one frequently cited case, a court found the agency erred in not finding a use when the selected alternative proposed "massive concrete support columns on the sidewalk along the entire length of the front of the [historic] Post Office Building."[18] Even if the building itself would not be touched directly, the court found that significant harm would occur because the columns would

> create an awning-like effect on the front of the building, shading the building during parts of the day, obscuring practically any view of the sky, obstructing a view of the facade for all but close passers-by, and giving people standing on the steps of the Post Office a view of the numerous and rather unattractive overhead support columns.[19]

Yet proximity to the impact can be highly relevant in determining whether a constructive use will occur. A federal court in Virginia, for example, found the agency was correct in concluding there was no constructive use of a significant Depression-era farm when a highway bypass would be located approximately 55 feet from its boundary.[20]

---

15. 23 C.F.R. § 774.9(a) (2025).

16. Citizens to Preserve Overton Park, Inc. v. Volpe, 401 U.S. 402, 415 (1971).

17. 5 U.S.C.A. § 706(2)(A) (West, Westlaw through Pub. L. No. 119-59); *see* Historic Bridge Found. v. Buttigieg, 22 F.4th 275, 281–82 (1st Cir. 2022).

18. Citizen Advocates for Responsible Expansion v. Dole, 770 F.2d 423, 427 (5th Cir. 1985).

19. *Id.*

20. Piedmont Env't v. U.S. Dep't of Transp., 159 F. Supp. 2d 260, 284 (W.D. Va. 2001).

E. SPECIAL CONSIDERATIONS FOR HISTORIC SITES

Congress did not define in Section 4(f) the term "historic site," but its regulations make clear that eligibility for the National Register of Historic Places is the key threshold.[21] Because Section 4(f) reviews typically occur in tandem with Section 106 review under the NHPA, that consultation is critical for identifying the resources at stake and their boundaries, which often can include the landscape surrounding the footprint of a historic building. Reliance on the NHPA is most evident in the public notification process. For instance, notice of the availability of a draft Section 4(f) evaluation must be given to the public for impacts to parks, recreation areas, and wildlife and waterfowl refuges. But notice and comment for impacts to historic properties are not required under the Section 4(f) regulations as those impacts are disclosed as part of the compliance process under Section 106 of the NHPA.[22]

Identifying which historic sites are eligible for protection within the Area of Potential Effect of a project is a fundamental part of NHPA review. In practice, the views of the State and Tribal Historic Preservation Officers are given considerable deference. These experts and their staffs have a critical role in consulting with the federal agency officials responsible for compliance to certify conclusions about the importance of a place and its boundaries. Note that in historic districts, the places that are "contributing" to the district will be considered a historic site for the purposes of Section 4(f). If the agency disagrees with the finding of the state or tribal authority, the NHPA regulations allow for a process by which the eligibility of a property can be formally resolved by the Keeper of the National Register.[23]

To determine whether properties are likely to be within the scope of Section 4(f), practitioners should be familiar with how eligibility is typically determined. The National Park Service maintains regulations at 36 C.F.R. pt. 60 that define the qualities that make a property eligible for listing.

21. 23 C.F.R. § 774.17 (2025).

22. 23 C.F.R. § 774.5(b)(1)(iii) (2025).

23. 36 C.F.R. § 800.4(c)(2) (2025). In *Stop H-3 Ass'n v. Coleman*, the Ninth Circuit enjoined the construction of a highway through Moanalua Valley, finding that it qualified for protection as a historic site despite a contrary finding by the state. 533 F.2d 434 (9th Cir. 1976).

Careful attention should be paid to the evaluation of a site's significance, particularly in making judgments about constructive use.

Archaeological sites discovered during construction may also be subject to Section 4(f).[24] In the event of a discovery made during project construction, the regulations require an evaluation of whether an exception applies under 23 C.F.R. § 774.13(b). That provision allows the Administrator to make a conclusion that an archaeological site is important "chiefly because of what can be learned by data recovery and has minimal value for preservation in place." The foreseeability of such a discovery is typically contemplated in a corresponding Section 106 agreement.

The First Circuit has upheld this provision as consistent with the regulation given the unique ways in which archeological sites can be distinguished. The court noted that Civil War battle artifacts at Gettysburg, for instance, would be the type of resource potentially worthy of preserving in place given their relation to a specific site.[25]

Notably, Congress has created a unique exemption in Section 4(f) for the 46,700 mile Interstate Highway System.[26] The Secretary of Transportation continues to have the authority to consider individual elements with national or exceptional historic significance that would trigger Section 4(f) protections. The FHWA has identified at least 132 specific features that meet this criteria.

F. EVALUATING AND SELECTING ALTERNATIVES UNDER SECTION 4(F)

1. Finding #1: Prudent and Feasible Alternative Adopted

Once a "use" is found, the agency must adopt "prudent and feasible" alternatives to those actions that threaten to cause harm.[27] The agency is required to select the avoidance alternative or, if it is found that no alternatives avoid all harm, the alternative that causes the least harm.

---

24. 23 C.F.R. § 774.9(e), 774.11(f) (2025).

25. Town of Belmont v. Dole, 766 F.2d 28, 33 (1st Cir. 1985).

26. 23 U.S.C.A. § 103(c)(5)(A) (West, Westlaw through Pub. L. No. 119-59).

27. 49 U.S.C.A. § 303(c)(1) (West, Westlaw through Pub. L. No. 119-59).

An alternative is not prudent if it does not meet the transportation needs of a project.[28] Agency crafting of project purpose, therefore, often done in conjunction with NEPA review, becomes a critical factor in whether or not the substantive requirements of Section 4(f) will demand the adoption of a harm-reducing alternative. For instance, in *Alaska Center for the Environment v. Armbrister*, the Ninth Circuit permitted the agency to move forward with a road cut project through two popular recreation areas as opposed to an alternative plan that would have improved existing rail service because that alternative would not have met the project purpose of meeting the demand for access.[29]

The Secretary is also free to choose among "alternatives which cause substantially equal damage to parks or historic sites."[30] In *Druid Hills Civic Association v. Federal Highway Administration*, the court held that

> Section 4(f)(2) requires a simple balancing process which totals the harm caused by each alternate route to section 4(f) areas and selects the option which does the least harm. The only relevant factor in making a determination whether an alternative route minimizes harm is the quantum of harm to the park or historic site caused by the alternative. Considerations that might make the route imprudent, e.g., failure to satisfy the project's purpose, are simply not relevant to this determination. If the route does not minimize harm, it need not be selected.[31]

The Section 4(f) regulations can assist agencies in determining what alternatives meet this threshold. A project is not feasible, for instance, "if it cannot be built as a matter of sound engineering judgment." An alternative is not prudent if it "results in additional construction, maintenance, or operational costs of an extraordinary magnitude," among other factors.[32]

---

28. Neighborhood Ass'n of the Back Bay, Inc. v. Fed. Transit Admin., 393 F. Supp. 2d 66, 78 (D. Mass. 2005); *see also* Honolulutraffic.com v. Fed. Transit Admin., 742 F.3d 1222, 1232 (9th Cir. 2013).

29. 131 F.3d 1285, 1289 (9th Cir. 1997).

30. Druid Hills Civic Ass'n v. Fed. Highway Admin., 772 F.2d 700 (11th Cir. 1985).

31. *Id.* at 716 (citing La. Env't Soc'y, Inc. v. Coleman, 537 F.2d 79, 85–86 (5th Cir. 1976)).

32. 23 C.F.R. § 774.17 (2025).

Further, in determining what alternatives are "prudent," the regulations allow the agency to reject preservation if costs will be of an "extraordinary magnitude" above a more harmful alternative. In *National Trust for Historic Preservation v. Buttigieg*,[33] the court determined that that the FHWA was permitted to reject a rehabilitation plan for the 1932 Frank J. Wood Bridge after the state DOT determined that it would cost 53% more than a new bridge. Previous litigation to save the bridge also resulted in a rejection of plaintiffs' claims that the Section 4(f) analysis was inadequate.

In some cases, agencies are afforded great deference in rejecting alternatives as imprudent due to efficiency and safety concerns.[34] The *Overton Park* case, discussed *supra*, described a variety of factors that can serve as a legitimate basis for an agency to reject alternatives. Yet other courts have looked at terminology used in Overton Park such as "unique problems" and "extraordinary magnitude" in finding that agencies erred in failing to study alternative solutions. In *Stop H-3 Assoc. v. Dole*,[35] the court found that the agency erred in ruling a no-build alternative imprudent.

2. Finding #2: All Possible Planning to Minimize Harm

Provided the agency has found no prudent and feasible alternative, it must make findings that all possible planning has been made to minimize harm to proceed with a harm-causing action. The regulations provide seven balancing factors the agency must consider, which include, among others, the significance of the resource, whether mitigation measures will reduce impacts, and relative costs.[36] After making a substantiated conclusion based on the balancing test, the agency is governed by a "reasonableness" standard, which is contained in the definition of "all possible planning" in the regulations.[37]

Courts have described agency duties under Section 4(f)(2) in reference to case law and FHWA publications. In the case of *Merritt Parkway Conservancy v. Mineta*,[38] the court emphasized the need to consider alternatives that result in less use or less drastic use of a resource first and mitigation

---

33. 125 F.4th 278 (1st Cir. 2025).

34. *See, e.g.*, Safeguarding the Hist. Hanscom Area's Irreplaceable Res., Inc. v. Fed. Aviation Admin., 651 F.3d 202, 213 (1st Cir. 2011).

35. 740 F.2d 1442 (9th Cir. 1984).

36. 23 C.F.R. § 774.3(c)(1) (2025).

37. 23 C.F.R. § 774.17 (2025).

38. 424 F. Supp. 2d 396 (D. Conn. 2006).

measures second.[39] The administrative record is critical to a court's evaluation as to whether the agency took the needed steps.[40]

3. De Minimis Finding

Congress has provided an important exception to the substantive requirements under Section 4(f) when the agency determines that an impact is "de minimis" in the associated review of the project under Section 106 of the NHPA. The de minimis finding is only appropriate when it is made under that review. The de minimis finding can be made if the Section 106 process results in either a determination of "no historic property affected" or "no adverse effect," terms defined in the NHPA regulations.[41] This conclusion must be backed up by a concurrence from the State or Tribal Historic Preservation Office. There are specific notice requirements for other categories of sites protected such as recreation areas and refuges. The legal impact of making a de minimis finding is that no further evaluation is required.

G. PROGRAMMATIC EVALUATIONS

The regulations implementing Section 4(f) allow for an alternative process to fast-track projects that meet certain criteria. These categories include projects with a net benefit to historic sites, bikeway or walkway construction projects, and when there are low-impact activities with "minor involvement" with historic sites. Such evaluation requires the agency to identify alternatives and describe measures to avoid harm. But the agency is not required to make the two critical Section 4(f) findings described above.

The following five programmatic Section 4(f) evaluations have been approved through the formal notice and comment process in the *Federal Register*:

- Section 4(f) Statement and Determination for Independent Bikeway or Walkway Construction Projects

39. *Id.* at 417–18.

40. *See* 23 C.F.R. § 774.7(a) (2025) (stating that the § 4(f) evaluation "shall include sufficient supporting documentation to demonstrate why there is no feasible and prudent avoidance alternative and shall summarize the results of all possible planning to minimize harm to the Section 4(f) property").

41. 36 C.F.R. §§ 800.4(d)(1), 800.5 (2025).

- Programmatic Section 4(f) Evaluation and Approval for FHWA Projects that Necessitate the Use of Historic Bridges
- Final Nationwide Section 4(f) Evaluation and Approval for Federally-Aided Highway Projects with Minor Involvements with Historic Sites
- Final Nationwide Section 4(f) Evaluation and Approval for Federally-Aided Highway Projects with Minor Involvements with Public Parks, Recreation Lands, Wildlife and Waterfowl Refuges
- Nationwide Programmatic Section 4(f) Evaluation and Approval for Transportation Projects That Have a Net Benefit to a Section 4(f) Property

H. STATE LAWS MODELED AFTER SECTION 4(F)

Several states have unique laws that apply to state transportation agencies and have been modeled after Section 4(f). In Kansas, for example, historic properties on a state register are protected unless "there is no feasible and prudent alternative to the proposal and that the program includes all possible planning to minimize harm to such historic property resulting from such use."[42] South Dakota also employs similar language except adding that "encroach[ing] upon" historic properties is prohibited.[43]

---

42. KAN. STAT. ANN. § 75–2724(a)(1) (West, Westlaw through laws enacted during the 2025 Regular Session of the Kansas Legislature effective on or before July 1, 2025).

43. S.D. CODIFIED LAWS § 1-19A-11.1(1) (Westlaw through the 2025 First Special Session and Supreme Court Rule 25-16); *see also* N.M. Stat. Ann. § 18-8-7 (West, Westlaw through chapters effective Dec. 31, 2025 of the 2025 First Regular Session the 2025 First Special Session of the 57th Legislature (2025); CAL. PUB. RES. CODE § 5024.5(a)–(b) (West, Westlaw through ch. 2 of 2026 Reg. Sess.); FLA. STAT. ANN. § 267.061 (West, Westlaw through July 1, 2025, of the 2025 first regular session); TEX. PARKS & WILD. CODE ANN. § 26.001 (West, Westlaw through the end of the 2025 Regular and Second Called Sessions of the 89th Legislature); S.C. CODE § 10-1-135 (Westlaw through 2025 Act No. 94) (requiring that easements, rights-of-way, or encroachments on state parks or historic areas must demonstrate "[t]here is important public necessity for the encroachment," alternatives are "neither prudent nor feasible," and "reasonable mitigation of impacts"); 20 ILL. COMP. STAT. ANN. 3420/4(c) (West, Westlaw through P.A. 104-459 of the 2025 Reg. Sess.); CONN. GEN. STAT. § 22a-19(a) (West, Westlaw through 2025 Regular Session and the 2025 November Special Session); MINN. STAT. ANN. § 116B.09 (West, Westlaw through legislation from the 2025 Regular and First Special Sessions); OR. REV. STAT. ANN. § 377.105(1), (5) (West, Westlaw through laws of the 2025 Regular Session of the 83rd Legislative Assembly).

Local Preservation Ordinances

6

A. INTRODUCTION

The bulk of legal protections for older and historic properties in the United States are conferred by municipal preservation ordinances. This chapter explores the varied character and scope of these rules, as well as differences in the practices of how they are implemented.

Traditional preservation regulation involves the establishment and operation of a local commission authorized by the governing body of a municipality with a specific scope of work. This review board has the authority to designate properties worthy of protection for their historic and aesthetic character. Tied to these designations is the board's discretionary power to approve, deny, or condition permits to ensure that modifications to a property or new development in its vicinity are "appropriate." Mindful of the due process rights of applicants, this commission must be qualified to make informed decisions and adhere to specific standards set by the ordinance.

Properties within the purview of the commission's authority are often dubbed "landmarks," in the case of individual properties, or "historic districts," in the case of a collection of properties that have a cohesive attribute, such as a related vintage or style within set geographic boundaries. Districts are composed of individual "contributing" properties and may be rated as to their relative importance in a survey document, as encouraged by federal guidance.

The degree of power a governing body vests in its preservation commission fluctuates from place to place. Every locality has unique political and cultural traditions. Ordinances typically allow community members or organizations to bring forward nominations to add properties to local registers. Confusion often stems around the relevance of designation on the National Register of Historic Places (NRHP). While a determination of significance under this federal criteria can be an aid in establishing local protections, municipalities have independent authority to designate properties using their own distinct criteria outside this federal process.

Support for preservation laws is widespread in America. All 50 states have enabling legislation and state preservation offices that have assisted over 3500 municipalities in establishing ordinances.[1] Places adopting protections for historic buildings have elected a policy trade-off, balancing unfettered economic growth with their interest in saving what is unique and distinct about their community.

The popularity of local preservation laws may be attributed to the following:

- Preservation decision-making often invites dialogue and an exchange of ideas focusing on how projects can be improved and harm avoided. Compromises may rarely be to everyone's full satisfaction, but local laws typically place priority on a process of conversation and dialogue with experts that can result in improvements to designs and treatments.
- Revitalizing historic places reflects a community's values in stewarding its history and protecting what is distinct about a place,

---

1. Sara C. Bronin and Leslie R. Irwin, *Regulating History*, 108 MINN. L. REV. 241, 312 (Nov. 2023), *available at* https://papers.ssrn.com/sol3/papers.cfm?abstract_id=4396040. There is no comprehensive inventory of these ordinances. An ambitious initiative called the Preservation Atlas aims to compile data on preservation ordinances at scale, including local designations and the code sections that confer protections. *See* NATIONAL PRESERVATION ATLAS, *Defining How We Protect Our Nation's Heritage, One Community at a Time*, www.preservationatlas.org (last visited Feb. 14, 2026).

thereby contributing to a municipality's economic development strategy. The function of a local preservation ordinance is to protect the places that differentiate one community from the next.

- Preservation is a tool to manage the impacts of an unrestrained private market that may not always value the historic context of a place. It aids the public's confidence that future generations can remain oriented to their place and its past by seeking ways to avoid permanent loss.[2]

The value of preservation ordinances is difficult to quantify because their mere existence in local codes alone likely deters proposals that cause harm. They add time, cost, and uncertainty the greater the damage proposed. Thus, action to revitalize and adapt significant older buildings gains a distinct advantage against projects that cause permanent harm to unique and irreplaceable historic places.

To retain political support, preservation commissions must be well-trained in procedures that ensure the due process of applicants. Besides having the obvious advantage of minimizing litigation risk, fair procedure is essential for maintaining public confidence. Final decisions should be articulated and rationalized clearly with close reference and attention to established legal standards. The success of the preservation movement rests on fair implementation of rules, the commission's adherence to ethical behavior, and administration of the law free of political influence.

B. BRIEF HISTORY OF LOCAL PRESERVATION PROTECTIONS

In 19th-century America, land-use regulation at the local level was rare. Saving distressed properties significant to the nation's story required outright acquisition. In 1818, the room where the Declaration of Independence was signed in Philadelphia's Independence Hall was scrubbed of its original features and in danger of being lost. Citizens mobilized to have the city purchase the site with public funds.[3] In the late 1850s, Virginians lobbied their

2. For a thorough review of the "why" of saving historic places, see Thompson Mayes, Why Old Places Matter: How Historic Places Affect Our Identity and Well-Being (2018).

3. Frank M. Etting, An Historical Account of the Old State House of Pennsylvania Now Known as the Hall of Independence 157 (1874).

state to purchase George Washington's Mount Vernon, which had fallen into serious disrepair. That effort proved unsuccessful, and the Mount Vernon Ladies Association was formed in response to acquire and steward the site.

In the 1890s the federal government began taking specific actions aimed at protecting national heritage on public lands. In 1892, the professional archaeological community succeeded in convincing President Benjamin Harrison to set aside one square mile of federal land in the Arizona Territory as a cultural reserve.[4] This action protected a site known as Casa Grande, a landmark that had stood for millennia, and still remains as evidence of the remarkable engineering skill of the Hohokam people.

The following year Congress passed a law to facilitate the acquisition of Gettysburg Battlefield through eminent domain. The landowner objected, and the case was ultimately resolved by the U.S. Supreme Court in favor of the acquisition as a "public use."[5] In 1889, the Preservation of Virginia Antiquities was founded and acquired Jamestown. It became the nation's first statewide preservation organization, now Preservation Virginia.

In 1931 Charleston, South Carolina, became the first municipality in America to use its zoning authority to protect historic properties.[6] Charleston gave its newly formed Board of Architectural Review (BAR) more than an advisory role, but the power to deny outright an application for alteration of an exterior façade from the public view. The nation's first historic district covered approximately 138 acres in the city's southeastern corner. Unlike other comparative colonial-era American cities like Boston, Philadelphia, and New York, Charleston had suffered far fewer losses of its older, character-defining buildings in the advent of the industrial era.

One driver of political momentum for the so-called Charleston Ordinance was the theft of ornamental features from its iconic antebellum buildings in the South of Broad neighborhood. By the early 1930s the Charleston Renaissance movement had fixed greater attention and pride on the uniqueness of the city's built environment. Yet increased visitation was resulting

---

4. This reservation of land was formally approved by Congress on March 8, 1889 (25 Stat. 961). The boundaries of the monument have subsequently been enlarged several times.

5. United States v. Gettysburg Elec. Ry. Co., 160 U.S. 668 (1896).

6. Previous legislative efforts in Santa Fe (1912) and New Orleans (1926) had resulted in boards with more limited advisory power. Louisiana was the first state to authorize the creation of a historic district, the Vieux Carre. *See* New Orleans v. Pergament, 5 So. 2d 129 (La. 1941).

in the insensitive removal of irreplaceable exterior and interior features of these architectural marvels, diminishing their historic integrity.

In April 1920, a local realtor, suffragette, and political activist named Susan Pringle Frost formed the Society for the Preservation of Old Dwellings, the nation's first grassroots preservation advocacy organization.[7] The membership organization's specific original aim was to save the 1803 Adam-style Joseph Manigault House, which was threatened with demolition for the development of an auto service station. This effort built the political momentum for the city to take an initiative never before made in America: affording rights to a local commission to deny property owners the right to tear down or make significant alterations to their property.

Working with the planning team Morris and Knowles and bolstered by the Supreme Court's endorsement of Euclidian zoning in 1926,[8] the city tailored the ordinance to a set of residences it described as the "Old and Historic District."[9] Charleston's BAR was granted the authority to deny a "Certificate of Appropriateness" for exterior changes to selected residential properties. The BAR had five citizen volunteer members, and its powers were limited to issuing denials only when a development was within public view and "obviously incongruous to the old historic aspects of the surroundings."[10]

Charleston's action was soon after followed by other historic communities including New Orleans (1937), San Antonio (1939), Alexandria (1946), Nantucket (1955), Annapolis (1959), and Santa Fe (1957). Many of these ordinances were facilitated by grassroots organizations at the state and local levels that maintained a close relationship with commissions to advocate for best practices.[11] These early efforts pioneered the ways in which advocates for historic buildings gained the tools to save older properties through land-use regulation.

---

7. Now known as the Preservation Society of Charleston, the organization has grown to include over 4000 members, *see* www.preservationsociety.org.

8. Euclid v. Ambler Realty Co., 272 U.S. 365 (1926).

9. Rules and Regulations of Board of Adjustment Under the Zoning Ordinance of the City of Charleston (1931), *available at* https://lcdl.library.cofc.edu/lcdl/catalog/266683.

10. *Id.* at 20–21.

11. The National Preservation Partners Network was formed in 2018 to advance the growth and effectiveness of the organized preservation movement through communication, education, training, and a common advocacy agenda. *See* National Preservation Partners Network, www.prespartners.org (last visited Feb. 14, 2026).

C. PRESERVATION ORDINANCES WITHIN THE STATE AND FEDERAL CONTEXT

Every municipal preservation law, by its nature, is a product of its place. Like zoning broadly, the terminology used and the mechanics of the review and appeal process reflect local policy choices. An ordinance can be tailored to protect the types of places a community values and the extent of political capital earned by the preservation community to constrain private action.

Local ordinances can be difficult to fully interpret without reference to the state and federal legal framework. The standards used for what places are worthy of designation are often guided by National Park Service rules. State governments may also constrain certain actions, particularly in places where municipal home rule is more limited.

1. State Enabling Laws

Provisions of state enabling laws governing preservation commissions should be reviewed concurrently with research into any local code. Typically, they contain specific procedures and criteria outlined for major threshold questions such as:

- How historic properties are designated (criteria and process including opportunities for objection from owners and/or state).
- The makeup of historic preservation commissions (professionals in the fields of architecture, history, art history, archeology, and real estate).
- Notification procedures.
- Review of requests for alterations and demolitions.
- The processing of appeals.
- Criteria for exceptions such as economic hardship.

Enabling laws may be more or less prescriptive depending on the degree of home rule afforded to municipalities. Some states grant broad powers that can allow commissions to adopt unique and creative approaches for protecting historic properties. Yet in most states local policymakers are guided by, and sometimes constrained by, specific state enabling legislation.

State enabling laws can have a beneficial role in protecting municipalities from due process challenges under the Fourteenth Amendment that allege that preservation standards are void for vagueness. The Pennsylvania Supreme Court, for instance, cited the provisions of its state enabling law in the face of such a challenge, referencing a requirement that preservation ordinances in the state must set "reasonably defined limits" for the scope of protections (e.g., visible exteriors) and contain specific considerations that "provide sufficient notice to property owners as to what will guide a governing body's decision-making process."[12]

Some states are even more prescriptive. North Carolina restricts the ability of its municipalities to deny an application for a certificate of appropriateness for more than a 365-day delay period.[13] The exception to this rule is if the resource to be demolished is deemed by the State Historic Preservation Officer to be of "statewide significance" without a showing of extreme hardship or permanent deprivation of all beneficial use or return.[14] Yet some caution is warranted in assuming the state plays a large role in whether and how preservation ordinances are devised. A recent comprehensive review of state enabling laws relative to the rates of adoption for new municipal preservation laws showed limited correlation.[15]

2. The Federal Framework

A common misunderstanding in the local context is that designation of historic properties at the federal level will automatically confer local legal protection. But federal designation only triggers reviews under federal law only when projects receive federal agency funding, permitting, or licensing. Even for a resource with the highest level of federal designation (i.e., a National Historic Landmark), a municipality must elect to use its discretion to confer legal protections. In this sense, local regulation is a key component of saving places that tell the nation's story.

Though local government processes for designation vary, it is common for communities to utilize the National Register of Historic Places (NRHP) as a planning tool. Prior to 1966 when Congress passed legislation establishing the NRHP, municipalities created ad hoc local inventories independent of federal criteria. The NRHP criteria added a more consistent, predictable

---

12. Park Home v. City of Williamsport, 680 A.2d 835, 838–39 (Pa. 1996).

13. N.C. GEN. STAT. ANN. § 160D-949(a) (West, Westlaw through S.L. 2025-97 of the 2025 Regular Session of the General Assembly).

14. *Id.* § 160D-949(c).

15. Bronin, Sara C. and Irwin, Leslie R., *Regulating History*, 108 MINN. L. REV. 241, 248 (Nov. 2023), available at https://papers.ssrn.com/sol3/papers.cfm?abstract_id=4396040.

procedure to govern how local historic designations are determined. Clear protocol and process for designations provide regulating authorities with greater insulation against challenges that designations are arbitrary.

Municipalities have wide latitude to make findings justifying historic designation. A recent example from the city of Chicago is typical of the way courts handle challenges, and the general deference provided to local government decision-making around the landmarking process. In designating the Arlington-Deming District, a state appeals court found the city did not run afoul of constitutional protections for a resident frustrated with what they felt was a lack of evidence supporting the district's designation.[16]

One of the key principles of the National Historic Preservation Act, which established the NRHP, was to assist state and local governments to "expand and accelerate their historic preservation programs and activities."[17] NRHP-listed sites can be significant at the national, state, or local level, unlike previous designations that focused only on National Historic Landmarks.[18] In the NHPA Congress authorized the Secretary of the Interior to establish criteria and promulgate regulations governing the NRHP and provide it a right to make determinations on nominations for listing at the federal level, which can be submitted by states, local governments, or private individuals.[19]

In drafting an ordinance, a local government may elect to use the federal NRHP criteria as a basis for nominating locally eligible sites.[20] Yet many localities accept NRHP designations but also extend protections to other places designated under either their own independent criteria or a statewide register. The basis for designation varies from place to place, but, unsurprisingly, communities use the NRHP criteria as a baseline and are additive to, for instance, better incorporate what is unique about local vernacular traditions. In this sense, each locality can take advantage of a federally approved designation program but also create one that is more homespun and rooted in the specific characteristics that make a place unique.

---

16. Robinson v. City of Chicago, 265 N.E.3d 440 (Ill. App. Ct. 2025).

17. 54 U.S.C.A. § 300101(6) (West, Westlaw through Pub. L. No. 119-59).

18. The National Historic Landmarks program was initially established in the Historic Sites Act of 1935.

19. 54 U.S.C.A. §§ 302103, 302104 (West, Westlaw through Pub. L. No. 119-59). These regulations are issued by the National Park Service at 36 C.F.R. pt. 60 and have been supplemented through a series of bulletins available on the NPS website.

20. The eligibility criteria for the NRHP are defined at 36 C.F.R. § 60.

The Dade County Florida Historic Preservation Ordinance is a representative example. Section 16A-10(1) of the Code establishes the designation process and procedure. Section (e) of the provision makes clear that any site listed in the NRHP is automatically included. The section also allows the County to consider "distinctive elements of the cultural, social, political, economic, scientific, religious, prehistoric, paleontological, or architectural history that have contributed to the pattern of history in the community, Miami-Dade County, south Florida, the State or the nation."[21] This addition is likely a result of the County's determination that the NRHP criteria were too restrictive for the full scope of what the County seeks to protect through its ordinance.

To ensure fair administration of rules for designated properties, the federal government also provides a toolkit for State and Tribal Historic Preservation Offices to "certify" local programs and provide technical assistance to local governments in their implementation of local preservation programs.[22] Adhering to the Certified Local Government (CLG) criteria is a requirement for eligibility for federal funding through the Historic Preservation Fund.[23] Local governments must meet certain standards in adopting local rules.[24] State-by-state CLG rules are set by Historic Preservation Offices, which receive federal funding and can be an important source of technical assistance, particularly for smaller towns and cities with less expertise.

To be eligible as a CLG, a municipality must commit that it:

(1) enforces appropriate State or local legislation for the designation and protection of historic property;
(2) has established an adequate and qualified historic preservation review commission by State or local legislation;
(3) maintains a system for the survey and inventory of historic property that furthers the purposes of chapter 3023 [54 U.S.C. §§ 302301 et seq.];
(4) provides for adequate public participation in the local historic preservation program, including the process of recommending properties for nomination to the National Register; and

21. Ch. 16A-10, METROPOLITAN DADE COUNTY CODE. The Code also makes it easier to designate resources from the recent past as that community does not adhere strongly to the NPS's 50-year rule. *See* Metropolitan Dade Cnty. v. P.J. Birds, Inc., 654 So. 2d 170 (Fla. App. 1995).

22. 54 U.S.C.A. §§ 302501–302505 (West, Westlaw through Pub. L. 115–95).

23. 54 U.S.C.A. § 302505(1); 36 C.F.R. § 61.7(a) (2025).

24. 54 U.S.C.A. § 302503.

(5) satisfactorily performs the responsibilities delegated to it under this division [54 U.S.C. §§ 300101 et seq.].[25]

The National Park Service has developed more detailed CLG regulations at 36 C.F.R. § 61.6(e). Other relevant statewide requirements may be defined by the SHPO in state-specific regulations.

CLGs are required to proactively survey and inventory historic properties. In that process, NRHP eligibility can be used as a basis for listing on a local register.[26] Yet, as in Miami-Dade County, described *supra*, NRHP eligibility may not be dispositive of whether it is protected at a local level. The terms of the municipal ordinance control whether and how the municipality affords protections, so local surveys have the greatest use when prepared mindful of the scope of existing local protections. Confusion can result when a historic site is determined eligible at multiple levels (i.e., local, state, and federal).[27] The terms of the ordinance control the scope of protection.

The value of professional and up-to-date historic resource surveys cannot be overstated. Regardless of how designations are determined, a survey creates for the commissions a strong basis for informed decision-making and for ensuring fair decision-making. Yet, in practice, surveys are often incomplete or in need of updates to reflect changed conditions and perspective on the relative historic importance of buildings, particularly those of more modern vintage.[28] For these reasons permit applicants are often advised by city staff of the need to accompany their requests for alteration or demolition with historic evidence of changes of a property through time. Robust

---

25. *Id.*

26. States typically maintain databases of NRHP-eligible sites through their SHPOs. Frequently, these determinations have been made as part of previous Section 106 compliance processes.

27. There may be reasons other than local protection to pursue formal designation of resources. The federal historic tax credit, for instance, applies only if the site seeking the credit has been listed on the NRHP.

28. The federal standard for the NRHP is that buildings 50 or more years old have an easier pathway to eligibility. 36 C.F.R. § 60.4 (2025). Places less than 50 years old must exhibit "exceptional importance." *Id.* § 60.4(g). This determination was made recently for the 2200-acre crash site of Flight 93 in Shanksville, PA. Some communities that are more concerned with places from the recent past have adjusted this period. For more on the origins of the 50-year threshold, adopted by many municipalities, *see* John Sprinkle, *Of Exceptional Importance: The Origins of the "Fifty Year Rule" in Historic Preservation*, 2 Public Historian 81–103 (Spring 2007).

historical information can be critical to consequential decisions about what can and cannot be changed and why. Sanborn insurance maps, for example, are often critical aids to demonstrate how a property can be adapted consistent with historic trends. If the map shows a building that once existed and has been removed, for instance, the commission may be more inclined to allow for a modern structure in its footprint.

D. LOCAL PRESERVATION REGULATIONS IN PRACTICE

As this chapter illustrates, local historic preservation ordinances vary considerably. The mechanics of how each law works reflect the policy choices of individual places and vary most directly on the degree to which the ordinance affects rights held in private property. This section will provide a framework for some of the key differentiating features of ordinances.

1. Local Commissions

A local review board or commission is pivotal to the administration of local preservation rules. In assuming a quasi-legislative role, this body typically evaluates applications for the change of a building that is either landmarked individually or contributes to a historic district. In some cases, a specific commission is set up for the administration of permits in one historic district, as in the Vieux Carre of New Orleans.[29]

The composition and quality of expertise on a preservation commission must be established to provide legitimacy to its decision-making power. Ordinances typically require representation from relevant fields such as architecture, history, planning, real estate, and law to ensure well-reasoned decisions. Without these requirements, commissions may be perceived as arbitrary or lacking important qualification. With defined qualifications, courts may be more inclined to afford deference to a commission's interpretation of statutory terms.[30]

---

29. *See* New Orleans, La., City Code ch. 166, §§ 31–38.

30. See Turchi v. Phila. Bd. of License & Inspection Review, 20 A.3d 586, 595 (Pa. Commw. Ct. 2011), finding that the historical commission was entitled to control administrative interpretation of the terms "in significant part" and "demolition" and that an appellate licensing board had exceeded its scope of review by offering a contrary interpretation.

The requirement to file a building or demolition permit is the most common way preservation review is triggered. Most states require municipalities to certify that construction is consistent with a building code.[31] In using its discretion to approve, deny, defer, or condition an application, a preservation commission is expected to apply a set of standards prior to issuing an approval, typically termed a "Certificate of Appropriateness." Commissions are often aided by the expertise of city staff, typically a planning department, and counseled by city legal representatives.

State planning laws often require consistency on how commissions are appointed, their relative size, rules, and the required expertise of members.[32] To ensure fair implementation of the law, code provisions typically include notice to the community, and neighboring property owners in particular, accompanied by hearing times and dates, and the opportunity for the applicant to present and the public to provide input. Motion practice customarily follows Robert's Rules of Order.

City attorneys will ensure that commissions are clearly authorized, have defined membership qualifications, and articulate rationales for decision-making in recorded findings consistent with clearly defined standards set by the ordinance. Close attention to procedural fairness prevents arbitrary decisions and provides the expertise necessary for evaluating preservation matters.

City staff generally have a leading role in screening applications prior to review by a full commission, which can also have the effect of streamlining projects with a small scope. The size of the impact may determine whether board review is necessary or whether permit approval can occur at the staff level. City staff are often delegated the authority to approve insignificant changes to avoid overburdening local preservation commissions. These less public decisions may be subject to appeal to the full board, though, in practice, community members who disagree with a staff decision may be unaware of the approvals. When full board review is required, staff often provide written recommendations to inform how motions are

---

31. The few states that do not require municipalities to adopt a state building code, such as Colorado, Delaware, and Texas, allow local jurisdictions to adopt their own rules.

32. In North Carolina, for instance, the majority of such commission members must have demonstrated "special interest, experience, or education in history, architecture, archaeology, or related fields" as well as live in the jurisdiction. N.C. Gen. Stat. Ann. § 160D-303 (West, Westlaw through S.L. 2025-97 of the 2025 Regular Session of the General Assembly).

framed. Permit applicants and members of the public are typically invited to make additional points in publicly noticed hearings through oral and written comments.

2. Scope of Review

a. Exterior Modifications

The purview of commissions is carefully defined by ordinance. The most common scope of review, by far, is the regulation of exterior modifications that are visible from the right-of-way. This includes removal of older material such as windows, roofs, doors, and siding as well as review of the design of additions and new buildings in close proximity.

Courts may be suspicious of vague or overly broad scope provisions, while upholding narrowly tailored ones that are supported by documented legislative intent. The scope must align with the community's preservation goals and provide clear guidance on how historic resources are best protected.

Most ordinances focus primary attention on regulating modifications to the exterior envelope of a building. The commission will analyze how a proposed scope of work could lead to the removal of original or older features that define the character of a building within the protected boundary. The ordinance may also aim to prevent alterations deemed insensitive to the original design intent of a historic structure.

The unique components worthy of particular attention to local commissions are known as the characteristics of a historic property that are the basis for its eligibility as a designated resource.[33] If an original roof has been replaced, but the original windows remain, for example, guidance from the commission may stress the importance of preserving the older materials above the newer. Greater leniency might be applied in approaching changes to more modern components. Municipalities may also look to concepts from National Park Service guidance in making judgment calls.[34] It may

33. In the federal context, the Section 106 regulations define an adverse effect as when an undertaking "may alter directly, or indirectly, the characteristics of a historic property that qualify the property for inclusion in the National Register in a manner that would diminish the integrity of the property's location, design, setting, materials, workmanship, feeling, or association." 36 C.F.R. pt. 800.5(a)(1) (2025).

34. The NPS maintains a comprehensive set of publications that can be of assistance including bulletins, best practices, and guidelines, available at www.nps.gov/subjects/nationalregister/publications.htm.

reference, for instance, the period of years of greatest relevance, or a "period of significance," in giving primacy to certain elements of a building or site.[35]

The City of Santa Fe's preservation ordinance is a representative example, stating in plain terms the intention of regulating exteriors and gives applicants a sense of the issues the Commission will look to in making decisions:

(a) Each structure to be recognized as a physical record of its time, place, and use. Changes that create a false sense of historical development, such as the addition of conjectural features or architectural elements from other buildings, shall not be undertaken;
(b) Changes to structures that have acquired historic significance in their own right shall be retained and preserved, recognizing that most structures change over time;
(c) Distinctive features, finishes, and construction techniques or examples of craftsmanship that characterize a structure be preserved; and
(d) New additions and related or adjacent new construction be undertaken in such a manner that if removed in the future, the original form and integrity of the historic property and its environment would be unimpaired.[36]

b. New Construction

In addition to review of historic building modifications, commissions are granted the power of design review for new buildings. These protections are intended to ensure the integrity of historic districts and limit incompatible development adjacent to designated landmarks. Decision-making relies on a study of the adjacent context, which can be a critical aspect of a site's importance.

Design guidelines and other supplementary material adopted by the board can be helpful for aiding review of new designs and to make the

---

35. National Park Service, *How to Complete the National Register Registration Form* (National Register Bulletin 16A), *available at* www.nps.gov/subjects/nationalregister/upload/NRB16A-Complete.pdf. Local registers may not include such a period, but it is standard practice when sites are nominated to the NRHP.

36. Santa Fe, N.M., Code of Ordinances § 14–5.2(C). In *City of Santa Fe v. Gamble-Skogmo, Inc.*, 389 P.2d 13 (N.M. 1964) the court upheld an earlier version of Santa Fe's ordinance against a plaintiff seeking to invalidate the regulation as an unlawful exercise of zoning authority citing the detailed description in the ordinance of "Old Santa Fe style."

permitting process more predictable for applicants. There is considerable regional variation in what is deemed appropriate for a new building in a historic context. In an early case in rural New Hampshire, a court found it sufficient for selectmen in the Town of Deering, to deny a prebuilt home within a quarter mile of its town green for being incompatible with the "atmosphere" of the town.[37] Similarly, an Ohio court upheld the city's right to deny a permit for a "radical departure" that would be caused by constructing a modern building in the City of Cleveland Heights.[38]

One of the most significant differences is that some jurisdictions may aim to create clear delineation and differentiation between new and old, as in Santa Fe's concern in its ordinance, discussed *supra*, indicating concern with creating a false sense of historical development.[39] Yet another community may embrace older styles and support the emulation of more traditional infill, stressing durability of materials and classical principles of design.[40] It might use its own guidance to encourage new construction that matches the dominant architectural style rather than be differentiated from it.[41]

The differentiation rule stemmed from the Venice Charter, developed in 1964 in the immediate years before the NHPA was passed. The drafters urged that any extra work that occurs on the restoration of a monument "be distinct" and "bear a contemporary stamp."[42] It then became the ideological predecessor to Secretary of the Interior's determination that contemporary

37. Town of Deering v. Tibbetts, 202 A.2d 232, 235–36 (N.H. 1964).

38. Reid v. Architectural Bd. of Review of Cleveland Heights, 192 N.E.2d 74, 77 (Ohio Ct. App. 1963) ("Not only does the house fail to conform in any manner with the other buildings but presents no identification that it is a structure for people to live in.").

39. *See* Secretary of the Interior Standard for Rehabilitation No. 9 which states, "New additions, exterior alterations, or related new construction shall not destroy historic materials that characterize the property. The new work shall be differentiated from the old and shall be compatible with the massing, size, scale, and architectural features to protect the historic integrity of the property and its environment." 36 C.F.R. § 67.7(b)(9) (2025).

40. The writings of Leon Krier are an excellent source in general. *See also* Christopher Alexander et al., A Pattern Language: Towns, Buildings, Construction (1977).

41. For instance, in 1957 Santa Fe passed an ordinance citing support for the "continued construction of buildings in the historic styles." City of Santa Fe v. Gamble-Skogmo, Inc., 73 N.M. 410, 413 (N.M. 1964).

42. International Charter for the Conservation and Restoration of Monuments and Sites, available at www.icomos.org/images/DOCUMENTS/Charters/venice_e.pdf.

work to historic buildings refrain from creating a "false sense of historical development."[43]

While the Secretary Standards can be uniquely important in the context of historic tax credit projects, they need not be followed by all jurisdictions in local preservation review processes. The National Alliance of Preservation Commissions maintains a representative library of design guidelines on its website.[44] Some showcase local judgment that more traditional design can and should be integrated into historic districts.

c. *Landscapes*

The adjacent surroundings of a historic building or district can often be the subject of attention in permitting decisions. In a 2002 case in Washington, D.C., the court upheld the city's decision to deny a permit for a new curb cut to facilitate the construction of a new garage.[45] Relevant to the decision was the city's conclusion that the streetside berms within the Kalorama Historic District were a unifying characteristic and showcased how central public transportation was in the original layout of the neighborhood. Some jurisdictions utilize preservation commissions to review changes to public resources, such as in San Francisco, which requires certificates of appropriateness for proposed alterations to "city-owned parks, squares, plazas or gardens on a landmark site."[46]

3. Guidelines for Review

A successful preservation ordinance should give property owners, architects, and commissions a shared framework for evaluating applications. Ordinance language can require commissions to adopt guidelines, policies, and procedures to help reduce subjective decision-making and improve consistency. The articulation of clear standards can better ensure that decisions are based on objective, published criteria rather than personal preference.

At a minimum, many commissions are guided by specific references in ordinance language to the federal Secretary of the Interior's Standards for

---

43. 36 C.F.R. § 68.3(b)(3) (2025).

44. *See* www.napcommissions.org/design-guidelines"www.napcommissions.org/design-guidelines.

45. Gondelman v. Dep't of Con. & Reg. Affairs, 789 A.2d 1238 (D.C. 2002).

46. City and County of San Francisco Code Planning Code art. X, § 1006(4).

the Treatment of Historic Properties.[47] These four sets of standards differ in the objectives set for any given project. A historic building being adapted for a new use will likely follow rehabilitation standards, the most frequently cited set in preservation practice. Standards are also set for preservation, restoration, and reconstruction, with terms carefully defined in the regulation.[48]

As an example, the Historic District Committee of Dover, Delaware, which advises the planning commission, is given wide latitude by ordinance to establish design standards for historic structures as well as new construction.[49] Pursuant to this authority, it has developed "Design Standards and Guidelines for the Dover Historic District Zone."[50] One court determined these guidelines so critical to the effective implementation of the ordinance that it overturned the issuance of a certificate of appropriateness approving new construction in the backyard of significant structure.[51]

There is a wide variety of tools any given municipality may employ in addition to or in lieu of design guidelines. Character studies and other contextual information can offer unique insight particularly for areas without up-to-date survey data. Applicants seeking to make the case for desired changes to their property in advance of a hearing also benefit from this information to tailor their case for change accordingly. Supplements can be critical to consistent, reasoned decision-making that can withstand judicial scrutiny in the event of a legal challenge.

4. Binding or Advisory Role

Not all local commissions have the power to issue permit denials. Some municipalities may feel ill equipped to defend against challenges and customize their ordinance to push applicants in the right direction without mandating action that requires staff to enforce those decisions. Commissions may be advisory to applicants themselves or other bodies of government, like a

47. 36 C.F.R. § 67.8 (2025).

48. *Id.* § 68.2.

49. City of Dover Code, pt. XII, tit. V, ch. 1341.04(a), (b).

50. Design Standards & Guidelines for the City of Dover Historic District (1992), available at www.cityofdover.gov/historic-district-guidelines.

51. Dover Hist. Soc'y v. City of Dover Planning Comm'n, C.A. No. 03A-06-002, 2004 WL 1790164 (Del. July 30, 2004). The special considerations included (1) style, (2) scale, (3) absolute size, (4) massing, (5) orientation, (6) proportions, (7) materials, (8) forms, (9) siting, (10) high density, and (11) secondary structures. *Id.* at *7.

planning commission or city council. Clearly defining the review type in the ordinance can help avoid disputes over the commission's authority and aid enforcement efforts.

As an example, the City of Harrisburg, Pennsylvania, has an Historic Architectural Review Board that makes recommendations to its city council on permit applications in its historic overlay zones. While specific procedures must be followed by the applicant, the code is clear that the council, so long as it takes into consideration specified criteria, has final say on whether to approve a certificate of appropriateness.[52]

5. Demolition Delay

One method to advance the objective of preserving older properties without establishing a local board at all is to enact procedural hurdles to deter harmful action. A common mechanism to support this type of policy is to require a delay period prior to issuing a demolition permit for buildings in a historic district, or simply of a certain age.[53] The justification for the time delay is to alert the community to a prospective loss and allow for time for private actors to negotiate a solution.

Weston, Massachusetts, has opted for a one-year demolition delay provision specifically for buildings built before 1945 with a provision for buildings otherwise determined significant. The law is "intended to encourage owners and townspeople to seek out persons who might be willing to purchase, preserve, rehabilitate or restore such buildings rather than demolish them."[54]

6. Designations

The process for designating landmarks and historic districts is a core function of many preservation commissions. Because these decisions can significantly affect the rights of an owner by limiting his or her ability to freely alter or demolish a structure, municipalities must afford the owner due process rights in making the designation. It is critical for local commissions to

---

52. City of Harrisburg, PA Code § 7-317.12.

53. *See* Julia H. Miller, *Protecting Potential Landmarks Through Demolition Review*, National Trust Preservation Law Publication (2006).

54. Weston By-laws & Regulations art. XXVI, available at www.westonma.gov/572/Text-of-Demolition-Delay-By-Law.

ensure their procedures for designation are procedurally sound, supported by objective criteria, and have boundaries that are well justified.[55] In designating properties, municipalities must ensure that proper notice is provided and have well-defined evidentiary standards.

a. *Types of Designations*

Some ordinances place great emphasis on the regulation of districts while others single out individual properties as part of a landmarks program. New York City's landmarks program was famously challenged in the most significant preservation law case to reach the U.S. Supreme Court. The Court upheld New York's regulation against a regulatory takings challenge under the Fifth Amendment and laid the groundwork for the expansion of local protection programs throughout the country.[56]

Notably, communities are not beholden to federal standards in creating local designation categories to confer protections. In Miami, Florida, for example, a court upheld a unique designation criterion for properties of exceptional significance that were less than 50 years old against a due process claim.[57] The court found persuasive that the county standard was patterned on the criteria delineated by the National Park Service for identifying such properties, that it was clarified by judicial and administrative interpretation, and that greater specificity would hinder the commission.

b. *Objections to Designation*

In the case that multiple properties are proposed for a district-level designation, some jurisdictions may allow a majority of affected property owners the chance to veto an effort. In Houston, Texas, for instance, two-thirds of the owners of property in a proposed historic district must consent.[58] A recent analysis also found that ten states require municipalities to allow for owner objection to designation.[59] Many large cities like New York, San

---

55. S. of Second Assocs. v. Georgetown, 580 P.2d 507 (Colo. 1978) (striking down a historic district designation that included all of the properties in the municipality as unconstitutionally vague as "nowhere in the ordinance is a delineation of the relevant areas to be found").

56. Penn Central Transp. Co. v. N.Y. City, 438 U.S. 104 (1978).

57. Metropolitan Dade Cnty. v. P.J. Birds, Inc., 654 So. 2d 170 (Fla. App. 1995).

58. Houston, Tex. Code § 33–222.1.

59. Bronin & Irwin, *Regulating History*, 108 Minn. L. Rev. 266–67 (2023).

Francisco, Chicago, and Washington, D.C., do not allow for owner objections to defeat the designation making them far more consequential.

7. Adjudicating Economic Hardship Claims

Absent specific authorization in a local code, local commissions are typically not empowered to consider factors of cost in permitting decisions. An applicant may, however, seek to take advantage of an economic hardship provision in the code to obtain administrative relief.

The presence of a hardship clause is generally intended to address in an administrative rather than a legal forum that the deprivation of value so significant that it would qualify as eminent domain, or a so-called regulatory taking. Technically, courts are inclined to uphold preservation ordinances against takings challenges absent a showing of complete economic loss. The Pennsylvania Supreme Court has held, for example, that a city can appropriately deny an applicant's economic hardship claim if they fail to demonstrate that they could not have made any practicable or possible economic use of the property they sought to demolish.[60]

Yet this does not mean municipalities may not be inclined to make exceptions for political purposes or to avoid the threat of litigation. Courts may look more favorably when an ordinance contains options for administrative relief. Not surprisingly, the definition of such relief in the form of economic hardship commonly tracks the U.S. Supreme Court's legal standard for an unconstitutional regulatory taking by requiring a property owner to establish that he or she has been denied "all economically beneficial or productive use of land."[61]

Jurisdictions vary in how claims are adjudicated. Some permit the preservation commission to make a final decision, sometimes with the aid of a hearing officer, while others allow for appeal to a city council. In some cases, a special economic review panel may be assembled.[62] They often vary considerably as to what materials are required of the applicant in the process.

---

60. City of Pittsburgh v. Weinberg, 676 A.2d 207 (Pa. 1995).

61. Lucas v. S.C. Coastal Council, 505 U.S. 1003, 1015 (1992).

62. Julia H. Miller, *Assessing Economic Hardship Claims Under Historic Preservation Ordinances*, ALLIANCE REVIEW 16 (Jan.–Feb. 2002).

For example, Detroit, Michigan, defines its exception for "undue hardship" simply when "governmental action, an act of God, or other events beyond the owner's control created the hardship, and all feasible alternatives to eliminate the financial hardship, which may include offering the resource for sale at its fair market value or moving the resource to an appropriate vacant site within the historic district, have been attempted and exhausted by the owner".[63]

In contrast, the city of Geneva, Illinois, requires applicants for the waiver to submit detailed personal financial information to the local commission and contains a laborious process of review.[64] Because a hearing will likely involve disputes between experts, the adjudicating body must be qualified to and prepared to make specific findings of fact after weighing the evidence.

8. Special Merit of the Replacement Project

On occasion preservation ordinances open the door for commissions to justify demolition of a historic structure based on the value of the building that might replace it. Washington, D.C., allows for the mayor's agent to issue a demolition permit when "necessary in the public interest," which includes cases when it is "necessary to allow the construction of a project of special merit."[65] Similarly, San Antonio allows the commission, in reviewing an application for demolition, to balance "the historic, architectural, cultural and/or archaeological value of the particular landmark or eligible landmark against the special merit of the proposed replacement project."[66]

In other cases, permitting decisions in historic districts may make exceptions for the quality of a replacement building. Detroit allows exceptions when "[t]he resource is a deterrent to a major improvement program that will be of substantial benefit to the community."[67] Beverly Hills, California, allows for demolition only in the case that a permit for the construction of a replacement building is simultaneously issued.[68]

---

63. Detroit, Mich. Code § 21-2-75(3).

64. Geneva, Ill. Code § 10-6-12.

65. D.C. Code Ann. §§ 6-1102(10), 6-1104(e).

66. San Antonio, Tex. City Code § 35-614(e)(1)(A).

67. Detroit, Mich. Code § 21-2-75(2).

68. Beverly Hills, Cal. Code § 10-3-4201.

9. Appeals

In some jurisdictions a municipality's elected body must certify designations of historic properties or provide aggrieved applicants an appeals process. In New York City, the city council has 120 days from the filing of a designation by its Landmarks Preservation Commission to modify or disapprove designations.[69] In South Carolina, appellants are authorized to file suit and request mediation, with settlements ultimately approved by local elected leaders.[70]

10. Penalties and Enforcement

Preservation ordinances must be enforceable to be effective. Codes employ a variety of approaches to define violations, set penalty amounts, and outline enforcement procedures. Stop-work orders, fines, and permit delays are often considered, though maximum penalties may be fixed by state law.

69. N.Y.C. Admin. Code § 25-303(g)2.

70. S.C. Code Ann. § 6-29-900 (Westlaw through 2025 Act No. 94).

Constitutional Law Issues 7

Many states might have state-specific avenues to challenge or defend local preservation laws. But in the vast majority of cases, contestants assert (often many) constitutional grounds. Those grounds cluster around the Fifth (takings), Fifth (due process), First (speech), and First (religion) Amendments. At least with regard to the freedom of religion arguments, there is a corresponding statutory issue.

A. FIFTH AMENDMENT (TAKINGS)

The Fifth Amendment's takings clause says, "[N]or shall private property be taken for public use, without just compensation."[1] Of course, the takings clause applies to state and localities—the far more likely source of historic preservation issues—in the same way it applies to the federal government.[2]

1. U.S. CONST. amend. V.

2. Sheetz v. County of El Dorado, 601 U.S. 267 (2024).

The takings clause of the Fifth Amendment prohibits the taking of private property for public use without just compensation.[3] The takings clause applies also to state and local actions through the Fourteenth Amendment.[4] Takings claims are of two types: (1) "physical takings," which are acquisitions of title to property for public use, and (2) "regulatory takings," which are regulations that prohibit private uses of property.[5] A takings classification depends on "whether the government has physically taken property for itself or someone else—by whatever means—or has instead restricted a property owner's ability to use his own property."[6] If the former is true, a per se taking has occurred.[7] The classic example of a taking is when the government actually replaces a private owner as the new deed holder. If the latter is true, analysis under *Penn Central Transportation Co. v. City of New York*[8] is required.[9] The government does not have to become the legal owner of property or physically occupy the property to take it under the Fifth Amendment; it can exert enough control over enough of the sticks in the bundle that it effectively becomes the owner.

Third, when the government withholds a right unless an owner does something, that can be a taking, too. For instance, if a city were to withhold permission to add a second unit to a parcel unless the owner agreed to restore the historic main building, that exaction could qualify as a Fifth Amendment violation. To use the phrasing of those bearing the burden of complying with the conditions, the terms of the "deal to get to refuse" are a sanitized form of extortion. To those on the other side, they are "leverage."

1. Physical Takings

a. Eminent Domain

Eminent domain refers to direct takings where the government uses its inherent power to acquire private property, pay just compensation for it, and put the property to use for a public purpose. The sovereign power to do so comes

---

3. U.S. Const. amend. V.

4. *See Sheetz*, 601 U.S. at 277.

5. Tahoe-Sierra Pres. Council, Inc. v. Tahoe Reg'l Plan. Agency, 535 U.S. 302, 323–24 (2002).

6. Cedar Point Nursery v. Hassid, 594 U.S. 139, 149 (2021).

7. *Id.* at 149–50.

8. 438 U.S. 104 (1978).

9. *Id.* at 149.

from the Fifth Amendment: "nor shall private property be taken for public use, without just compensation."[10] States (and often component parts of states such as counties, cities, and public utilities) very frequently have the power to condemn private property flowing from state constitutions. And while each state might have slight variations on the right, most track the federal analysis.

Typically, a government will notify an owner of its plans to take private property, and the owner and the government then negotiate a price. If the taking itself is challenged or if no price can be agreed upon, state laws provide for different legal proceedings in which the owner may challenge the government's decisions.

Notice that eminent domain can be used not just to acquire land or buildings to preserve them; it can also be used to acquire (and possibly terminate) conservation easements. The Uniform Conservation Easement Act "neither limits nor enlarges the power of eminent domain" regarding either condemning easements or the eased property.[11]

Note that "condemnation" is often used to describe a government's direct taking of property. "Condemnation" in connection with the takings clause leads to the ownership of the property passing from the owner to the government. "Condemnation" is also used to describe scenarios when the government cuts off an owner's access or use of private property—for example, when the government condemns a dilapidated house—but in those cases, the ownership of the property does not change. In those cases, the government is exercising its police power, not its power to take private property.

The Fifth Amendment requires that takings be for "public use." Public uses obviously include such things as highways and airports, but the restriction has been very generously read to include "public purpose" even when the public will not actually put the land to affirmative use or have access to it. Instead, such public purposes include eliminating blight[12] and promoting economic development.[13]

In *Berman v. Parker*, the Court upheld Congress's plan to redevelop a blighted part of Washington, D.C., by taking private property and then passing along that same property to developers. Congress began its act with a

10. U.S. Const. amend. V.

11. UCEA, Commissioners' Prefatory Note ¶ 11.

12. Berman v. Parker, 348 U.S. 26, 29 (1954) (approving plans to eliminate slums and blighted areas in Washington, D.C.).

13. Kelo v. City of New London, 545 U.S. 469 (2005).

statement that blighted areas and substandard housing were injurious to public health, safety, and welfare. Entire areas had to be replanned, and the private marketplace would be unable to tackle the problem at a large enough scale, and "public participation" was needed. First, a planning commission was charged with developing a comprehensive plan, which would then be certified to the District of Columbia Redevelopment Land Agency to be carried out. The agency had been vested with the power of eminent domain. The owner of a department store in the affected area challenged the taking on the basis that it did not comply with the public use requirement: The store was not even residential to start with, and reconveying title to a private developer to carry out the agency's plan was not a public use, according to the store's owner.

The Court began by describing the very broad scope of the government's police power: "Public safety, public health, morality, peace and quiet, law and order—these are some of the more conspicuous examples of the traditional application of the police power to municipal affairs. Yet they merely illustrate the scope of the power and do not delimit it."[14] The language of the Court made clear that there could be no broad and objective test for the edges of the police power: "The values it represents are spiritual as well as physical, aesthetic as well as monetary. It is within the power of the legislature to determine that the community should be beautiful as well as healthy, spacious as well as clean, well-balanced as well as carefully patrolled."[15] Having then defined the breadth of the government's appropriate aims, the Court noted that the takings clause was just the means to achieve those broad purposes. The ability to use it was "clear."[16] The Court basically washed its hands of the dispute and deferred to Congress to decide how to achieve its goals. If, in the view of Congress, swapping out owners with new developers was a good idea, then so be it. Judicial oversight was extremely narrow: "If those who govern the District of Columbia decide that the Nation's Capital should be beautiful as well as sanitary, there is nothing in the Fifth Amendment that stands in the way."

In the decades that followed, the Supreme Court has not drifted away from the hands-off approach to takings challenges. In *Kelo v. City of New London*,[17] the Court confirmed that the Fifth Amendment's "public use"

---

14. *Berman*, 348 U.S. at 32.

15. *Id.* at 33.

16. *Id.*

17. 545 U.S. 469 (2005).

requirement can be very broadly interpreted. Instead, responding to a series of hypotheticals spinning out possible abuses, the Court simply replied that states were able to further limit the use of eminent domain. Many have. State statutes and constitutional amendments have limited public purposes in different ways such as prohibiting redevelopment takings or takings to cure blight.

Eminent domain is a two-edged sword: While land can be taken to promote historic preservation, it can also be taken to flatten historic resources. For every government seizure of land to protect a historic battlefield, there is a government seizure of land to build a highway through a historic neighborhood. While there are obviously limits, the courts have deferred to more democratically responsive parts of government to decide whether particular uses of land are wise.

b. Physical Takings Not Involving Eminent Domain

A diminution of property value, standing alone, will not establish a taking.[18] In the textbook example of eminent domain, the government takes a tract of land for use as a highway, airport, or some other traditional government project. In those cases, the landowner might object to the compensation being paid by the government or perhaps whether there is public purpose being served by the taking.[19] However, the existence of a taking is not in debate: When the taking happens, a new deed is recorded making the government fee simple owner of the property with the full range of ownership rights.

Not every case of eminent domain involves such a clear example. When the government physically takes property without going through the normal eminent domain process, the owner pursues a claim of "inverse condemnation" where the main issue is likely to be whether the government has even *taken* property at all.

The most important case involving an inverse condemnation claim is *Loretto v. TelePrompter Manhattan CATV Corp.*[20] In that case, an owner sued when a New York law allowed a cable company to install equipment on property while excluding compensation for the physical occupation

---

18. *See* Ragucci v. Metropolitan Dev. Comm'n, 702 N.E.2d 677, 683 (Ind. 1998).

19. *See, e.g.*, Kelo v. City of New London, 545 U.S. 469 (2005).

20. 458 U.S. 419 (1982).

above a nominal $1 payment. TelePrompter installed a 30-foot cable slightly less than one-half inch above the top of the building, directional taps that were about four-inch cubes, and some metal boxes along the cables using screws, bolts, and nails.[21] The possession was minimal to be sure given that the building was a five-story apartment building. Nevertheless, when government action results in the loss of physical space more than just temporarily, a compensable taking happens: "In short, when the 'character of the governmental action' is a permanent physical occupation of property, our cases uniformly have found a taking to the extent of the occupation, without regard to whether the action achieves an important public benefit or has only minimal economic impact on the owner."[22]

Even when the physical possession is small, the analysis is simple. "When the Government physically takes possession of an interest in property for some public purpose, it has a categorical duty to compensate the former owner . . . regardless of whether the interest that is taken constitutes an entire parcel or merely part thereof."[23] Moreover, the same result occurs whether the government itself occupies a small piece of the property or authorizes a third party to. In fact, a taking occurs in part precisely because "an owner suffers a special kind of injury when a *stranger* directly invades and occupies" his property.[24]

Some scholars have argued that *Loretto* should be read broadly and used as a sword to *attack* preservation laws. To them, there is no difference between a law that makes an owner tolerate a cable box on his land and a law that prohibits an owner from removing a building he owns from this land. In both cases, some space that is owned by the objector is being involuntarily filled with tangible material he does not want: "It defies logic to say that a permanent physical occupation of property only exists—and is therefore a taking—when the government places the object on the land but not when it compels the upkeep of an unwanted object."[25]

---

21. *Id.* at 422.

22. *Id.* at 434–35 (quoting *Penn Central*, 438 U.S. 104, 124 (1978)).

23. Brown v. Legal Found. of Wash., 538 U.S. 216, 233 (2003) (citation omitted).

24. Loretto v. Teleprompter Manhattan CATV Corp., 458 U.S. 419, 436 (1982) (emphasis in original); Building Owners & Managers Ass'n Int'l v. FCC, 254 F.3d 89, 97 (D.C. Cir. 2001).

25. Kraz Greinetz, *Historic Preservation: Launched from Grand Central Terminal, but Derailing*, 18 Duke J. Const. L. & Pub. Pol'y Sidebar 365, 380 (2023).

In a very recent case, the Fifth Circuit became the first court to use *Loretto* to find that forcing an owner to *keep* a portion of a building is theoretically indistinguishable from a law that permits the government to *build* one. In *Money v. City of San Marcos*,[26] the façade of a home in the Burleson Historic District of San Marcos, Texas, had a Juliet balcony to which Frank Zimmerman, a former owner, had attached a letter Z. The current owners wanted to remove Mr. Zimmerman's initial from their house; Mr. Zimmerman had notoriously been associated with the Ku Klux Klan.

The owners' house was not itself historic, but it was located within a historic district. In fact, the Texas Historical Commission had rejected an application to designate the house as historic. Nevertheless, by being within the historic district, the owners faced a fine if they removed the Z without the proper permission. The commission denied their application for permission to remove the Z, and the homeowners sued, alleging a taking.

The district court determined that the takings claim was not ripe and then *sua sponte* dismissed all claims for failure to state a claim. On appeal, the bulk of the Fifth Circuit's opinion was spent explaining why the lower court should not have dismissed the case on ripeness grounds before getting to the substance of the owners' case. The court quickly determined that, on remand, the *Loretto* case was indeed controlling. The court wrote:

> We see no meaningful distinction between the allegations in the Moneys' complaint and *Loretto*. Both here and there, a government ordinance prohibited a building owner from removing an object that was already attached to the exterior of his building when he purchased it. Likewise, both the Z and the cable equipment were installed at a former owner's discretion, not pursuant to government action or regulation, but subsequently enacted public ordinances prohibited removal.[27]

The implication of *Money* is possibly very significant. It would seem that a local preservation law which compelled an owner to continue possessing even tiny pieces of a building is a per se taking entitling the owner to compensation. It is unclear how the Fifth Circuit ruling might be limited to

26. No. 24-50187, 2025 WL 429980, at *5 (5th Cir. Feb. 7, 2025).

27. *Id.*

the one case before it. The owner in *Money* not only asserted a Fifth Amendment violation but also asserted that his rights under the Texas Constitution and been violated; unlike the federal constitution, the Texas constitution had long forbidden restrictions of property for "purely aesthetic purposes."[28] Most preservation laws are solidly grounded in not purely aesthetic purposes, so a challenge even in Texas might be unlikely to work. But, the Fifth Amendment analysis equating a preservation requirement to *Loretto* remains.

One recent Supreme Court case involving inverse condemnations deserves some attention for its possible impact on a narrow subset of preservation laws. In *Cedar Point Nursery v. Hassid*,[29] the Supreme Court ruled that a California regulation giving union organizers access to farms to talk with employees about supporting a union is unconstitutional. The regulation granted access up to three hours a day over a 30-day period for a total of 120 days each year. Chief Justice John Roberts wrote that when "the government physically acquires private property for a public use," the Fifth Amendment's takings clause "imposes a clear and categorical obligation to provide the owner with just compensation." The access regulation created a right to invade the growers' property and, therefore, was a physical taking.

The case was significant for using the same analysis for temporary intrusions that *Loretto* had used for permanent ones. In other words, whereas *Loretto* shrank the size of the intrusion to which the Fifth Amendment applied, *Cedar Point* shrank the duration of the intrusion to which the First Amendment applied. As Chief Justice Roberts saw the regulation, employers lost the ability to exclude others. Reacting to the concerns of the minority, he added that the government can still require temporary intrusions such as health and safety inspections as a condition of receiving permits and licenses.

How might *Cedar Point* impact preservation laws? Going forward, preservation laws that include public access might be attacked as a physical taking automatically requiring at least some compensation. Most preservation laws do not *require* any public access. For instance, nothing in the National Register listing process requires that the doors to a historic house ever be thrown open to tour groups or that campers be allowed to hike

28. *Id.* at *4–5 (citing Spann v. City of Dallas, 235 S.W. 513, 513, 518 (Tex. 1921)).

29. 594 U.S. 139 (2021).

across a historic battlefield. Instead, many preservation laws extract public access as part of the deal for financial benefits and tax breaks to owners. In those cases, if an owner wants to receive a tax benefit for donating a conservation easement, there must be at least some sort of public access, even if that means simply being visible from a public street. After all, the tax benefits for preserving a historic building are in exchange for some public benefit; if the public cannot access the piece of history their public funds have gone toward securing, has there really been a public benefit?[30]

There are exceptions, though, where public access is required without a corresponding benefit to the owner. Many states outlaw the removal of grave markers on private property without first working through an approval process.[31] But because of the peculiar interests involved in burial grounds, many states' laws go a step further and allow certain groups of people to visit those burial grounds on private land. The common law has already created a legal doctrine that allows interested parties to access burial sites even on private land.[32] When an owner permits a burial on private land, an easement of access is created that flows down through the family of the deceased. About 20% of states have codified that right to access.[33] Some statutes expand the scope of access beyond the common law to include genealogical researchers and others.[34] In West Virginia, even "close friends" may use the statute to visit graves on private land.[35]

30. www.nps.gov/orgs/1739/upload/brochure-easements-historic-properties.pdf ("In order to claim the Federal income tax deduction for a historic preservation easement, at least some visual public access to the property must be available.").

31. *See, e.g.*, S.C. CODE § 27-43-10 (Westlaw through 2025 Act No. 94).

32. *See* Alfred L. Brophy, *Grave Matters: The Ancient Rights of the Graveyard*, 2006 B.Y.U. L. REV. 1469, 1497 (2006).

33. *See, e.g.*, ALA. CODE § 35-1-4 (Westlaw through Act 2026–15); FLA. STAT. ANN. § 704.08 (West, Westlaw through July 1, 2025, of the 2025 first regular session); MO. ANN. STAT. § 214.132 (West, Westlaw through the end of the 2025 First Regular and First and Second Extraordinary Sessions of the 103rd General Assembly); N.C. GEN. STAT. ANN. § 65-102 (West, Westlaw through S.L. 2025-97 of the 2025 Regular Session of the General Assembly); S.C. CODE ANN. § 27-43-310 (Westlaw through 2025 Act No. 94); VA. CODE ANN. § 57-27.1 (West, Westlaw through the 2025 Regular and Reconvened Sessions); W. VA. CODE ANN. § 37-13A-1 (West, Westlaw current with legislation of the 2025 Regular Session).

34. VA. CODE ANN. § 57-27.1.

35. W. VA. CODE ANN. § 37-13A-1 (recognizing right of access by "close friends").

2. Regulatory Takings

Even when the government does not become the new title owner of real property, a taking can still occur through a "regulatory taking." In a regulatory taking, the government exercises so much control over a parcel that it is effectively its owner. Cases challenging regulatory takings often come down to just how much control the government can exercise before tipping into a taking. On the one hand, government would grind to a halt if every law that weakened a stick in the bundle of property rights required payment to all the owners affected by the law. On the other hand, when the government controls the owner's use of the property so much that it might as well be the registered owner, the government has constructively taken the property.

In *United States v. Dickinson*,[36] the Supreme Court held that an action is still a taking "when inroads are made upon an owner's use of it to an extent that, as between private parties, a servitude has been acquired either by agreement or in course of time."

a. *Partial Takings*

The Supreme Court created the doctrine of regulatory takings in *Pennsylvania Coal Co. v. Mahon*[37] in 1922. Pennsylvania passed a law that outlawed coal mining that would cause the ground to sink beneath houses. In 1878, the Pennsylvania Coal Co. had sold land—but just the surface—to H.J. Mahon; the sale had expressly reserved the right to extract all of the coal from underground. When the coal company wanted to mine the coal from under Mahon's surface, Mahon invoked the Kohler Act, a 1921 statute that forbade mining that would cause the surface to sink under houses, and argued that any rights to mine the coal retained by the coal company had been taken away by the Kohler Act. In finding that the Kohler Act had effected a taking of the coal company's right to extract coal (as it had specifically reserved unto itself), Justice Holmes penned a one-sentence summary of takings clause law that has remained true a century later: "The general rule at least is that while property may be regulated to a certain extent, if the regulation goes too far it will be recognized as a taking."[38]

The Court began by noting, "Government hardly could go on if to some extent values incident to property could not be diminished without

---

36. 331 U.S. 745 (1947).

37. 260 U.S. 393 (1922).

38. *Id.* at 415.

paying for every such change in the general law."[39] Where a regulation places limitations on land that fall short of eliminating all economically beneficial use, then under a *Penn Central* taking, the court considers several factors to examine the severity of the government burden on private property rights.[40] These factors include "the economic impact of the regulation[;] its interference with reasonable investment backed expectations[;] and the character of the governmental action."[41] As before, the analysis must focus on the "parcel as a whole," not discrete segments.[42] It is insufficient to establish a taking "by showing that [plaintiff has] been denied the ability to exploit a property interest that [it] heretofore had believed was available for development" (*id.*).

The Court never set an exhaustive list of factors to weigh. Still, it identified three factors described as of "particular significance"[43] that have been reviewed by myriad courts ever since, often with no consideration of any other factor:

> The economic impact of the regulation on the claimant and, particularly, the extent to which the regulation has interfered with distinct investment-backed expectations are, of course, relevant considerations. So, too, is the character of the governmental action. A "taking" may more readily be found when the interference with property can be characterized as a physical invasion by government than when interference arises from some public program adjusting the benefits and burdens of economic life to promote the common good.[44]

i. Character of the Government Action

One factor is universally called the "character of the government action." "Character of the government action" examines the nature of the government's action, such as whether it is a broad program that applies across

39. *Id.* at 413.

40. *Lingle*, 544 U.S. at 539.

41. Pittsburg Cnty. Rural Water Dist. No. 7 v. City of McAlester, 358 F.3d 694, 718 (10th Cir. 2020).

42. *Penn Cent.*, 438 U.S. at 130.

43. Embassy Real Est. Holdings, LLC v. District of Columbia, 944 A.2d 1036, 1052 (D.C. 2008) (explaining that "[t]here is no single test" for a partial taking and that the Penn Central factors merely describe "general considerations") (internal quotation marks omitted).

44. *Penn Cent.*, 438 U.S. at 124.

an entire city or state or whether, instead, it is a targeted action meant to address a specific, unique problem. An action that works broadly, like those that promote historic preservation across a region, are on safer ground from being ruled a taking than one-off actions that address a single historic house.

The *Lingle* Court stated that courts should focus on whether a regulation "amounts to a physical invasion" or "adjusts the benefits and burdens of economic life to promote the common good" when the character of the government action is evaluated.[45] If a regulation that "promote[s] the common good" is important, then courts will have to consider the extent to which the challenged program in fact supports the common good.[46]

Penn Central's discussion of the "character" factor is hard to distill from the other factors. Justice Brennan, on the factor, wrote that a "'taking' may more readily be found when the interference with property can be characterized as a physical invasion by government . . . than when interference arises from some public program adjusting the benefits and burdens of economic life to promote the common good."[47] But, the Court seems to have been saying that a variety of considerations are relevant: Does the regulation treat the matter comprehensively, or is it a targeted response to a specific instance? Does the regulation use neutral, general criteria? Does the regulation act as a form of spot-zoning? Does the public at large benefit?

In *New Albany Historic Preservation Commission v. Bradford Realty, Inc.*,[48] the owner of a historic building in New Albany, Indiana, filed a challenge to a new preservation ordinance by asserting, among other grounds, an uncompensated taking. In 2002, New Albany designated its downtown as protected under the new preservation ordinance. In 2008, the plaintiff performed work on a two-and-one-half-story frame house that he used as a rental property without first having obtained the necessary certificate of appropriateness for the work.[49] When the owner finally applied (under protest) for the certificate, the local preservation board decided that replacing the wood siding with vinyl siding was inappropriate and denied the certificate, and the plaintiff sued.[50]

45. Lingle v. Chevron U.S.A. Inc., 544 U.S. 528, 539 (2005) (quoting *Penn Cent.*, 438 U.S. at 124).

46. *Id.*

47. *Penn Cent.*, 438 U.S. at 123.

48. 965 N.E.2d 79, 89 (Ind. Ct. App. 2012).

49. *Id.* at 82–83.

50. *Id.* at 83.

On appeal, the Indiana Court of Appeals weighed the "character of the government action" factor against the owner. The court opened its discussion of the factor by noting that a spectrum exists where physical invasions are more likely to be takings while takings are less likely when the "interference arises from some public program adjusting the benefits and burdens of economic life to promote the common good."[51] The court then decided that the ordinance at issue was one that enhanced the quality of life by preserving the character and desirable aesthetic features of a city. Specifically, the purpose of the municipal preservation ordinance was to promote the educational, cultural, and general welfare of the citizens of New Albany and ensure the viability of the downtown and other historic commercial activities and to enhance tourism. The court ended the review of the factor with this: "As such, the ordinance serves a substantial public purpose."[52] At least for that court, the factor would seem to be another way of asking about the substantiality of the public purpose.

The focus within the "character" factor is on the justification for the regulation and whether the regulation is designed to confer a broad public benefit. Of course, *Penn Central* was itself a preservation ordinance, which the Court ruled is, in and of itself, for the benefit of the public at large. *Penn Central* might well be applied in dissimilar cases that find that some regulation is not really for the broad public benefit and instead is more akin to a personalized response to an individual case.[53] And even within the context of historic preservation, the wide variety of approaches might have a greater or smaller economic impact. But, as for the interplay of the "character" factor and historic preservation, such regulations would seem to start with the three-factor analysis up 1–0 until the Supreme Court changes its mind.

ii. Economic Impact on the Claimant

In *Penn Central*, the Court embraced the idea that a historic preservation ordinance could hold down the value of property. The inability of the

---

51. *Id.* at 89 (quoting Ragucci v. Metro. Dev. Comm'n of Marion Cnty., 702 N.E.2d 677, 683 (Ind. 1998)).

52. *Id.* at 89.

53. *See, e.g.*, CAA Assocs. v. United States, 91 Fed. Cl. 580, 602 (2010) (using the "character of government action" factor to find that a low-income housing regulation worked a taking because the regulation put what should have been a societal burden on the shoulders of just a subset).

station's owner to add an office tower above the Beaux-Arts building meant that the owner could not maximize its profits, but more was required for a taking: The site of the terminal, after all, "must, in its present state, be regarded as capable of earning a reasonable return, and that the transferable development rights afforded appellants by virtue of the [site's] designation as a landmark are valuable, *even if not as valuable as the rights to construct above the Terminal*."[54]

Even when an ordinance lowers the value—and doesn't just prevent its increase—the result is the same. "The Fifth Amendment prohibition against taking without compensation does not guarantee the most profitable use of property, and a diminution in value, standing alone, does not establish a taking."[55] In the D.C. case below, the economic impact of the regulation also supported a finding that no taking occurred. When governmental action "does not interfere in any way with the present uses" of the property, and when that action allows the owner "not only to profit from the [property] but also to obtain a reasonable return on its investment," there is an insufficient economic effect to warrant compensation.[56]

Note that the existence of a negative economic impact is not dispositive. For example, in *Gordon v. District of Columbia*,[57] no one debated that the preservation ordinance in Washington, D.C., led to a diminished fair market value for the owner's house, but there was nevertheless not a taking. In that case, the owners of 3020 Albemarle Street in the Forest Hills neighborhood of northwest D.C. decided to sell their house. When neighbors became concerned about how the large lot might be redeveloped, they decided to try to have the house declared historic by the Historic Preservation Review Board. What followed was a scheme that certainly did not, in the court's telling, paint the neighbors in a flattering light. They worked with a consultant who snuck into the house while pretending to be a legitimate potential buyer and then leveraged their ruse to get other access while documenting the house as historic. The sellers had an offer for $1.55 million, which was withdrawn after the house was designated as historic; the same buyer made a new offer for $1.2 million, expressly citing the historic designation as

54. *Penn Cent.*, 438 U.S. at 138.

55. Jackson Ct. Condos., Inc. v. City of New Orleans, 874 F.2d 1070, 1080 (5th Cir. 1989) (citations omitted).

56. *Penn Cent.*, 438 U.S. at 136 (citations omitted).

57. 309 A.3d 543, 562 (D.C. 2024).

the reason for the lowered offer. In addition to other claims, the owners claimed that the designation had worked a taking on their house, but the court disagreed. Despite a reduction in value based on the drop in the offers of about $300,000 because of the designation, the owners "still had an offer to purchase the home, albeit at a reduced price—$1.2 million as opposed to $1.5. [*sic*] million."[58]

iii. Reasonable Investment-Backed Expectations

The "economic impact on the claimant" is very closely related to the "reasonable investment-backed expectations" factor. The former is more a matter of number crunching: Before the regulation, the owner had property worth a certain figure, but after the regulation, the fair market value has dropped to a lower figure. As with any traditional real estate appraisal, reasonable minds might disagree about how much a potential buyer might knock off an offer because of the regulation or what it would cost an owner to maintain the property under the regulation's requirements.

The "reasonable investment-backed expectations" takes a different view and questions, basically, just how foreseeable the regulatory losses were. The requirement "limits recovery to owners who can demonstrate that they bought their property in reliance on the non-existence of the challenged regulation."[59] The owner's expectations must be reasonable.[60] Common sense would reveal that "one who buys with knowledge of a restraint assumes the risk of economic loss. In such a case, the owner presumably paid a discounted price for the property. Compensating him for a 'taking' would confer a windfall."[61]

"The existence of a regulatory regime does not per se preclude all investment-backed expectations for development."[62] Rather, "the regulatory regime in place at the time the claimant acquires the property at issue helps shape the reasonableness of those expectations."[63] As one federal circuit court explained:

---

58. *Id.* at 563.

59. Creppel v. United States, 41 F.3d 627, 632 (Fed. Cir. 1994).

60. *See* Ruckelshaus v. Monsanto Cnty., 467 U.S. 986, 1005–06 (1984).

61. *Creppel*, 41 F.3d at 632 (citations omitted).

62. Palm Beach Isles Assocs. v. United States, 231 F.3d 1354, 1364 (Fed. Cir. 2000).

63. *Palazzolo v. Rhode Island*, 533 U.S. 606, 633 (2001) (O'Connor, J., concurring).

> The purpose of consideration of plaintiffs' investment-backed expectations is to limit recoveries to property owners who can demonstrate that "they bought their property in reliance on a state of affairs that did not include the challenged regulatory regime." This factor also incorporates an objective test—to support a claim for a regulatory taking, an investment-backed expectation must be "reasonable." . . . The critical question is whether a reasonable developer confronted with the particular circumstances facing the Owners would have expected the government [action]. . . . This is an objective, but fact-specific inquiry into what, under all the circumstances, the Owners should have anticipated.[64]

In *Embassy Real Estate Holdings, LLC v. D.C. Mayor's Agent for Historic Preservation,*[65] Embassy Real Estate Holdings, LLC planned to partly demolish the former Italian embassy[66] and redevelop the property with condos. The owner had applied for pre-construction and construction permits before the Historic Preservation Office applied to have the embassy declared a historic landmark. A prior owner sought the advice of an architectural design team that said, although the property was not in a historic district or designated as a historic landmark, it was "clearly eligible for designation," and that "should anyone file a designation application, it was our opinion that application would succeed."[67] What followed was a tactical choice where the owner and his team met with the preservation officer for the District of Columbia and decided to attempt to negotiate with members of the local preservation community to buy their silence and not attempt to have the property designated as historic. The preservation officer himself did not have present plans to pursue the designation but left the door open. The prior owner's plans changed when September 11 shifted the real estate landscape. After meeting with new investors, the prior owner again met with the city's preservation officer. This time, the response was chillier because of a new part of the plans for a 90-foot tower. Still, the prior owner left thinking that the preservation officer would not be seeking landmark status.

---

64. Cienega Gardens v. United States, 331 F.3d 1319, 1345–46 (Fed. Cir. 2003) (citations omitted).

65. 944 A.2d 1036, 1040 (D.C. 2008).

66. The embassy was located at 2700 16th Street, N.W. and 1651 Fuller Street, N.W.

67. *Id.* at 1041.

The owner proceeded with development plans, and the historic preservation officer responded with an application for designation of the property, which was eventually granted. A lawsuit followed asserting a taking. The court found that not all redevelopment possibilities had been foreclosed. But, even if they had, the investment-backed expectations were not reasonable.[68] Instead, the court listed several facts that undercut the idea that the developer could have reasonably expected to be able to push forward with the revised plans:

> That finding [that the expectations were not reasonable] is supported by substantial evidence: the vague assertions made by [the city's preservation officer] coupled with the absence of assurances (requested or given) that no landmark application would be filed, as well as [the consultant's] caution to [the owner] that the option the owner] chose—to bypass [Historic Preservation Review Board] review and rely on private negotiations and agreements—entailed "some risk." [The owner], as well as the [preservation officer], were well aware of the historic significance of the property, and [the consultant] had advised that if a landmark application were filed, it would be granted. As the Mayor's Agent remarked, one who is about to embark on such an expensive and complex project requiring significant demolition, alteration and new construction of a known historic property would require more than a casual statement that the [preservation officer] had "no intent at the time" to designate the property as an historic landmark before proceeding on that premise. That statement by all accounts was made in 2001, in connection with the first proposed design, but in Spring 2004, when the design was changed to add the tower the [Historic Preservation Review Board] found to be especially incongruous, [the preservation officer] made no secret of his objection. Moreover, although [the owner] negotiated and entered into agreements with the private parties more likely to file for landmark designation, it was well aware that under the Act the [preservation officer] was entitled to initiate designation proceedings, and that [the owner]'s agreement with

---

68. *Id.* at 1054.

> [a preservation advocacy group] did not preclude the [preservation officer] from doing so. Thus, this case is unlike [*Pennsylvania Coal Co. v. Mahon*, 260 U.S. 393 (1922)], where the land owners had no way of knowing that unforeseen new regulations would affect their property rights, after having taken reasonable precautions in their private negotiations with the only parties known to have an interest. Here, petitioner took a calculated (and, as it turned out, unwise) risk and commenced the project in the face of [the preservation officer]'s expressed concerns without either returning to [him] to obtain a firm assurance that it would not seek to designate [the owner]'s property as an historic landmark, or [the owner] itself initiating the application process in order to dispel any uncertainty.[69]

Whether a government action is regulatory turns, in part, on the "economically beneficial use test."[70] A court must consider if all economically beneficial use is prohibited for the entire parcel.[71] If a beneficial use of the "parcel as a whole" remains, there is no taking under the economically beneficial use test.[72]

In *Banker's Choice, LLC v. Zoning Board of Appeals of Cincinnati*,[73] a developer bought the Davis Furniture Building at 1119–1121 Main Street in downtown Cincinnati with plans to demolish the building the developer characterized as an "eyesore" to protect its investment in other property across the street. The Historic Conservation Board, however, denied the necessary permit; the board found that there were at least three buyers who would purchase the building for an amount that would allow the developer to recoup its purchase price. Thus, the board found that the matter was not a case of the loss of all economic value. On appeal, a magistrate decided that the offers were not bona fide, that the building was not historic anyway, and that there was no economically viable way to restore the building.

---

69. *Id.* at 1055.

70. Clajon Prod. Corp. v. Petera, 70 F.3d 1566, 1577 (10th Cir. 2013).

71. *Id.* (citing Penn Cent. Transp. of City of N.Y., 438 U.S. 104 (1978), for this statement: "'Taking' jurisprudence does not divide a single parcel into discrete segments and attempt to determine whether rights in a particular segment have been entirely abrogated.").

72. *Id.* at 1577.

73. 170 N.E.3d 923, 926 (Ohio Ct. App. 2021).

One of the factors the court had to consider was "Will the reasonable investment-backed expectations of the property owner be maintained without approval of a Certificate of Appropriateness"?[74]

The appellate court began by writing off the decision below that an economically viable use remained. Although the appellate court did not deny that there were offers to buy the building that would have generated a profit for the developer, the court ruled that selling a building is not an economically viable use of the building. However, an owner's ability to sell an affected property does not constitute an economically beneficial use; "[t]ypical economic uses enable a landowner to derive benefits from land ownership rather than requiring a landowner to sell the affected parcel."[75]

As to the investment-backed expectations, the developer had paid $125,000 at a sheriff's sale for the building. When the developer bought the building, the Cincinnati ordinance said that permission for demolition could be granted as long as certain showings were made, such as an economic hardship. The appellate court found that, when the developer bought the historic building, it had the intention of restoring it if it could do so, but that if the numbers did not work out, that the developer intended to raze the building.

In *District Intown Properties Ltd. Partnership v. District of Columbia*,[76] the court looked at the expectations of the owner not just at the moment the law sprang into effect, but also at the time the owner purchased the property. In that case, the owner of some land wanted to add some townhouses. The fact was that the owner had long owned and used the property with a heightened sense of possible profit only arriving much later. When the development expectations were created by the owner, it was reasonably foreseeable that the preservation would be needed because the relevant law predated the formation of the plans.

b. Total Takings

Deciding whether the government has caused a taking of property requires the decision-maker to look at a spectrum. On one end of the spectrum are pure, classical physical appropriations such as taking title to real estate to

74. CINCINNATI, OHIO MUNICIPAL CODE 1435–09–2(b).

75. *Lost Tree Village Corp. v. United States*, 787 F.3d 1111, 1117 (Fed. Cir. 2015).

76. 23 F. Supp. 2d 30, 37 (D.D.C. 1998), *aff'd*, 198 F.3d 874 (D.C. Cir. 1999).

build a road. On the other end are traditional laws that admittedly impact ownership rights but only as a consequence of some exercise of the government's police power, such as outlawing smoking in restaurants. Whether a specific action falls closer to one end of the spectrum or the other is a difficult task, but the Supreme Court has made the analysis simpler in at least a few cases. The Court has recognized that certain categories of government action qualify as total takings even though they do not result in the transfer to fee simple title. Among the "categorical" takings are police power actions that result in a total deprivation of economic use to an owner and those that involve even de minimis physical occupation of an owner's land.

Historic preservation enjoys a bias in favor of constitutionality because preservation of historic buildings does not remove value in the same way that an environmental regulation might. Preservation laws generally have nothing to do with the actual use of a structure and involve only what the exterior shell (and sometimes the interior too) look like. They do not forbid using a building at all. Especially considering how creative architects and developers can be (sometimes, perhaps, involuntarily), there will almost always be a remaining use of the property giving it economic value.

Churches, grain silos, elevated subway lines, and factories have all been adaptively reused as offices, commercial spaces, recreational facilities, and other facilities. One recent example of an award-winning adaptive reuse happened at Google's Los Angeles facility at 16 South Campus Drive. During World War II, industrialist Howard Hughes commissioned Henry L. Gogerty to build a huge hangar in which Hughes's famous *Spruce Goose* could be built. The hangar was, like the plane, built from wood because of war shortages and is one of the largest wooden structures in the world.[77] After decades of decline, the Cargo Building—as the hangar was titled—was redeveloped as a gigantic office for Google. Instead of demolishing the hangar, Google restored its exterior, reopened windows, and essentially built large office buildings inside the old hangar. Certainly not every building will have as many potential uses as one of the world's largest wooden structures. Still, the range of imaginative reuses demonstrates that having to keep a building is unlikely to sap a parcel of economic possibilities.

And while the owner of a preserved building might not have Google's financial wherewithal, the court does not look only at whether a redevelopment is economically possible by the property owner himself or herself.

77. www.laconservancy.org/learn/historic-places/google-playa-vista/.

Rather, an owner can still find value in property as a rental, for example, to a third party that can undertake restoration while also paying an owner an acceptable rent. Before finding that an owner lacks a remaining valuable use, a court would have to find that the owner could not practicably sell the property, could not earn a reasonable return through rent, and lost the ability to generate income otherwise.[78]

In *Penn Central*, the Supreme Court held that the economic impact caused by a law was one of the three enumerated factors for deciding whether a taking had happened just from having to live with the law. However, in 1992, the Court addressed an extreme example of just that one factor and decided that if the regulation eliminates *all* economically beneficial uses, then no balance is even necessary. Instead, the regulation is a taking per se. The owner, Lucas, challenged a law as it applied to two coastal residential lots he bought in 1986. The owner had paid $975,000 for two parcels on the Isle of Palms, an oceanfront island a few miles northeast of Charleston, South Carolina.[79] Two years later, South Carolina enacted the South Carolina Beachfront Management Act, which prevented the owner from building inhabitable structures on the parcels. The Act prevented Lucas from constructing a single-family house on each lot. Lucas claimed that he had no economically viable use for his land because of the Act's limits and that a taking resulted for which he should be compensated.

The case really did hinge on the completeness of the economic loss. In his dissent, Justice Stevens criticized the majority for an arbitrary rule requiring 100% loss of economic value. He questioned how a person sustaining a 95% deprivation could be left out of the mix but that someone hitting 100% would be covered. In a footnote response, Justice Scalia noted that the 100% loss is just an extreme example of the *Penn Central* factor about economic impact. He noted that someone suffering such high diminutions could take advantage of the *Penn Central* analysis and still show a taking even if the regulation did not result in a per se taking. One might wonder if Justice Scalia even himself really would require a true, 100% loss of value. For example, even in *Lucas*, is seems unlikely that no one would have paid even $1 for title to two beachfront parcels just for the benefit of having a known spot to put a beach chair and umbrella while visiting the beach.

---

78. Maher v. City of New Orleans, 516 F.2d 1051, 1066 (5th Cir. 1975).

79. Lucas v. S.C. Coastal Council, 505 U.S. 1003, 1006–07 (1992).

If a complete loss of value is literally the trigger for a per se taking under *Lucas*, then it is hard to imagine what preservation law might meet that standard. Preservation laws are, by definition, meant to preserve buildings mainly. While a property owner might very well wish that he or she could demolish a structure to build back a larger or more profitable building, having to retain a historic improvement seems to ensure that there would be at least some value left, possibly very large. Commentators in the wake of *Lucas* routinely assumed the same thing:

> In the context of historic preservation, it is highly unlikely that a property owner could ever show that a landmark designation has made her property completely valueless. As most landmarking statutes are currently written, it is hard to imagine a landmark designation that would be permissible under the preservation-enabling legislation and could also be described under *Lucas* as "physically appropriating and eliminating all beneficial use of" a property.[80]

Even so, there have been cases making the claim, with at least one success. For instance, in *District Intown Properties Ltd. Partnership v. District of Columbia*,[81] a partnership bought an apartment building across the street from the National Zoo in 1961. In 1988, the land was subdivided into nine contiguous lots, and all of them were declared historic landmarks the next year.[82] The owner's request for permission to build townhouses on eight of the newly created subdivisions was rejected as inconsistent with the landmark status. The eight lots on which the townhouses were to be built were divisions of the landscaped lawns while the apartment house itself occupied the ninth lot. In a challenge, the court began by considering the subject property and opted to consider the entire nine parcels together based on their having been a unified piece for more than 20 years that not even the

---

80. Nicholas Caros, *Interior Landmarks Preservation and Public Access*, 116 Colum. L. Rev. 1773, 1805 n.96 (2016) (citation omitted); *see also* Daniel T. Cavarello, Comment, *From Penn Central to United Artists' I & II: The Rise to Immunity of Historic Preservation Designation from Successful Takings Challenges*, 22 B.C. Env't Aff. L. Rev. 593, 618 (1995) ("[S]ince this phenomenon is highly unlikely to occur in the historic preservation designation context, the *Lucas* rationale would seem to have little or no effect on the current state of immunity from takings challenges in American historical preservation jurisprudence.").

81. 198 F.3d 874, 877 (D.C. Cir. 1999).

82. *Id.* at 876.

owner treated separately after the subdivision. As a result, the "denominator problem" analyzed whether there had been a taking of a much larger parcel than any one subdivided lot.[83]

Having decided the relevant property, the court had no trouble in finding that there had not been a per se taking under *Lucas*. To trigger *Lucas*, the property would have to have been rendered "valueless," yet the owner presented no evidence to prove that the regulation had stripped all economically beneficial use from the land.[84] The majority specifically pointed out that total loss of value was the standard for *Lucas* to apply and that the majority was not addressing the related issue of whether a traditional *Penn Central* case would fly.[85] The majority pointed out that, even had it considered the new, vacant landscaped lots apart from the parcel with the apartment house, they would have reached the same result. The majority noted that the city agreed that "any construction that destroyed the lawn" would be incompatible but that the owner had failed to produce any evidence that all value had been removed from the vacant lot.[86]

The opposite outcome was seen in *Keeler v. Mayor & City Council of Cumberland*.[87] In that case, the Catholic Church owned a chapel and monastery it deemed a "draining financial liability" and wanted to demolish for smaller, modern facilities with gardens and parking. The demolition required permission from the Cumberland Historic Preservation Commission, which denied the request. Not only could the church not demolish the buildings, but it had to stabilize them at a safe standard. Doing so would cost, according to one witness, nearly $400,000 with a complete renovation costing about $2 million.[88] For unspecified reasons, the city stipulated that "no economically feasible plan can be formulated," and the court simply declared that "there is no doubt the application of the Cumberland Historic Zoning Ordinances to the Church has rendered the Church property economically useless, and has worked a regulatory taking."[89] It is unclear whether the same outcome would have resulted had the owner been able

83. *Id.* at 882.

84. *Id.*

85. *Id.*

86. *Id.*

87. 940 F. Supp. 879 (D. Md. 1996).

88. *Id.* at 888.

89. *Id.*

to simply mothball the building and possibly eke out tiny proceeds from renting out parking spaces instead of having to spend at least several hundred thousand dollars. But, given the uncontested testimony that the value minus the maintenance outlay would lead to a huge loss, the court found that *Lucas* justified a per se taking.

In Charleston, South Carolina, in 2021, the owner of a very dilapidated circa 1873 cottage sought permission to demolish the house. At a meeting of the Board of Architectural Review, the owner claimed that no one would purchase the property with the lodestone of a house in place. Thus, he sought to demolish it so that he could sell the land. If true, Charleston's ordinance against demolition of buildings more than 50 years old without approval by the Board of Architectural Review could possibly have set the stage for a takings suit. Happily, however, a local lawyer purchased the house as a passion project to restore without any interest in making a profit—just in not *losing* money—and restored the house.[90]

One recent case employed a clever workaround to avoid a finding that *Keeler* might produce. In *DC Preservation League v. Mayor's Agent for Historic Preservation*,[91] the Washington Metropolitan Area Transit Authority (WMATA) owned the Foundry Branch Trestle, a trolley bridge that was no longer in use, as well as two associated parcels.[92] The owner wanted to demolish the trestle, but it was covered by the D.C. historic preservation law. When permission was granted, a preservation advocacy group appealed.

The appellate court dodged the *Keeler* analysis by pointing out that the preservation law itself did not actually cause the loss of value. The trestle had no current use, was in dangerous disrepair, and would cost $2 million to $4 million to restore, plus at least $100,000 more in annual upkeep.[93] To the reviewing court, it was not the law that led to the financial bind: "In other words, the denial of a demolition permit would not cause the Trestle to lack an economically viable use; rather, WMATA seeks a demolition permit precisely because the Trestle already has no economically viable use."[94] The property was valueless whether or not it was protected.

---

90. Robert Behre, *How Do You Make Money Fixing Up a Charleston Home? Start with Even More Money*, Post & Courier (Charleston, S.C.), Mar. 3, 2024, at A11.

91. 282 A.3d 578, 582 (D.C. 2022).

92. *Id.* at 579.

93. *Id.* at 581.

94. *Id.*

In *Lucas*, Justice Scalia went out of his way to note one exception. If the land could not have been used for the purpose even apart from the regulation because of nuisance laws, then the law itself was not really the cause of any taking. For example, even if it reduced the value of Blackacre to $0, a prohibition against such improvements that would deflect floodwaters onto neighboring property would not be a taking. The Court has long sustained state actions that prevent public nuisances against constitutional challenges.[95]

3. Exactions

When the government wants to control the use of property, it might consider exacting a concession from the owner for something that it could not directly require without triggering constitutional checks. In other words, the government can make the owner an offer he or she can't refuse.[96] In one example, the government sought to exact a concession (viz., the dedication of some of the parcel to a community greenspace) in return for something controlled by the government but needed by the owner (viz., a permit for the development of the land).[97] Two Supreme Court cases, *Nollan v. California Coastal Commission* and *Dolan v. City of Tigard*, limited the government's ability to impair property interests with land-use regulations: Exactions from owners need a "nexus" and "rough proportionality" between the government's demand and the effects of the proposed land use. The *Nollan* nexus test asks whether the government is trying to achieve some goal related to the health, safety, and welfare of the community that is connected to the private party's actions and to the exactions being sought. The *Dolan* proportionality test asks whether the burden placed on the owner is roughly proportional to the burden the owner would impose on the community.

a. Essential Nexus

Interestingly, the landmark *Nollan* case itself arose from a case involving historic preservation. In the 1980s, the Nollan family owned an oceanfront

95. *See, e.g.*, Mugler v. Kansas, 123 U.S. 623 (1887) (law prohibiting manufacture of alcoholic beverages); Hadacheck v. Sebastian, 239 U.S. 394 (1915) (law barring operation of brick mill in residential area); Miller v. Schoene, 276 U.S. 272 (1928) (order to destroy diseased cedar trees to prevent infection of nearby orchards); Goldblatt v. Hempstead, 369 U.S. 590 (1962) (law effectively preventing continued operation of quarry in residential area).

96. THE GODFATHER (Paramount Pictures 1972).

97. Nollan v. California Coastal Commission, 483 U.S. 825 (1987).

bungalow that had fallen into disrepair. When the Nollans sought to demolish the house and build a three-bedroom house in its place, the California Coastal Commission agreed to approve the request, but only if the Nollans created a public easement to connect two public beaches on either side of their land. The commission claimed the easement protected the public's legitimate interests in having views of the beach and beach access. The Nollans sued the commission on the grounds that the easement constituted an uncompensated taking.

The Court ruled in favor of the Nollans. The Court agreed that the commission had a legitimate public interest in assuring that the public had views of the beach and access to the beach. However, there was no connection between those interests and the Nollans' development activity or adding an easement for people who were already on public beaches. In other words, there must be an "essential nexus" between the legitimate public interest and the condition imposed upon the property owner to achieve that interest.

b. Roughly Proportional

Florence Dolan owned a 1.67-acre parcel bordering Fanno Creek in Tigard, Oregon, with a 9700-square-foot store and a gravel parking lot.[98] Dolan petitioned to nearly double the size of the store and to pave a parking lot for 39 cars. Tigard's comprehensive plan prohibited development within the 100-year floodplain and called for properties within the floodplain to dedicate that area as a "greenway." It also called for new development to create bicycle paths where possible or to pay for their creation offsite if necessary.

The city accepted the proposed development plan provided that the owner dedicated land in the floodplain to a greenway and dedicated a 15-foot-wide strip next to the floodplain for a bike path; the trade would mitigate storm-water runoff and would mitigate added traffic caused by the development.[99] The concession amounted to 10% of the parcel but would count toward the 15% open space requirement already in place.

The owner contested the exactions. The Supreme Court agreed that there was a connection between the "problem" being caused by the use of the land and the concession being sought. After all, increasing the size of the store would increase runoff, and the expanded store would lead to more

---

98. Dolan v. City of Tigard, 512 U.S. 374 (1994).

99. *Id.* at 378.

traffic. Thus, asking for greenway space to mitigate the runoff and a bike path to alleviate vehicular traffic made sense.

But then the Court distinguished the "legislative" nature of the land-use controls in *Agins* against the "adjudicative" nature of the conditions applied to Dolan's particular property.[100] The difference is that a "legislative" control is one that applies across the board, whereas an "adjudicative" control is one that is specific to the particular case. Furthermore, the dedication of land (deeding the land to the city) was not a limitation on use but a required divestiture of land.

However, the Court then went on to "determine whether the degree of the exactions demanded by the city's permit conditions bears the required relationship to the projected impact of petitioner's proposed development."[101] The court noted that some courts relied on generalized statements by jurisdictions regarding the relationship while others required "a very exacting correspondence, described as the 'specifi[c] and uniquely attributable' test."[102] The Court chose a middle ground and required findings that the conditions imposed on development bore a "reasonable relationship" between the impact of development and the burden of the required dedication.

Therefore, the Court chose "rough proportionality" to indicate that a jurisdiction must make an individual determination about proportionality for each burdened property without requiring the jurisdiction to provide exact mathematical proof. The burden of proof rests with the jurisdiction. The Court justified this shift by noting that generally applicable legislative regulations should be treated with more deference than property-specific adjudicative determinations.

B. FIRST AMENDMENT (RELIGIOUS LIBERTY)

When a religious group or adherent wants to demolish, build, or alter a building to advance its religious purposes, the group's First Amendment rights and the government's interest in preservation can conflict. Conflicts typically arise in two ways when preservation is used either as a shield or

100. *Id.* at 385 (contrasting the regulations at issue in *Agins v. City of Tiburon*, 447 U.S. 255, 260 (1980)).

101. *Id.* at 388.

102. *Id.* at 389.

a sword. First, use laws can be used ostensibly to protect buildings but asserted in such a way that they trammel religious uses. Second, a property can be "landmarked" and thereby have alterations or demolitions limited, thus making it more expensive for the religious group to function.[103]

When a contestant raises religious freedom as a basis for an attack of historic preservation, it typically takes one of three forms:

- First, contestants might assert that a historic preservation regulation limits their ability to practice religion as they want. For example, imagine a preservation ordinance that prevents a congregation from building a steeple or removing an earlier occupant's religious symbols. A congregation might use the familiar vehicle of a Section 1983 suit to litigate the merits of its claim that its free exercise rights have been violated.
- Second, although the traditional Section 1983 method continues to exist, most contestants would sidestep that process in favor of a statutory claim and assert that a regulation violates a federal statute such as the Religious Freedom Restoration Act or its successor—Congress's attempt to codify a particular constitutional analysis that it saw the Court changing.
- Third, a less frequent challenge is that some government action or regulation actually is the government's attempt to establish a religion in violation of the establishment clause.

Of these three, challenges based on a federal statute are the most common given the expansive coverage of the statutes and the easier burdens for plaintiffs. However, because the statutes were an attempt to codify constitutional analysis—and because technically, constitutional challenges can still be brought outside the statutes—a review of the law as it developed before the statutes makes sense. At the other end, challenges asserted that a preservation law violates the establishment clause are infrequent, so they will be covered last.

1. Free Exercise

The First Amendment provides that "Congress shall make no law respecting an establishment of religion, or prohibiting the free exercise thereof."[104]

---

103. www.churchlawandtax.com/pastor-church-law/church-property/landmarking/.

104. U.S. Const. amend. I.

By incorporation into the Fourteenth Amendment, this applies to state governments.[105]

Understanding how the free exercise clause is used in historic preservation cases requires a long view of history. The law has swung back and forth as to how the clause should be applied, and eventually Congress interceded not just once, but twice. And, when Congress did act, it did so in very express reaction to the state of the law at the time, even heavily borrowing judicial concepts. Most challenges asserting religious infringement are brought pursuant to that second congressional reaction, but to fully understand that statute, one must wade through its swampy background.

The first free exercise challenges began in the mid-19th century with the famous *Reynolds* case in which a law against polygamy was upheld without having to permit an individual to defend that he was just doing what his religion required. In *Reynolds v. United States*,[106] a member of the Church of Jesus Christ of Latter-day Saints named George Reynolds agreed to serve as the test case in a challenge to the Morrill Anti-Bigamy Act and even worked with the U.S. Attorney to document his violation of the act by having married two women. At trial, Reynolds sought to charge the jury that there would be no violation if the jury found he had only been seeking to follow his religion. The trial court refused that instruction, and Reynolds was convicted.

The case worked its way to the Supreme Court in 1878 where Reynolds raised several issues involving the jury and the admission of evidence. But, the case is historically significant as the first foray of the Court into the free exercise clause. The Court relied upon the writing of Thomas Jefferson heavily[107] and accepted Jefferson's statement that religion is "a matter which lies solely between man and his God." Actions, however, were a different matter and could be regulated by the state:

> Laws are made for the government of actions, and while they cannot interfere with mere religious belief and opinions, they may with practices. Suppose one believed that human sacrifices were

105. Employment Div., Dep't of Human Res. v. Smith, 494 U.S. 872, 876–77 (1990).

106. 98 U.S. 145 (1878).

107. *Id.* at 154 ("Coming as this [quoted passage authored by Jefferson] does from an acknowledged leader of the advocates of the measure, it may be accepted almost as an authoritative declaration of the scope and effect of the amendment thus secured.").

> a necessary part of religious worship; would it be seriously contended that the civil government under which he lived could not interfere to prevent a sacrifice? . . . So here, as a law of the organization of society under the exclusive dominion of the United States, it is provided that plural marriages shall not be allowed. Can a man excuse his practices to the contrary because of his religious belief? To permit this would be to make the professed doctrines of religious belief superior to the law of the land, and, in effect, to permit every citizen to become a law unto himself. Government could exist only in name under such circumstances.[108]

During the decades that followed, the Court heard a series of famous free exercise cases in which the Court essentially rewrote the pro-regulation *Reynolds* approach and replaced it with what became known as one of the most difficult tests for the government to meet. Most famously, in *Sherbert v. Verner*,[109] a Seventh-day Adventist was denied unemployment benefits because she refused to accept a job which would have required her to work on Saturdays, her faith's day of worship. The Supreme Court sided with the plaintiff in *Sherbert* and set up a three-part, pro-religion test for free exercises challenges: (1) Once claimants demonstrate their religious exercise has been burdened, either directly or indirectly, by government action, then (2) the burden shifts to the government to establish (A) that the burden is justified by a compelling state interest (an interest of the "highest order") and that (B) there are no lesser means open to the government to achieve that critical state interest but by burdening claimant's religious exercise.

The pro-religion analysis of *Sherbert* controlled free exercise claims for many years until free exercise jurisprudence had a reboot in 1990 with *Employment Division v. Smith*, where a fractured Court ruled that, in most instances, there is no free exercise clause protection for religious objectors to neutral laws of general applicability. The "rational basis test" is met if the law is merely rationally related to a legitimate government purpose. This discussion will leapfrog over the long, complex history of free exercise analysis that began even as early as Thomas Jefferson and James Madison and instead start with the long, complex history starting in 1990. In

108. *Id.* at 166.

109. 374 U.S. 398 (1963).

1990, the Supreme Court shook First Amendment analysis to its core when it decided *Employment Division v. Smith*.[110] In that case, Oregon denied unemployment benefits to two Native American men who had been fired for using peyote for sacramental purposes during a religious ceremony.[111] The Supreme Court surprised most scholars by upholding the government's decision; the government did not have to show a compelling state interest, just even-handedness. As long as the subject law applied across the board, then the government could regulate the *conduct* whether or not it happened in a religious setting without regulating the religious beliefs. It would be the conduct itself that was outlawed, and the fact that the ban happened to impact a religious practice was secondary. One notable exception to the more forgiving standard was that strict scrutiny would apply when exceptions were available on a case-by-case basis but had been denied in the subject case.[112]

Rather than the strict scrutiny standard, the government needed only to meet a "rational basis" test. The regulation had to be rationally related to a legitimate government purpose.[113] If parties were otherwise entitled to avoid generally applicable laws just because their religious beliefs happened to violate the regulation, unless the government could show that it had a compelling interest in the regulation, then the analysis would be "permitting [them], by virtue of [their] beliefs, to become a law unto [themselves]" which would "contradict[] both constitutional tradition and common sense."[114] As Justice Scalia famously explained: "[T]he right of free exercise does not relieve an individual of the obligation to comply with a 'valid and neutral law of general applicability on the ground that the law proscribes (or prescribes) conduct that his religion prescribes (or proscribes).'"[115]

When the Court breathed new life into *Reynolds* with the *Smith* case (a pro-government ruling favoring a regulation against drug use over an individual's religiously based violation), Congress reacted. Congress was so displeased with the Court's return to a pro-regulation stance in *Smith* that it passed the Religious Freedom Restoration Act (RFRA) in 1993, which

110. 494 U.S. 872 (1990).

111. *Id.* at 874.

112. *Id.* at 884.

113. *Id.* at 872.

114. *Id.* at 885 (citations omitted).

115. *Id.* at 879 (quoting United States v. Lee, 455 U.S. 252, 263 (1982) (Stevens, J., concurring).

reimposed the pre-*Smith* free exercise clause jurisprudence on the federal government when it or its actors behave.[116] Its first attempt to unwind *Smith* (viz., the RFRA) was ruled unconstitutional, coincidentally in a case involving historic preservation. In *City of Boerne v. Flores*,[117] a 1923 Catholic church in Boerne, Texas, built in the style of historic missions, had far outgrown its historic church. The city of Boerne had a preservation ordinance that required approval for the church's expansion, and the city denied the expansion's building permit.[118] When the archbishop sued, the suit was based mainly on a claimed violation of the RFRA.[119]

The Supreme Court explained that, while Congress has broad legislative powers, they are not without limit. In particular, the Court ruled that legislation created pursuant to Section 5 of the Fourteenth Amendment had to be "remedial" and not create new rights. Because the clear purpose of RFRA was to expand (and create) new rights that would have otherwise been outside the scope of the First Amendment (as interpreted by *Sherbert*), Congress had attempted to do too much. By broadly seeking to prohibit substantial interfering with religious exercise by the federal government and states, Congress crossed a line.[120] RFRA was unconstitutional and could not be used to challenge the city's historic preservation law.

Congress responded again in an effort to revert the analysis to a strict scrutiny basis. But before that happened, there was at least one significant case that demonstrates how preservation laws would have fared under the less demanding "rational basis" analysis. In *St. Bartholomew's Church v. City of New York*,[121] the Second Circuit upheld the New York City Landmarks Preservation Law. St. Bartholomew's Church and Community House were designated as historic landmarks in 1967. The church was built in

116. The Court quickly ruled that RFRA was unconstitutional as applied to local and state government. In *City of Boerne v. Flores*, 521 U.S. 507 (1997), an archbishop sued the city of Boerne for the denial of a building permit. The church was within a historic district, which created a presumption to deny the permit to uphold the historical district's characteristics. The Court found the RFRA unconstitutional due to Congress's abuse of power in defining the substantive religious right, but it still applies to federal laws today. After *Boerne*, the tide had turned again, and religious institutions had far less protection than they had enjoyed before *Smith*.

117. City of Boerne v. Flores, 521 U.S. 507 (1997).

118. *Id.* at 512.

119. *Id.*

120. *Id.* at 532–36.

121. 914 F.2d 348 (2d Cir. 1990).

1917 according to plans by Bertram G. Goodhue to incorporate portions of an earlier building by McKim, Mead, and White. The Community House was built in 1928. The Second Circuit ruled that the preservation law was neutral and generally applicable with no intent to discriminate against religion; therefore, the less demanding test applied. The court rejected the argument that the law was not, in reality, generally applicable since an outsized number of protected buildings were religious; that sort of gerrymandering might have triggered the higher standards,[122] but the court explained the percentages by observing that grand structures like churches were more likely to trigger the preservation law not because of their religion, but only because of their fancy details.

Not every decision during the short *Smith* reign favored preservation. For example, in *First Covenant Church v. City of Seattle*,[123] the Washington Supreme Court fully recognized what the Supreme Court had decided in *Smith* when First Covenant challenged its designation as a landmark. However, the Washington Supreme Court ruled that the law fell into the exception for individualized assessments in *Smith*, which left strict scrutiny intact. Because each building had to be considered individually and because the law even included a religious exception, strict scrutiny applied.

While the short reign of *Smith* produced a few academically interesting cases, Congress was more successful on its second attempt to flip the analysis back to being pro-religion. Congress's first try, RFRA, was followed seven years later by RLUIPA (the Religious Land Use and Institutionalized Persons Act) of 2000. The RLUIPA was narrower than RFRA in that it was limited to land use issue (and, oddly, institutionalized persons) whereas the RFRA had applied generally to religious burdens. The new law, however, applied not just to federal actors, but to everyone. Congress's second attempt to unwind *Smith* (viz., the RLUIPA) has stuck and has basically returned free exercise analysis in property cases (such as historic preservation) to a pre-*Smith* status favoring an individual's religious rights. Congress avoided the fate of RFRA by focusing its new law on land use, an area where discrimination against religion was most flagrant.[124]

---

122. *See* Church of Lukumi Babalu Aye, Inc. v. City of Hialeah, 508 U.S. 520 (1993).

123. First Covenant Church v. City of Seattle, 840 P.2d 174 (1992).

124. Guru Nanak Sikh Soc. of Yuba City, 456 F.3d 978, 986, 994 (9th Cir. 2006) (citing H.R. Rep. No. 106-219, at 18–24 (1999)) (summarizing the evidence from these hearings)).

A case brought under the RULIPA is technically not a direct claim for a constitutional violation; rather, it is a claim for a statutory violation where the statute reacted to constitutional violations and broadened protections. Moreover, a challenger should certainly at least start with a statutory claim under the RULIPA and possibly plead direct constitutional violations as a backstop. Courts avoid addressing constitutional issues when a case may be resolved by statutory interpretation.[125]

However, when the RLUIPA does not apply, the actual status of constitutional law is still the pro-government *Smith* case and its progeny. The strict scrutiny test was not wholly discarded. It remains the test when the religious exercise of a party has been impacted by a law that is either not generally applicable or not neutral. The First Amendment does not exempt an individual from compliance with a "valid and neutral law of general applicability."[126] If a law's object is not to infringe or restrict religious practices, the law is neutral.[127] As restated recently by the Tenth Circuit, "Neutral rules of general applicability normally do not raise free exercise concerns even if they incidentally burden a particular religious practice or belief."[128] However, if a law that is not neutral or generally applicable yet burdens a religious practice, it is subject to strict scrutiny.[129]

If a law is not generally applicable, the courts will *strictly scrutinize* the regulation. The government may not substantially burden the free exercise of religion without showing the burden furthered a "compelling government interest." A compelling government interest is one "of the highest order" and "paramount."[130] No court has found historic preservation to be a compelling government interest.[131]

Because the RLUIPA will apply to most preservation law challenges, that will be the focus of the following discussion.

---

125. Lyng v. Nw. Indian Cemetery Protective Ass'n, 485 U.S. 439, 445–46 (1988).

126. Emp't Div. v. Smith, 494 U.S. 872, 877 (1990).

127. Grace United Methodist Church v. City of Cheyenne, 451 F.3d 643, 649–50 (10th Cir. 2006).

128. *Id.* at 649.

129. *Id.*

130. United States v. Hardman, 297 F.3d 1116, 1127 (10th Cir. 2002); *see also* Wisconsin v. Yoder, 406 U.S. 205, 215 (1972); Sherbert v. Verner, 374 U.S. 398 (1963).

131. Keeler v. Mayor & City Council of Cumberland, 940 F. Supp. 879, 886 (D. Md. 1996) (noting that "courts and commentators are apparently unanimous in opining that [historic preservation] is not [a compelling government interest]" and listing cases and articles).

2. Application to Historic Preservation

a. *Identifying the Free Exercise*

The first step in a challenge is to identify whether the regulation actually impacts an aspect of free exercise at all. Only religious beliefs are protected by the free exercise clause, which gives special protection to the exercise of religion.[132] For example, a denial of permission to clad a historic church in aluminum siding might very well have burdened the church, but there was no burden on any religious practice at all caused by the generally applicable regulation: "The commission's decision, however, has not interfered with the right of the plaintiff or its members to express their religious views, or associate or assemble for that purpose. Further, the restrictions within the historical district apply to all other property owners within the district."[133] To have any conceivable case for a First Amendment challenge, a regulation must at least have some religious impact.

One might ask: Because of the regulation, what about the owner's religion might be different? The test could be broad. For instance, a church[134] might put a premium on caring for the poor and might be hampered in its ability to fund a food program to pay for more expensive, historically appropriate windows. In that case, the threshold for showing a religious impact will have probably been met, leading to the substantive analysis. On the other hand, a regulation that requires some historic font on signage would not trigger a First Amendment challenge even if the regulation somehow was disfavored by a congregation. As a threshold matter, a regulation might be subject to many challenges, but if the only impact on a church is a wholly secular one, the free exercise clause will not work.

The fact that there are any cases at all in which courts discounted the contestant's argument as based on a mere secular impact is surprising. The Supreme Court has been very clear that it is not the position of the courts to assess the honesty of an adherent's belief or the significance of some belief. In *Lakewood, Ohio Congregation of Jehovah's Witnesses, Inc. v. City of Lakewood, Ohio*,[135] the Sixth Circuit heard an appeal of a congregation

---

132. Thomas v. Rev. Bd. of Ind. Emp. Div., 450 U.S. 707, 713 (1981).

133. First Church of Christ, Scientist v. Historic Dist. Comm'n, 738 A.2d 224, 231 (Super. Ct. Conn. 1998), *aff'd*, 55 Conn. App. 59, 737 A.2d 989 (1999).

134. Most cases involve churches. Although that term excludes mosques and synagogues, it will be used in its secular sense to denote any sort of religiously purposed structure.

135. 699 F.2d 303, 307 (6th Cir. 1983).

whose request for a building permit in a residential neighborhood had been denied. A central tenet of the faith was "the distribution of literature to homes and on the street, and the conduct of in-home Bible studies for the purpose of instructing and encouraging people to apply biblical teachings to daily life."[136] But, building a religious building in the exclusively residential area violated the zoning of the city. The Sixth Circuit ruled that the impact on the congregation was secular and not religious. It explained:

> The Congregation's "religious observance" is the construction of a church building in a residential district . . . . [T]he activity has no religious or ritualistic significance for the Jehovah's Witnesses. There is no evidence that the construction of Kingdom Hall is a ritual, a "fundamental tenet," or a "cardinal principle" of its faith. At most the Congregation can claim that its freedom to worship is tangentially related to worshipping in its own structure. However, building and owning a church is a desirable accessory of worship, not a fundamental tenet of the Congregation's religious beliefs. The zoning ordinance does not prevent the Congregation from practicing its faith through worship whether the worship be in homes, schools, other churches, or meeting halls throughout the city. The ordinance prohibits the purely secular act of building anything other than a home in a residential district.[137]

The increased financial burden caused by redirecting the congregation to more expensive commercially zoned property and the "violation of the Congregation's aesthetic choices" did not amount to pressuring the congregants to change their religious belief. Hence, the court rejected the constitutional attack.

b. Identifying and Applying the Appropriate Test

In *St. Bartholomew's Church v. City of New York*,[138] a New York City church and its community building were designated as landmarks without objection from the church in 1967. In 1983, the church wanted to demolish the 7-story community house and replace it with a 59-story office

---

136. *Id.* at 304.

137. *Id.* at 306–07.

138. 914 F.2d 348, 351 (2d Cir. 1990).

tower. When the certificate of appropriateness was denied by the Landmarks Preservation Commission of the City of New York, the church tried again with a 47-story office tower; it too was rejected.[139] The church then applied for permission under a separate provision for "hardship exceptions" based on the financial implications of living with and repairing the existing structure. Again, the commission rejected the church's request.

Next, the church went to court and sued for a civil rights violation alleging several supposed violations. As for the free exercise claim, the Second Circuit identified the supposed incidence of free exercise that the regulation had impacted:

> [T]he Church contends that by denying its application to erect a commercial office tower on its property, [the City has] impaired the Church's ability to carry on and expand the ministerial and charitable activities that are central to its religious mission. It argues that the Community House is no longer a sufficient facility for its activities, and that the Church's financial base has eroded. The construction of an office tower similar to those that now surround St. Bartholomew's in midtown Manhattan, the Church asserts, is a means to provide better space for some of the Church's programs and income to support and expand its various ministerial and community activities . . . . [T]he revenue generated by renting commercial office space will enable the Church to move some of its programs—such as sheltering the homeless—off-site. The Church concludes that the Landmarks Law unconstitutionally denies it the opportunity to exploit this means of carrying out its religious mission.[140]

The circuit court nevertheless found that the law was a regular law of general application. Supreme Court decisions indicated that neutral regulations that diminish the income of a religious organization do not implicate the free exercise clause.[141] The critical question is whether the claimant has

139. *Id.* at 351.

140. *Id.* at 353–54.

141. *See* Jimmy Swaggart Ministries v. Bd. of Equalization, 493 U.S. 378 (1990); Hernandez v. Comm'r, 490 U.S. 680 766 (1989).

been denied the ability to practice his religion or has been coerced in the nature of those practices.

In another case arising in New York City, the court determined that there was no basis for a free exercise challenge when the city's preservation ordinance merely had a secular impact limiting the windfall from redevelopment. The New York Society for Ethical Culture challenged the landmark designation of its Meeting House, an Art Nouveau building. One writer from the time of construction noted the building was "certainly quite the best piece of Art Nouveau architecture yet designed in this country, and compares well with the magnificent German department store buildings whose excellence is so great as to almost promise a future for this style."[142] The Society asserted that protecting the building from demolition unconstitutionally interfered with their religious, educational, and charitable purposes.

The court found that the challenge lacked a religious aspect: "[T]he Society does not seek simply to replace a religious facility with a new, larger facility. Instead, using the need to replace as justification, it seeks the unbridled right to develop its property as it sees fit. This is impermissible, and the restriction here involved cannot be deemed an abridgement of any First Amendment freedom, particularly when the contemplated use, or a large part of it, is wholly unrelated to the exercise of religion, except for the tangential benefit of raising revenue through development." The court added that, if the society ever needed to demolish the building to actually better advance its purpose with a different building, that might be a different outcome, but even then the court noted that such a subsequent request would be suspicious.[143]

3. Religious Land Use and Institutionalized Persons Act

In 1993, Congress enacted the Religious Freedom Restoration Act (RFRA) to restore the "compelling interest" test employed by the Supreme Court in free exercise cases prior to *Smith*. The *express purpose* of the statute was to restore the "compelling interest" test that had been used before *Smith*. In 1997, however, the U.S. Supreme Court struck down RFRA as applied to the states.[144] Now, RFRA applies only to challenges of federal regulations, and

---

142. Soc'y for Ethical Culture in City of N.Y. v. Spatt, 416 N.Y.S.2d 246, 248 (1979), *aff'd*, 415 N.E.2d 922 (1980).

143. *Id.* at 253.

144. City of Boerne v. Flores, 521 U.S. 507 (1997).

very few challenges to historic preservation come at the federal level. As to state and local laws, the pre-RFRA cases are still controlling.

Congress took another swing at the ball in 2000 when it passed by unanimous consent the Religious Land Use and Institutionalized Persons Act (RLUIPA) to ensure that religious uses were not unduly burdened by land-use laws. The RLUIPA provides that "[n]o government shall impose or implement a land-use regulation in a manner that imposes a substantial burden on the religious exercise of a person, including a religious assembly or institution, unless the government demonstrates that imposition of the burden on that person, assembly, or institution (A) is in furtherance of a compelling governmental interest; and (B) is the least restrictive means of furthering that compelling governmental interest." The RLUIPA also prohibits laws that treat religious uses on less than equal terms to similarly situated secular uses. In other words, if a regulation places a "substantial burden" on religious exercise, the constitutional analysis again returns to the strict scrutiny analysis that existed before *Smith*. Most importantly for historic preservation cases, the law specifically provides that "[t]he use, building, or conversion of real property for the purpose of religious exercise shall be considered to be religious exercise."[145]

Despite its being a federal statute, the RLUIPA applies very broadly to all levels of government, from federal action (such as approving a property for the National Register of Historic Places) down to municipal boards and their individual members.[146] The RLUIPA is one of the very few federal statutes that unambiguously and directly limits state and local land-use decisions. Likewise, "land-use regulation" is itself very broadly defined to mean:

> a zoning or landmarking law, or the application of such a law, that limits or restricts a claimant's use or development of land (including a structure affixed to land), if the claimant has an ownership, leasehold, easement, servitude, or other property interest in the regulated land or a contract or option to acquire such an interest.[147]

Although eminent domain obviously impacts the use of one's property, the taking of land by the government impacts the use in a very different way

145. 42 U.S.C.A. § 2000cc-5(7)(B) (West, Westlaw through Pub. L. No. 119-59).

146. *Id.* § 2000cc-5(4).

147. *Id.* § 2000cc-5(B)(5).

than a zoning change or the imposition of historic or architectural reviews; therefore, eminent domain is a safe harbor for governments from RLUIPA coverage.[148] Within the context of historic preservation, of course, essentially every government imposition will trigger coverage by the RLUIPA as a form of either zoning or landmarking law.

Because zoning and land-use laws are local matters, parties must normally at least try to resolve their issues through the normal permitting process. But, when such laws conflict with federal protections, the federal rights prevail. Nearly a quarter of a century after RLUIPA's passage, the Department of Justice recognized that many state and local governments still are unfamiliar with the protections the law offers.[149]

a. Overview

The land-use provisions of the Religious Land Use and Institutionalized Persons Act of 2000 (RLUIPA) protect individuals, houses of worship, and other religious institutions from discrimination in zoning and landmarking laws. The RLUIPA prohibits zoning and landmarking laws that "substantially burden" the religious exercise of churches or other religious assemblies or institutions absent the "least restrictive means" of furthering a compelling governmental interest. This prohibition applies in any situation where (1) the state or local government entity imposing the burden receives federal funding; (2) the burden affects, or removal of the burden would affect, interstate commerce; or (3) the burden arises from the state or local government's procedures for making individualized assessments of a property's uses. It is difficult to imagine a religious challenge to a state or local regulation that fails to trigger an RLUIPA review.

In addition, the RLUIPA prevents different treatment for religious and non-religious owners. The RLUIPA prohibits zoning and landmarking laws that (1) treat churches or other religious assemblies or institutions on less than equal terms with nonreligious assemblies or institutions; (2) discriminate against any assemblies or institutions on the basis of religion or religious denomination; (3) totally exclude religious assemblies from

---

148. Faith Temple Church v. Town of Brighton, 405 F. Supp. 2d 250 (W.D.N.Y. 2005); Sandstrom v. Wendell, No. 1:23-CV-00405 EAW, 2024 WL 1242415, at *8 (W.D.N.Y. Mar. 22, 2024).

149. www.justice.gov/d9/2024-03/2024_doj_letter_-_rluipa-final.pdf.

a jurisdiction; or (4) unreasonably limit religious assemblies, institutions, or structures within a jurisdiction.

b. Cases under the RLUIPA

While many religious contestants to historic preservation cite the RLUIPA, the law was never intended to provide a general immunity to preservation laws.[150] Many cases brought under the RLUIPA do not involve historic preservation but are instead traditional land-use cases. For example, in one case brought very soon after the law's passage, the court ruled in favor of a man in Connecticut who had sued under the RLUIPA when his city issued a cease and desist letter to stop him from using his house as a meeting place for prayer sessions of 25–40 attendees.[151] Other cases followed where there were no preservation issues raised, just the use of buildings.[152]

The law applies to cases where the government makes "individualized assessments of the proposed uses for the property involved," such as case-by-case exceptions to use ordinances or waivers of zoning requirements.[153] Note that this provision codified the carve-out from *Smith* that left the earlier strict scrutiny standard in place for some cases.

The RLUIPA does not define "compelling interest," but the Supreme Court has explained that compelling interests are only "interests of the highest order."[154] Further, local governments cannot rely on generalized, "broadly formulated interests," but instead must "show that the compelling interest test is satisfied through application of the challenged law to . . . the particular claimant whose sincere exercise of religion is being substantially burdened."[155]

---

150. *See* 146 CONG. REC. S7774–81 (daily ed. July 27, 2000) (joint statement of Senator Hatch and Senator Kennedy on the Religious Land Use and Institutionalized Persons Act of 2000).

151. Murphy v. Zoning Comm'n of New Milford, 148 F. Supp. 173 (D. Conn. 2001).

152. *See, e.g.*, Fifth Ave. Presbyterian Church v. City of N.Y., 293 F.3d 570 (2d Cir. 2002) (enjoining the city from removing homeless people from sleeping on a church's steps with the permission of the church).

153. 42 U.S.C.A. § 2000cc(a)(2)(C) (West, Westlaw through Pub. L. No. 119-59).

154. Church of the Lukumi Babalu Aye, Inc. v. City of Hialeah, 508 U.S. 520, 546 (1993).

155. Holt v. Hobbs, 574 U.S. 352, 363 (2015). When the U.S. Supreme Court later vacated the judgment of the Minnesota Court of Appeals in a different RLUIPA case, which had upheld a county's requirement that Amish households install modern septic systems despite assertions that their religion forbade the use of such technology, one justice emphasized that "the question in this case 'is not whether the [County] has a compelling interest in enforcing its [septic

The RLUIPA applies widely not only to diverse places of worship, but also to religious schools, camps, retreat centers, cemeteries, and social service facilities such as group homes, homeless shelters, and soup kitchens, as well as to individuals or families exercising their religion through the use of property, such as home prayer gatherings or Bible studies.[156]

Cases brought under the federal law fall into two categories: those alleging a substantial burden on religious practices and those alleging discrimination against religion.

i. "Substantial Burden" for the RLUIPA

"Substantial burden" is not defined in the RLUIPA. The RLUIPA cosponsors, Senator Orrin Hatch and Senator Ted Kennedy, explained the lack of a definition:

> The Act does not include a definition of the term "substantial burden" because it is not the intent of this Act to create a new standard for the definition of "substantial burden" on religious exercise. Instead, that term as used in the Act should be interpreted by reference to Supreme Court jurisprudence.[157]

According to the statute, the government will not impose a land-use regulation that imposes a "substantial burden" unless the government can demonstrate that the burden being imposed (1) furthers a compelling governmental interest and (2) is the least restrictive means of furthering that interest.[158]

Not every minor inconvenience triggers RLUIPA review, even if the activity does not have to be a central part of the practice. The Act protects

---

system requirement] *generally*, but whether it has such an interest in denying an exception' from that requirement to the Swartzentruber Amish *specifically*." Mast v. Fillmore Cnty., 141 S. Ct. 2430, 2432 (2021) (Gorsuch, J. concurring) (emphasis in original).

156. RLUIPA broadly defines religious exercise as "any exercise of religion, whether or not compelled by, or central to, a system of religious belief." 42 U.S.C.A. § 2000cc-5(7)(A) (West, Westlaw through Pub. L. No. 119-59). Courts have found that a host of religious activities are protected by RLUIPA, including charitable acts by religious institutions. *See, e.g.*, Micah's Way v. City of Santa Ana, No. 8:23-CV00183, 2023 WL 4680804, at *5 (C.D. Cal. June 8, 2023) (finding that, under RLUIPA, faith-based ministry's food distribution to those in need was religious exercise).

157. 146 Cong. Rec. S7779 (daily ed. July 27, 2000) (statement of Sen. Hatch and Sen. Kennedy).

158. 42 U.S.C.A. § 2000cc(a)(1) (West, Westlaw through Pub. L. No. 119-59).

"religious exercise," which is defined as "any exercise of religion, *whether or not compelled by, or central to*, a system of religious belief."[159] By expressly removing the centrality of some action from the calculus, the Act lightens the burden on those raising a challenge.[160] More than an inconvenience must be shown.[161]

To date, the majority of RLUIPA cases have been brought by individuals seeking to practice their religions; there has been very little guidance on how to extrapolate a meaning of "substantial burden" from cases of individuals that can be used to assess whether a congregation has been substantially burdened. The Department of Justice has explained that whether something qualifies as a substantial burden is a fast-intensive matter that can turn on many factors:

> Courts have looked at factors such as the size and resources of the burdened party, the actual religious needs of an individual or religious congregation, the level of current or imminent space constraints, whether alternative properties are reasonably available, the history of a complainant's efforts to locate within a community, the absence of good faith by the zoning authorities, and many other factors.[162]

As yet, there is no clear test for when a burden crosses the line into substantiality. The Eleventh and Fourth Circuits have taken approaches that seem different only by the degree of the burden and not any objective, bright-line distinctions.

In *Sherbert*, the Court defined the term as making someone choose "between following the precepts of her religion and forfeiting benefits, on the one hand, and abandoning one of the precepts of her religion in order

---

159. 42 U.S.C.A. § 2000cc-5(7)(A) (West, Westlaw through Pub. L. No. 119-59) (emphasis added).

160. *Cf.* Hernandez v. Comm'r, 490 U.S. 680, 699 (1989) (framing a free exercise challenge around whether the government has imposed a substantial burden on the observation of a central religious belief or practice).

161. Smith v. Allen, 502 F.3d 1255, 1278 (11th Cir. 2007), *overruled by* Hoever v. Marks, 993 F.3d 1353 (11th Cir. 2021), *and abrogated by* Sossamon v. Texas, 563 U.S. 277 (2011).

162. Statement of the Department of Justice on the Land Use Provisions of the Religious Land Use and Institutionalized Persons Act (RLUIPA), available at www.justice.gov/crt/page/file/1071246/dl?inline=.

to accept work, on the other hand." Later, in *Thomas*, the Court added that when a state grants or withholds an important benefit upon conduct proscribed or required by one's faith, the Hobson's choice puts a substantial pressure on the adherent to modify his behavior and to violate his beliefs, meaning a substantial burden.[163]

Given the frequency they are mentioned in the same breath, a near companion case was *Wisconsin v. Yoder*,[164] where the Court ruled that a law requiring Amish children to attend school placed an undue burden on their religious practice. For Wisconsin to require attendance beyond eighth grade, the state had to either demonstrate that it is not actually denying free exercise with its law or that "there is a state interest of sufficient magnitude to override the interest claiming protection under the Free Exercise Clause."

When a secular law is thrown up as a pretext for interfering with a church's plans, the case is easiest. Especially since the RLUIPA very clearly applies in the case of outright discrimination, such treatment triggers "substantial impact." For example, in *Grace Church of North County v. City of San Diego*,[165] the city would not approve a church's short-term permit without a provision that the church not reapply in the future. Moreover, the church faced "outright hostility" to its application and faced decision-making that was "seemingly arbitrary or pretextual."

Otherwise, cases where the heart of the matter involves a balance between preservation and religious exercise are rare. Almost every reported case involves a general urban plan with use restrictions that is challenged by a congregation that wants to conduct worship services in an area with unsympathetic zoning. However, in *Zubik v. City of Pittsburgh*,[166] the issue was front and center when Pittsburgh designated a Catholic church as historic, thereby preventing exterior alterations. The church had decided to vacate the structure as a church because of the great expense in maintaining it.

The parties saw the burden on the church's religious exercise quite differently. For the church, the designation would "burden the Diocese with delay, uncertainty, and expense in seeking permission to control its disposition of church property, all of which imposes a substantial burden on the

---

163. *Thomas v. Rev. Bd. of Ind. Emp. Sec. Div.*, 450 U.S. 707, 717 (1981).

164. 406 U.S. 205 (1972).

165. 555 F. Supp. 2d 1126 (S.D. Cal. 2008).

166. No. CV 20–1809, 2025 WL 461533, at *14 (W.D. Pa. Feb. 11, 2025).

Diocese's religious exercise." The city, on the other hand, predicted a "minimal effect of limiting how [the Diocese] could alter the street facing façade" while doing "nothing to prevent services, interior alterations, or transfer of ownership of the property, [or] restrict religious beliefs." Between those choices, the Diocese had the burden of persuasion that the preservation ordinance imposed a "substantial burden" on its religious exercise.

The federal district court noted that a Third Circuit case had already laid out the meaning of "substantial burden" but that the cases had involved the religious exercise of an individual and not a land-use case. The district court expressly added that pulling the analysis from the context of an individual adherent in personal religious exercise and applying it to an institutional land-use case was an awkward fit.

Reexamining the term in the context at hand, the district court began with an objective analysis of the words and phrases, looking to grammatical construction and ordinary dictionary definitions. The substantial burden had to be on a religious exercise, and a religious exercise was unambiguously defined as including the use of a building for religious purposes. Thus, the court looked to the dictionary definition of "substantial" and out-of-circuit cases to arrive at the idea that a burden was substantial when it was more than just inconvenient and was closer to making the use effectively impracticable.[167] The court relied on the removal of stained glass windows as a substantial burden; the church was forbidden from removing the stained glass windows and moving them to another church, and that replaced the church with the city as the party in control of "external religious ornamentation and symbols affixed to the Church Building." The court very strongly rejected the city's reply and argued that a "basic tenet of the faith cannot be so fragile as to be substantially burdened by a requirement to keep the appearance of their building as it has appeared since its construction." The court easily swatted that argument away by explaining that the statute did not require any central tenet to be considered at all, just the exercise of religion. It was not up to the court to decide how central a particular tenet was in a party's faith.

Having decided the threshold issues of "substantial burden," the district court then turned to whether the city could establish a "compelling interest." The city argued that its interest was "enhance[ing] the quality of

167. *Id.* at *17.

life by preserving the character and desirable aesthetic features of a city," "preserv[ing] and restor[ing] the qualities of the City . . . relating to its history, culture, and traditions," "preserv[ing] and restor[ing] harmonious outward appearance of structures," and "afford[ing] the City . . . the opportunity to acquire or arrange for the preservation of designated districts or structures," among other things. One might easily imagine any or all of those same interests being identified by any government to defend historic preservation—there was nothing in the city's list that was specific to Pittsburgh. And while the city correctly identified other cases in other contexts identifying such concerns as "permissible" or even "significant," it did not point to cases finding them to be "compelling." So far, historic preservation has not been classed as a compelling interest.[168] Thus, the court ruled against the city for not having a compelling interest.[169]

Very clearly, not every landmarking decision violates a group's religious rights. In 2018, the Department of Justice released a non-binding explanation of the RLUIPA in lay terms, which included a series of questions and answers. Among them was this:

> Can places of worship still be landmarked? Yes, places of worship can be landmarked. However, like any other land use regulation, landmarking designations that impose a substantial burden on religious exercise must be justified by compelling governmental interests and pursued in the least restrictive ways possible. Landmarking regulations also must be applied in a nondiscriminatory manner.[170]

---

168. *See, e.g.*, Church of Lukumi Babalu Aye, Inc. v. City of Hialeah, 508 U.S. 520 (1993); WR Prop. LLC v. Twp. of Jackson, No. CV173226MASDEA, 2021 WL 1790642, at *12 (D.N.J. May 5, 2021) ("Given this high bar, courts have held that 'aesthetics,' traffic, and 'community character' are normally not compelling interests."). In *Keeler v. Mayor & City Council of Cumberland*, the court found that the city had failed to "assert[ ] that historic preservation is a compelling interest of government" where "[c]ourts and commentators are apparently unanimous in opining that it is not." 940 F. Supp. 879, 886 (D. Md. 1996); First Covenant Church of Seattle v. City of Seattle, 840 P.2d 174, 185 (Wash. 1992) ("The possible loss of significant architectural elements is a price we must accept to guarantee the paramount right of religious freedom.").

169. *Zubik*, 2025 WL 461533, at *19–20.

170. Statement of the Department of Justice on the Land Use Provisions of the Religious Land Use and Institutionalized Persons Act (RLUIPA), available at www.justice.gov/crt/page/file/1071246/dl?inline=.

ii. Discrimination under the RLUIPA

In addition, RLUIPA prohibits zoning and landmarking laws that discriminate against religious uses. Specifically, the RLUIPA forbids regulations that "(1) treat churches or other religious assemblies or institutions on less than equal terms with nonreligious assemblies or institutions; (2) discriminate against any assemblies or institutions on the basis of religion or religious denomination; (3) totally exclude religious assemblies from a jurisdiction; or (4) unreasonably limit religious assemblies, institutions, or structures within a jurisdiction."[171] Most challenges alleging an unlawful discrimination under the federal law involve zoning matters about where churches are allowed and do not raise preservation issues. As the sponsors of the law, Senators Kennedy and Hatch said upon its signing:

> Zoning codes frequently exclude churches in places where they permit theaters, meetings halls, and other places where large groups of people assemble for secular purposes . . . . Churches have been denied the right to meet in rented storefronts, in abandoned schools, in converted funeral homes, theaters, and skating rinks—in all sorts of buildings that were permitted when they generated traffic for secular purposes.[172]

Simply being designated as a historic property does not mean that the contestant's religious practices have been burdened, certainly not substantially.

When a church acts as a private real estate developer, its case for RLUIPA protection is at its lowest. Cases where a church plans to rebuild on its own land generally fare better. Cases where the church plans to take the money from a sale and run are not well received. Even when the proceeds are going to be used to engage in a church's mission, the result is the same.

4. Establishment Clause

The First Amendment has two religious provisions. While the free exercise clause protects one's ability to exercise one's religion, the establishment

---

171. 42 U.S.C.A. § 2000cc(b)(1) (West, Westlaw through Pub. L. No. 119-59).

172. 146 Cong. Rec. S7774–75 (daily ed. July 27, 2000) (joint statement of Senators Hatch and Kennedy).

clause simultaneously prevents the government from going so far as to establish an official religion. Of course, the establishment clause has been understood as preventing far more than just the actual creation of a national faith.

As with the free exercise clause, the law under the establishment clause has also seen wild swings. Most recently, in *Kennedy v. Bremerton School District*,[173] the Supreme Court cut the remaining ties with the well-worn *Lemon* test and entanglement tests and instead adopted a new—and still unexplained—historical evaluation in their place. Even before *Kennedy*, historic preservation cases raising establishment clause challenges were exceedingly rare. Since *Kennedy*, there have been none. Given the lack of direction, this section will simply recap the overall development of the current law with broad brushstrokes. Then, it will recap the very few cases decided pre-*Kennedy* to give some sense of how challenges might arise in the future, albeit to uncertain results.

In *Lemon v. Kurtzman*,[174] the Supreme Court held that states violated the establishment clause by publicly funding supplemental pay for teachers in religious schools who taught secular subjects. To pass the resulting *Lemon* test, a law had to (1) have a secular purpose, (2) have a principal effect that neither advances nor inhibits religion, and (3) not foster excessive government entanglement with religion. Although the *Lemon* test was generally viewed as simply bringing together various threads from earlier cases, the case was almost immediately criticized as hard to apply. Technically the case remained good law for decades, but it suffered one of the slowest deaths of any famous Supreme Court case. Variations sprouted, and soon there was a coercion test and an endorsement test[175] to fill in gaps and clarify (supposedly) the contours of *Lemon*. Even by 1993, Justice Scalia poked fun at the *Lemon* test and described it as "some ghoul in a late-night horror movie that repeatedly sits up in its grave and shuffles abroad after being repeatedly killed and buried."[176] By the time the last nail was driven into its coffin, the Supreme Court declared that the analysis had been "long ago abandoned."[177]

---

173. 597 U.S. 507 (2022).

174. 403 U.S. 602 (1971).

175. Lynch v. Donnelly, 465 U.S. 668, 688 (1984) (O'Connor, J., concurring).

176. Lamb's Chapel v. Ctr. Moriches Union Free Sch. Dist., 508 U.S. 384, 398 (1993) (Scalia, J., concurring).

177. Kennedy v. Bremerton Sch. Dist., 597 U.S. 507, 510 (2022) (citing *Am. Legion*, 588 U.S. 29 (2019) (plurality opinion) and *Town of Greece v. Galloway*, 572 U.S. 565, 575–77 (2014)).

In *Kennedy v. Bremerton School District*,[178] a public high school football coach was fired after praying midfield after three football games. The only reason the school district gave for his firing was a concern that his repeated behavior exposed the district to lawsuits. The Supreme Court, as to the establishment clause, explained that because the district restricted the coach's activities precisely because of their religious character, the district's action was not neutral. Moreover, they were not generally applicable; they had been specifically crafted just for the one employee. Given that no one on the Court thought that *Smith* applied for those reasons, it was no surprise that a free exercise violation had happened (as well as a free speech violation for other reasons), leaving the Court to decide whether the district was rightly concerned that any other response would have triggered a countervailing establishment clause concern.

The Court held it was not because there was "only the 'mere shadow' of a conflict" based on the lower courts' reliance on *Lemon* and the endorsement test. The Court stated that *Lemon* and the endorsement test had been supplanted by a test based on "historical practices and understandings."[179] What does that historical test look like? That's a good question. However, *Kennedy* gave a hint by citing directly to another very recently decided case also based on the establishment clause where Justice Gorsuch, in a concurring opinion, listed these factors: (1) "the government exerted control over the doctrine and personnel of the established church"; (2) "the government mandated attendance in the established church and punished people for failing to participate"; (3) "the government punished dissenting churches and individuals for their religious exercise"; (4) "the government restricted political participation by dissenters"; (5) "the government provided financial support for the established church, often in a way that preferred the established denomination over other churches"; and (6) "the government used the established church to carry out certain civil functions, often by giving the established church a monopoly over a specific function."

In other words, the focus now seems to be on honestly creating an official religion and steering people into the faith through sticks and carrots. Mere entanglement with religion is no longer enough. It is hard to imagine a scenario where government would try to create an official religion by way of landmarking religious buildings, but in time, the *Kennedy* test might

178. 597 U.S. 507 (2022).

179. *Kennedy*, 597 U.S. at 535–36.

morph into a different analysis that could be used to challenge historic preservation. For the time being, the following is a short recap of some of the cases that tried to use the *Lemon* establishment clause test to fight historic preservation.

In *Rayellen Resources, Inc. v. New Mexico Cultural Properties Review Committee*,[180] a challenge was filed to the registration of about 400,000 acres as a cultural property. The case was primarily about technical issues about notice, inspection rights, and state ownership of some of the lands. Among the many grounds asserted for the contest, the plaintiff-landowners charged that designating land which was culturally significant to Native Americans violated the establishment clause. Lumped together with other odds and ends into a section of opinion about other issues that were "without merit," the New Mexico Supreme Court flatly asserted that the purpose of the action was "to promote historic preservation, not to advance religion."[181]

A few cases have argued that the preservation of religious structures—mainly monuments like crosses and statues of the Ten Commandments—run afoul of the establishment clause. The historical presence of the structures was used to establish a time-honored condition that should be left well enough alone. As repeatedly found, a reasonable observer who was familiar with the history of the spot would not likely understand that the structure was endorsing a particular faith.[182]

In another case, *East Bay Asian Local Development Corp. v. State*,[183] the plaintiffs challenged an exception in California's preservation law that allowed religious properties to opt out. The Supreme Court of California engaged in a lengthy discussion of why *Lemon* did not make sense as the correct analysis but used it anyway in the absence of any other direction from the Supreme Court. The California court decided that the state wrote the statute with legitimate secular purposes by crafting a law that would avoid potential—not just actual—free exercise claims. Additionally, the state

---

180. 319 P.3d 639, 656 (N.M. 2014).

181. *Id.*

182. *E.g.*, Modrovich v. Allegheny Cnty., 385 F.3d 397 (3d Cir. 2004) (involving a statue of the Ten Commandments); Freedom from Religion Found., Inc. v. Weber, 951 F. Supp. 2d 1123, 1125 (D. Mont. 2013), *aff'd sub nom.* Freedom from Religion Found. v. Weber, 628 F. App'x 952 (9th Cir. 2015) (involving a 1953 statue of Jesus).

183. 13 P.3d 1122, 1134 (Cal. 2000).

acted with a secular purpose by lessening a potential heavy financial burden of maintenance on churches.

In *American Atheists, Inc. v. City of Detroit Downtown Development Authority*,[184] a nonprofit organization challenged a program by which property owners received public funds to fix up their properties' exteriors. While slightly more than 6% of the public funds went to religious properties, the vast majority did not. The program did not on its face favor religious projects, and nothing about the program suggested that it had been crafted to favor religious properties even less conspicuously.

In conclusion, there are certainly cases in which the establishment clause has been included as a basis for contesting some aspect of a historic preservation action. They have uniformly fared badly even under the former *Lemon* test. It is too early to know how the current *Kennedy* analysis for establishment clause cases will change the law, but considering that *Kennedy* is universally understood as religion friendly, it is hard to see how *Kennedy* will lead to successful challenges.

C. FIRST AMENDMENT (FREE SPEECH)

The First Amendment simply states, "Congress shall make no law . . . abridging the freedom of speech."[185] However, no part of the amendment is interpreted literally or narrowly: It applies to more than just laws, it is not limited to actual "speech," and the Fourteenth Amendment expands its restraints to well beyond just Congress. What counts as speech? That abstract question has come up in many, many cases but has avoided an answer. The Supreme Court has written this: "In deciding whether particular conduct possesses sufficient communicative elements to bring the First Amendment into play, we have asked whether '[a]n intent to convey a particularized message was present, and [whether] the likelihood was great that the message would be understood by those who viewed it.'"[186]

184. No. 07-2398, 2009 WL 1478961 (6th Cir. May 28, 2009).

185. U.S. Const. amend. I.

186. Texas v. Johnson, 491 U.S. 397, 404 (1989) (quoting Spence v. Washington, 418 U.S. 405, 410–11 (1974)).

1. Supreme Court Interpretations

The Supreme Court's cases regarding the First Amendment have not been perfectly consistent, and the volumes of precedent just from the High Court have generated libraries worth of legal scholarship. While a comprehensive review of those cases is impossible, some threads consistently run through them. First, when a "law" is content based—that is, its application hinges on what the message being conveyed is—the Court has employed "strict scrutiny" of the law. Second, when a regulation is content neutral—that is, knowing what the message being conveyed is does not matter—the Court uses a more forgiving "intermediate scrutiny" standard. Additionally, the Court will look behind the actual text of a regulation to see whether, despite facial neutrality, the law was, in reality, motivated by favor or disfavor for the message being conveyed.

Whether a regulation is content neutral is not always clear. The main inquiry is whether the government is regulating speech because of disagreement with its message.[187] A regulation might have an incidental effect on some particular speakers or messages more than on others, but the regulation is still content neutral if it serves some purpose unrelated to the content of regulated speech.[188] Likewise, the mode of delivery is not the same as a content-based restraint.[189]

Deciding whether a regulation impacts different speech differently because of the message being conveyed is not the end of the analysis; even some content-based speech can survive judicial scrutiny as long as it is (1) justified by a compelling government interest and (2) narrowly tailored (sometimes the least restrictive means) to achieve the government interest. The burden of proving those two prongs of the test falls on the government, not the one challenging the regulation.

When a regulation does not turn on the content of the speech (i.e., it is content neutral), the Court uses a more forgiving "intermediate" standard. In such cases, the application of the regulation does not require knowledge of the content of the message, but instead regulates the "time, place, or manner" of the message. For example, a regulation that bans loud noises in a residential neighborhood on weekends is concerned only with the time,

---

187. Ward v. Rock Against Racism, 491 U.S. 781 (1989).

188. *Id.*

189. Chesapeake & Potomac Tel. Co. of Va. v. United States, 42 F.3d 181 (4th Cir. 1994).

place, and manner and would apply equally to a protestor with a bullhorn as it would to a leaf blower.

The "intermediate scrutiny" standard requires (1) a narrow tailoring (even if not the least restrictive means) of the regulation to achieve a "substantial" government interest (not necessarily a compelling one) and (2) ample alternative channels for expressing the message. In other words, as long as there are ample other ways to express the same message, the regulation will survive if the government interest is "substantial" instead of "compelling," and the tailoring of the regulation can be somewhat more loosely fit to achieve that end.[190]

When a regulation is a content-neutral regulation of manner, the "less restrictive alternative analysis" test does not apply;[191] instead, the appropriate inquiry is whether the regulation "is not substantially broader than necessary."[192]

2. Application to Historic Preservation

Most preservation work happens at a local level, so it is important to note at the start that the First Amendment has very clearly and repeatedly been applied to state and local governments through the Fourteenth Amendment.[193]

One of the most thorough discussions of the interplay of historic preservation and the First Amendment arose in Charleston, South Carolina.[194] While the district court judge's opinion was reversed by the Fourth Circuit for lack of standing, the trial court's analysis remains a well-regarded discussion worthy of review. The owner of 348 King Street decided to operate a nightclub known as the "Treehouse Night Club" in the historic building. The circa 1830 federal building stands in the Old and Historic District—the largest collection of historically significant buildings in America, with 2800 of them in 2.7 square miles.[195] The plaintiff/artist sued when the city rejected a mural painted at sidewalk level on the first floor, front side of the build-

190. *Ward*, 491 U.S. at 798.

191. *Id.* at 781.

192. *Id.* at 800.

193. Gitlow v. New York, 268 U.S. 652 (1925).

194. Burke v. City of Charleston, 893 F. Supp. 589 (D.S.C. 1995).

195. *Id.* at 592.

ing. The judge's description of the art was cool, at best: "'[A] colorful cartoon of imaginary characters, including smiling mountains, flying creatures with impractically small wings and tiny yellow bipeds.' . . . Plaintiff's work carries some artistic message emphasizing the importance of diversity and tolerance in society. This message may, however, not be readily discernible by all persons."[196]

Both sides submitted volumes of evidence. Documents and experts convinced the judge that the Board of Architectural Review did an excellent job at maintaining the style, form, and materials of the historic area; detailed the long history of the subject building; and documented the many examples of murals in Charleston. After a lengthy review of architecture in Charleston, when the judge finally turned to the law, one of her first conclusions of law was that "[a] city has the constitutional power to regulate the use of private property in the interest of historic preservation."[197] Next, the court decided that the artwork should be reviewed as "pure speech" and not just as "commercial speech," which is far more regulable by the government.[198] Finally, the court decided that the proper test was for "time and manner" restrictions of pure speech, which, again, require (1) the regulation must be neutral, (2) the regulation must be narrowly tailored to serve a significant governmental interest, and (3) the regulation must leave open ample other channels for communication.[199]

Of course, painting has long been considered a form of protected speech, so the *Burke* court's analysis was easier to justify. But what about the simple appearance of a building itself? Is architecture an expressive message entitled to full First Amendment protection? As much as dance or music, the appearance of a building can convey a message. Anyone familiar with even just 20th-century architecture can clearly understand the "message" of Frank Lloyd Wright's Usonian houses and contrast that with competing ideas conveyed by fanciful Queen Anne houses and contrast both with brutalist buildings. On the other hand, quite obviously, buildings have functional aspects (e.g., securing one's belongings and keeping the rain off one's bed) that distinguish architecture from language. At the edges, some

196. *Id.*

197. *Id.* (citations omitted).

198. *Id.* at 607–08.

199. *Id.* at 608.

aspects of a building—the number of bedrooms it contains and its distance from the sidewalk—are better left to traditional zoning laws.

If a regulation is found to apply differently based on the content of the speech, then the regulation will likely fail. After all, "[A]bove all else, the First Amendment means that government has no power to restrict expression because of its message, its ideas, its subject matter, or its content."[200] When a regulation prevents design that is "too different," the regulation might veer into content-based restrictions. For example, if a property owner wanted to build a thoroughly modern house on a street of consistently Greek Revival rowhouses, he or she might argue that a regulation requiring that new buildings maintain the character of a neighborhood is vetting new houses based on what the architecture of the new houses are "saying."

The government has the constitutional power to regulate the use of private property in the interest of historic preservation.[201] In *Penn Central Transportation Co. v. New York*,[202] the owner of a railroad terminal challenged under the takings clause—not under the First Amendment—the New York City Landmarks Preservation Commission's refusal to approve plans to build an office tower atop Grand Central Terminal. The Supreme Court very clearly laid out the justification for the government's interest in preservation:

> Over the past 50 years, all 50 States and over 500 municipalities have enacted laws to encourage or require the preservation of buildings and areas with historic or aesthetic importance. These nationwide legislative efforts have been precipitated by two concerns. The first is recognition that, in recent years, large numbers of historic structures, landmarks, and areas have been destroyed without adequate consideration of either the values represented therein or the possibility of preserving the destroyed properties for use in economically productive ways. The second is a widely shared belief that structures with special historic, cultural, or architectural significance enhance the quality of life for all. Not only do these buildings and their workmanship represent the

200. Police Dep't of Chi. v. Mosley, 408 U.S. 92, 95 (1972).

201. Penn Cent. Transp. Co. v. New York, 438 U.S. 104 (1978). *See generally* Dale R. Agthe, Annotation, *Statutes Protecting Historical Landmarks*, 18 A.L.R.4th 991 (1982).

202. 438 U.S. 104 (1978).

> lessons for the past and embody precious features of our heritage, they serve as examples of quality for today. "Historic conservation is but one aspect of the much larger problem, basically an environmental one, of enhancing—or perhaps developing for the first time—the quality of life for people."[203]

Likewise, in a challenge brought under the equal protection clause, the Court again recognized New Orleans' power to determine that activities of street peddlers might interfere with the charm of a historic district.[204] The Court wrote:

> The City Council plainly could further that objective [to preserve the appearance and custom valued by the Quarter's residents and attractive to tourists] by making the reasoned judgment that street peddlers and hawkers tend to interfere with the charm and beauty of a historic area and disturb tourists and disrupt their enjoyment of that charm and beauty, and that such vendors in the Vieux Carre, the heart of the city's tourist industry, might thus have a deleterious effect on the economy of the city. They therefore determined that to ensure the economic vitality of that area, such businesses should be substantially curtailed in the Vieux Carre, if not totally banned.[205]

However, no federal court has ruled that historic preservation is a "compelling government interest."

The very few cases that have squarely involved First Amendment issues and architecture have concerned new construction. That is, is a government regulation that prevents an owner from building anything too dissimilar to the character of an area consistent with the First Amendment? Those cases do not necessarily come up in preservation scenarios and can even arise in challenges to limitations in brand-new gated communities.

While the analysis might apply to a historic preservation case, a more interesting case involves a related topic. When an owner is prevented from

---

203. *Id.* at 107 (citations omitted).

204. *See* New Orleans v. Dukes, 427 U.S. 297 (1976).

205. *Id.* at 303.

demolishing a historic structure, a claim might be made that the government is compelling speech with which the owner does not agree. If an owner is forced to continue "speaking" through his or her ownership of an architectural style (e.g., a whimsical Victorian house) or history (e.g., a 19th-century slave dwelling), the owner might have an even stronger case.

In the same way that the government may not generally prevent someone from saying what he or she wants, neither can the government force a person to communicate an idea with which he or she disagrees. "[T]he right of freedom of thought protected by the First Amendment against state action includes *both* the right to speak freely and the right to refrain from speaking at all."[206] In either case, the test for validity of the regulation follows the same analysis and looks for content neutrality and the type of interest the government has.[207]

In *Board of Managers of Soho International Arts Condominium v. City of New York*,[208] the topic of compelled speech in a preservation context was squarely confronted. The 12-story condominium building at 599 Broadway was built in 1917 and abutted an 8-story building until the shorter building was demolished in the 1940s, leaving only the southern wall of the razed building anchored to 599 Broadway for structural reasons.[209] In 1973, the support structure was used as the skeleton of an artistic work by American artist Forrest Myers. Almost three decades later, the owner of 599 Broadway sought permission to removal the artwork/structural supports from the New York City Landmarks Preservation Commission, but the Commission denied the request: "[T]he sculpture contributes to the special architectural and historic character of the historic district and that its permanent removal will adversely affect the district's special sense of place."[210]

The owners sued for what was claimed to have been First Amendment violations, among other grounds. The Southern District of New York

206. Wooley v. Maynard, 430 U.S. 705, 714 (1977) (emphasis added).

207. Antonyuk v. Hochul, 639 F. Supp. 3d 232, 344 (N.D.N.Y. 2022), *aff'd in part, vacated in part, remanded sub nom.* Antonyuk v. Chiumento, 89 F.4th 271 (2d Cir. 2023), *cert. granted, judgment vacated sub nom.* Antonyuk v. James, 144 S. Ct. 2709 (2024), *and reinstated in part by* Antonyuk v. James, 120 F.4th 941 (2d Cir. 2024), *and aff'd in part, vacated in part, remanded sub nom.* Antonyuk v. James, 120 F.4th 941 (2d Cir. 2024).

208. No. 01 CIV. 1226 (DAB), 2004 WL 1982520, at *10 (S.D.N.Y. Sept. 8, 2004).

209. *Id.* at *1.

210. *Id.* at *4.

began its analysis by characterizing the preservation ordinance as content neutral.[211] The threshold issue for the court was whether the regulation was adopted because of disagreement with the messages being conveyed. The court sided with the commission since the Landmarks Law was clearly enacted for purposes wholly unrelated to speech. The law even specifically said, "[A]s a matter of public policy . . . the protection . . . of improvements . . . of special historical or aesthetic interest or value is a public necessity and is required in the interest of the health, prosperity, safety and welfare of the people." The court continued: "The Law does not target or focus on speech or expressive activity, and its restrictions on First Amendment rights are merely incidental. Plaintiff has cited to no provision in the Landmarks Law which directly refers to speech or expressive conduct or even implies that the law exists or was enacted to regulate First Amendment activity."[212]

Next, the district court turned to the more specific issue of compelled speech. Many times the Supreme Court has struck regulations that compel someone to broadcast government-approved messages such as the Pledge of Allegiance or an op-ed to counterbalance a newspaper's editorial.[213] Because the characterization as compelling speech would trigger almost unassailable strict scrutiny, the parties unsurprisingly differed. The owner claimed that it was being made to ostensibly demonstrate to the public its approval of the artwork's message. The commission, on the other hand, distinguished "compelled speech" cases as those involving actually forced speaking of discrete and ideological messages. The court agreed with the commission and wrote that "the doctrine of compelled speech encompasses only actual speech."[214]

Having rejected the compelled speech argument, the court easily found at least a substantial state interest to justify the regulation. The Supreme Court has repeatedly found such an interest in aesthetics.[215] And, while there

---

211. *Id.*

212. *Id.*

213. *Id.* at *13 (citations omitted).

214. *Id.*

215. City Council v. Taxpayers for Vincent, 466 U.S. 789, 805 (1984) ("It is well settled that the state may legitimately exercise its police powers to advance esthetic values."); Metromedia, Inc. v. San Diego, 453 U.S. 490 (1981) (seven justices finding a ban on billboards for aesthetic purposes a substantial government interest); Penn Cent. Transp. Co. v. New York, 438 U.S. 104, 129 (1978) ("States and cities may enact land-use restrictions or controls to enhance the quality of life by preserving the character and desirable aesthetic features of a city . . . and appellants do not contest that New York City's objective of preserving structures

might have been other ways to advance the substantial interest, the government need not pursue every imaginable, less burdensome approach. It is not the role of the court to sit as a super-legislature to pick the best possible option.[216]

D. DUE PROCESS

The government does not have to give specific rules for making case-by-case decisions, even when the history of the administrating body is less than consistent.[217]

In *Mayes v. Dallas*,[218] the plaintiff, a residential homeowner in a historic preservation district in Dallas, sought to paint his brick home and construct a walkway with pylons across his front lawn. He alleged denial of due process because the ordinances did not provide objective, specific standards that would prevent the arbitrary exercise of power by the city. The court found that the ordinances' mandates that "all building facade material shall be architecturally and historically appropriate" and "the manner in which materials are used . . . and the fashion in which elements . . . are utilized shall be compatible and harmonize with the existing structures in the block" provided adequate guidelines to satisfy due process. The court concluded:

> [T]he ordinance is precise where possible—such as in delineating the district, and in defining the nature of the alterations that require approval, including the principles and often specific criteria by which alterations are to be determined as appropriate or not—while the regulatory process is accomplished through personnel with proper qualifications, and an elaborate decisionmaking and appeal process provides for ultimate review by the City Council.[219]

---

and areas with special historic, architectural or cultural significance is an entirely permissible governmental goal."); Berman v. Parker, 348 U.S. 26, 33 (1954) (noting that "[t]he concept of the public welfare is broad and inclusive" and includes the power of the state to legislate for the "spiritual as well as physical, aesthetic as well as monetary") (citation omitted).

216. *Id.*

217. Maher v. New Orleans, 516 F.2d 1051 (5th Cir. 1975).

218. 747 F.2d 323 (5th Cir. 1984).

219. *Id.* at 325.

Persons who must conform their conduct to the law are entitled to fair notice of what is permitted and proscribed.[220] Fair notice serves several interests: It prevents those who might stray into an area from running into obstacles and penalties, it prescribes standards for those who must enforce the law, and it protects the general interest of the public in preventing other speech from being chilled.[221]

Due process comes in two varieties: substantive and procedural. The difference was summarized well in a case challenging the designation of the plaintiff's property within a city's historic district:

> Construing the Complaint liberally, the Court interprets Plaintiff's claims to allege that the adoption and implementation of the Ordinance were so fundamentally unfair, and such an abuse of the Defendant's power, that Plaintiff's constitutional rights were violated. In constitutional jargon, this is an allegation of violation of a Plaintiff's "substantive" due process rights, as opposed to his "procedural" due process rights. Whereas substantive due process rights guarantee fundamentally just and fair governmental action, procedural due process rights protect one's access to adequate process when deprived of a right in which one has a property interest.[222]

One's substantive due process rights are not violated simply because the owner disagrees with the government's action. Rather, substantive due process protects against those government actions that are carried out to oppress, which are so abusive as to shock the conscience, or that are illogically connected to the government's supposed goal.[223] While it might seem odd, the courts have repeatedly recognized that small missteps in zoning matters do not rise to the level of a due process violation; otherwise, because of the sheer number of miscues and flubs in the complex zoning process, federal courts would be turned into glorified zoning boards.[224]

---

220. Vill. of Hoffman Ests. v. Flipside, Hoffman Ests., 455 U.S. 489 (1982).

221. Grayned v. Rockford, 408 U.S. 104 (1972).

222. Van Horn v. Town of Castine, 167 F. Supp. 2d 103, 106 (D. Me. 2001) (citation omitted).

223. PFZ Props., Inc. v. Rodriguez, 928 F.2d 28, 31 (1st Cir. 1991), *overruled by* San Geronimo Caribe Project, Inc. v. Acevedo-Vila, 687 F.3d 465 (1st Cir. 2012).

224. *Van Horn*, 167 F. Supp. 2d at 107; Coniston Corp. v. Vill. of Hoffman Ests., 844 F.2d 461, 467 (7th Cir. 1988) ("Something more is necessary than dissatisfaction with the rejection of

When the parameters for coverage are ill defined, the result might be a due process challenge. In *Hanna v. City of Chicago*,[225] owners of property in two historic districts created by the Commission on Chicago Landmarks challenged the Chicago ordinance on due process grounds both on its face and as applied to them in particular. The trial court granted the city's motion to dismiss, and the owners appealed. The Illinois Court of Appeals began by summarizing the Chicago ordinance, highlighting that it specified seven factors to consider before designating a property: (1) a critical part of the city's heritage, (2) a significant historic event, (3) a significant person, (4) important architecture, (5) an important architect, (6) a distinctive theme as a district, and (7) a unique visual feature. A designated property needed at least two of those factors.

The owners challenged the law, saying that it was an improper delegation of the city council's authority and was too vague to guide them. The trial court disagreed, ruling that the final approval had to come from the city council of designations and that there was enough guidance to survive challenges.

Plaintiffs were correct that "'[a]n ordinance or statute violates due process guarantees when its terms are so incomplete, vague, indefinite and uncertain that men and women of ordinary intelligence must necessarily guess at their meaning and differ as to their application.'"[226] "The law is clear that a legislative act that is so vague, indefinite, and uncertain that the courts are unable, by accepted rules of construction, to determine with any reasonable degree of certainty what was intended will be declared void."[227] In the owners' view, words such as "historic," "significant," and "value" were so undefined that any property in Chicago could be covered.[228] The city countered that, when read in the context of the preservation ordinance, especially by professionals in that field, the meaning was clear.[229] The court found that the approval of similar language in another ordinance was not binding on the court in that case and that even the definition of a

---

a site plan to turn a zoning case into a federal case; and it should go without saying that the something more cannot be merely a violation of state (or local) law.").

225. 907 N.E.2d 390 (Ill. App. Ct. 2009).

226. *Id.* at 395 (quoting City of Wheaton v. Sandberg, 574 N.E.2d 697 (Ill. Ct. App. 1991)).

227. *Id.* (quoting *City of Wheaton*, 574 N.E.2d 697).

228. *Id.* at 395.

229. *Id.*

professional was itself open to too much interpretation.[230] The court did, however, note that it was simply ruling on the satisfactory pleadings to withstand a motion to dismiss.[231]

The case has a happy ending for preservationists. After the case was remanded by the appellate court, the owners again lost in the trial court on summary judgment even on amended pleadings.[232] The owners began by arguing that the appellate court had already decided the constitutional issues, but the appellate court disagreed; it pointed to language in its first opinion that it was deciding only that the allegations were sufficient to survive a motion to dismiss. The appellate court had merely ordered that the case be remanded for—both ironically and vaguely—"further proceedings" and was not meant as a final ruling on the merits:

> The bottom line is this: while plaintiffs are correct that, at the time the cause was before us, we made some remarks suggesting our feelings that the Ordinance could be seen as unconstitutional for vagueness and improper delegation, they are wholly incorrect that these remarks amounted to strict holdings or instructions to the trial court to so find or be bound upon remand.[233]

Turning to the merits of the owners' arguments about vagueness, the appellate court had a change in tune and began with a recap of just how low the standard is for precision. All that is required is that a reasonable person could understand the meaning, not that it have perfect precision and clarity. The entire ordinance had to be considered as a whole, and it was not enough to imagine hypothetical cases where the meaning could be confusing. Even susceptibility to misapprehension and misapplication would not submarine an ordinance because of the "great tolerance" for vagueness in civil laws.

The most important discussion involved the supposed vagueness of the factors used in deciding to designate a property. Despite the same court having earlier ruled that the terms were ill defined and that their use in

230. *Id.* at 397.

231. *Id.*

232. Hanna v. City of Chicago, 2013 IL App (1st) 121701-U.

233. *Id.* ¶ 21.

other cities' ordinances was not persuasive, now the court came to the exact opposite outcome:

> Without having to define each and every word challenged (which the trial court has already done at length in this cause), in our view, we find that all of them have popular understandings and are used commonly enough to not be considered vague in the context of a constitutional challenge. In addition, we would note that the terms plaintiffs cite from the Ordinance are terms that have been challenged before in the arena of historic preservation law and, significantly, have consistently been upheld by courts of law as constitutional.[234]

234. *Id.* ¶ 40.

Protections for Archaeological Sites, Traditional Cultural Places, and Burial Sites

8

A. OVERVIEW

This chapter focuses on the laws that aim to protect cultural property that is distinct from the architecture of historic buildings. Often, but not exclusively, these resources are below ground and associated with the practice of archaeology.

Unique treatment in the context of the law is warranted because the objective of protection is a scientific understanding of the past as well as cultural continuity. These purposes can function in tandem. They can also conflict. Significant differences of opinion emerged between descendant tribes and scientists in considering the appropriate treatment and disposition of the remains of Kennewick Man, a 9000-year-old skeleton discovered in Washington state in 1996.[1]

Regulatory review of this category of sites is required of federal agencies under many of the same laws that protect

[1] For a background on the dispute, see *Bonnichsen v. United States*, 367 F.3d 864 (9th Cir. 2004).

buildings and structures.[2] This chapter adds additional context for how this subset of cultural resources are treated under those legal processes. One practical reason for distinct treatment is that non-structural resources, by their nature, are often not as apparent at the time a project is initiated. To satisfy federal law requirements, federal agencies typically set forward a process agreed to by the State Historic Preservation Office to by making a reasonable effort to identify sites in advance and engage in harm avoidance strategies. The law also works to ensure that sites encountered in the process of construction are evaluated for protection, and that proper notification is sent to state and local groups with a stated interest.

Archaeological sites are commonly misunderstood as isolated individual objects beneath the soil. Yet materials typically fit into a broader context. It is often the role of archaeologists to contextualize individual pieces of information within a larger geographic area to make sense of the information it provides us. When someone carelessly removes these objects, whether or not with an attempt to harm, it becomes more difficult to tell an accurate story and convey its significance. Losing site context deprives us and future generations of the ability to understand the full history of human interaction with the land.

As stressed herein, the rationale for the protection of non-structural cultural property is not simply scientific research. It is also because these sites are linkages for modern-day communities to their past and often hold unique significance to living people. The meaning ascribed to them can be religious in nature as well as symbolic to advance cultural continuity. Many Indian tribes use their consultation rights to stress these purposes. Notably, the federal government has legal requirements to consult with tribes extending beyond the scope of this chapter.[3]

---

2. NHPA, NEPA, and Section 4(f) all contemplate protections for sites eligible for the National Register of Historic Places.

3. *See* Advisory Council on Historic Preservation, Consultation with Indian Tribes in the Section 106 Review Process: The Handbook (June 2021), available at https://pmiphx.org/presidents-corner/adaptive-reuse-bridging-the-gap-between-historical-preservation-and-modern-architectural-practices (last visited Feb. 15, 2026) ("The federal government's unique relationship with each and every Indian tribe is embodied in the U.S. Constitution, Indian treaties, court decisions, federal statutes, and executive orders. This relationship is deeply rooted in history, dating back to the earliest contact between colonial and tribal governments. As the colonial powers did, the United States acknowledges federally recognized Indian tribes as sovereign nations; thus, federal government interaction with federally recognized Indian tribes takes place on a 'government-to-government' basis.").

B. EVOLUTION OF THE STUDY OF ARCHAEOLOGY IN AMERICA

Archaeology as a professional field has experienced significant evolution over the last century. The term *archaeology* to define a field of study is borrowed from the Greek concept of *arkhaiologia* or the "study of ancient things."[4] It is typically associated with the academic endeavor of piecing together evidence of past lives from material objects found beneath the soil.

Educational institutions and museums have long had a prominent role in shaping how archaeology is practiced in America. The National Museum (predecessor of the Smithsonian Museum) was pivotal in establishing the early framework for legislation to protect archaeological sites. The Antiquities Act of 1906 was the first major federal legislation in the United States to protect archaeology on federal lands and gave both the executive and legislative branches the power to make reservations through national monuments. The political momentum that resulted in its passage is credited to academics that had comparative experience working with much more highly regulated systems of exploration and investigation of antiquities abroad.[5]

In recent years, archaeological practice has come to embrace methods of inquiry more anthropological in nature, respecting that cultures often ascribe meaning to objects found from the past. While a more traditional approach to archaeology centered on the careful removal of objects and curation in a museum, modern eyes may see this removal as culturally insensitive at a minimum, if not deeply sacrilegious.

Perhaps nowhere are the divergent perspectives about archaeology more intense than in the case of human remains. One particularly fraught example came in the wake of the investigation of a late 17th-century and early 18th-century burial ground for persons of African descent in New York City. A team of archaeologists working for the General Services Administration encountered hundreds of sets of human remains during construction of a federal office building in the early 1990s in Lower Manhattan. Historic maps had shown the probability of the discovery, yet the agency proceeded against the advice of researchers urging caution prior to excavation.

---

4. Online Etymology Dictionary, www.etymonline.com (last visited Feb. 15, 2026).

5. *See* National Park Service, *The Antiquities Act, 1900–1906*, www.nps.gov/articles/lee-story-antiquities.htm (last visited Feb. 15, 2026).

When remains began to be exhumed, significant blowback ensued, and the affected descendant community pressed to reset the process. Researchers ultimately were persuaded to closely engage with this community at significant cost and delays. Ultimately, the dialogue resulted in a more sensitive research process centered on a biocultural approach to research for the over 400 sets of remains that had been discovered and continued encapsulation of the undisturbed cemetery site.[6] Today the site is commemorated as the African Burial Ground National Monument.

There is wide consensus that the work of archaeologists has evolved to require engagement with modern-day communities with associations with sites prior to settling on a course of action for research. The shift is enabled by the focus on "consultation" in the National Historic Preservation Act, the unique procedural requirement defined in its implementing regulations.[7] Courts interpreting the NHPA have paid particular attention to the good faith dialogue required with Indian tribes as a means of identifying historic properties, assessing the effects of a project, and resolving those effects that are adverse through harm avoidance, minimization, and mitigation measures.[8] The premise of these procedural requirements is that consultation in good faith with affected parties can aid the agencies in making these determinations and implement Congress's will to protect heritage sites.

---

6. General Services Administration, *The New York African Burial Ground: Unearthing the African Presence in Colonial New York* (2009), https://npshistory.com/publications/afbg/unearthing-v5.pdf (last visited Feb. 15, 2026). The revised research method took into account the areas the people came from, the languages they spoke, and other historical and cultural information.

7. "Consultation" is defined by the Section 106 implementing regulations as "the process of seeking, discussing, and considering the views of other participants, and, where feasible, seeking agreement with them regarding matters arising in the section 106 process." 36 C.F.R. § 800.16(f) (2025).

8. *See generally* 36 C.F.R. pt. 800 (2025). *See also* Pueblo of Sandia v. U.S. Forest Serv., 50 F.3d 856 (10th Cir. 1995) (admonishing the U.S. Forest Service for failing to make a reasonable or a good faith effort to identify historic properties after having been put on notice by a concerned tribe that the project area contained places of religious and cultural significance); Muckleshoot Indian Tribe v. U.S. Forest Serv., 177 F.3d 800 (9th Cir. 1999) (finding that the Forest Service erred in its obligation to minimize the adverse effects of transferring intact portions of the culturally significant Huckleberry Divide Trail to a logging company); Pit River Tribe v. U.S. Forest Serv., 469 F.3d 768 (9th Cir. 2006) (finding that the Forest Service violated the NHPA by not consulting with tribes prior to authorizing the extension of a lease for a geothermal facility near the Medicine Lake caldera).

In recent years, the term *cultural resources management*, or CRM, has become embraced as a more accurate descriptor for protection of the suite of resources traditionally grouped as archaeology. The CRM concept is more fitting because the objects of protection may not be perceived as "historic" in its conventional sense by descendant communities. CRM firms are typically engaged by private sector permit applicants to perform compliance work that might be necessary under federal and state law. This includes employing certified archaeologists as well as specialists in legal authorities related to tribal consultation, burial grounds, and cultural property in a sense broader than the built environment.

The shifted terminology is an important signal to applicants. It is a common assumption that archaeology as a scientific practice is the only form of mitigation for an impact. But this may not be the preferred approach for resolving adverse effects for those afforded input through consultation, particularly descendants with ties to the communities that produced the material culture at issue.

Looking forward, the practice of archaeology, as it is conventionally described, is more than a process for excavating and removing important objects of antiquity to a museum. For important reasons, it has come to embrace a more ethical and inclusive practice that takes into account the perspective of living, traditional communities. With this shift, the field has more frequently regarded avoidance of harm, or preservation in place, as preferential to extraction and research.

C. ELIGIBILITY OF ARCHAEOLOGICAL SITES FOR THE NATIONAL REGISTER OF HISTORIC PLACES

Objects, materials, and landscapes distinct from, though sometimes closely related to, the built environment are recognized by the National Park Service as eligible for designation on the National Register of Historic Places. The eligibility designation has legal significance under federal law by considering the site worthy of protecting.[9] The NPS regulation most common for archaeological sites is criterion D, which states that eligible places are

9. In 1976, Congress amended Section 106 of the NHPA to specifically instruct that properties eligible for the National Register be considered in project planning in addition to those formally listed.

those "that have yielded, or may be likely to yield, information important in prehistory or history."[10]

The criterion D basis for eligibility is often used by practitioners as a catch-all for materials encountered below ground on project sites. The concept of "importance" is a critical determinant in assessing eligibility in consultation with regulatory bodies such as the applicable State or Tribal Historic Preservation Officer. All human material encountered below ground contains information about the past, but eligible sites must meet a higher threshold. States typically employ a qualified archaeologist to review the determinations made by permit applicants.

Criterion D is the most common route for a determination of eligibility for archaeology, but it is not the only pathway. Criterion A (association with events), Criterion B (association with individuals), and Criterion C (of a distinctive type or period or have artistic value, or a component of an identifiable historic district) can also be pathways for establishing importance. Professional archeologists are trained to recognize these other aspects of significance, and input from communities associated with these sites can provide important context in making these determinations.[11]

The basis for eligibility can be particularly important in the context of mitigation for projects subject to Section 106 of the NHPA. If scientific understanding is the only reason a place is significant, it reasons that harmful effects can still be avoided through removal and interpretation. Yet caution is warranted. Time and time again in Section 106 consultations, groups that ascribe meaning to these sites object to that rationale and have urged avoidance and minimization measures with a preference for preservation in place. The regulations require agencies to evaluate harm avoidance measures prior to sanctioning the removal of objects from the landscape and imposing mitigation measures.[12]

---

10. 36 C.F.R. § 60.4(d) (2025).

11. *See* National Park Service, *Guidelines for Evaluating and Registering Archaeological Properties*, www.nps.gov/subjects/nationalregister/upload/NRB36-Complete.pdf (last visited Feb. 15, 2025).

12. Often in Section 106 consultations agencies will immediately jump to mitigation measures as a way to resolve harm without evaluating harm avoidance and minimization measures. Yet the Section 106 regulations state that the goal of consultation is to "avoid, minimize and mitigate any adverse effects on historic properties." 36 C.F.R. § 800.1(a) (2025). The inclusion of three distinct, specific actions and the ordering suggests a priority for agency action that consulting parties may stress as they work within the NHPA process.

There has also been a growing trend of deference to the self-governing rights of Indian tribes in U.S. courts and as reflected in multiple policies at the federal and state levels. Explicit recognition of tribal views on historic resources was emphasized by Congress in 1980 in its amendments to the NHPA.[13] The added statutory text clarifies that "[p]roperty of traditional religious and cultural importance to an Indian tribe or Native Hawaiian organization may be determined to be eligible for inclusion on the National Register."[14] Further, in 2007 the United Nations Declaration on the Rights of Indigenous Peoples (UNDRIP) expanded on the rights of indigenous peoples. Article 11 states:

> Indigenous peoples have the right to practice and revitalize their cultural traditions and customs. This includes the right to maintain, protect and develop the past, present and future manifestations of their cultures, such as archaeological and historical sites, artefacts, designs, ceremonies, technologies and visual and performing arts and literature.[15]

As a result, archaeological training and certification programs increasingly focus on ensuring that methods for study of cultural objects are mindful of those who ascribe them meaning. This can be true for Indian tribes with sovereign rights, but also for other descendant groups that may not have as strong a material record of their contributions reflected in the built environment.[16]

---

13. 54 U.S.C.A. § 302706(a) (West, Westlaw through Pub. L. No. 119-59) (asserting that "[p]roperty of traditional religious and cultural importance to an Indian tribe or Native Hawaiian organization may be determined to be eligible for inclusion on the National Register").

14. 54 U.S.C.A. § 302706 (West, Westlaw through Pub. L. No. 119-59). For more information on how Native Hawaiian Organizations are identified, see www.achp.gov/sites/default/files/2017-02/NHOPolicy.pdf.

15. United Nations, United Nations Declaration on the Rights of Indigenous People (2007), available at www.un.org/development/desa/indigenouspeoples/wp-content/uploads/sites/19/2018/11/UNDRIP_E_web.pdf. The United States announced its support for the Declaration on January 12, 2011. U.S. Department of State, *Announcement of U.S. Support for the United Nations Declaration on the Rights of Indigenous Peoples*, https://2009-2017.state.gov/s/srgia/154553.htm (last visited Feb. 15, 2026).

16. *See, e.g.*, Advisory Council on Historic Preservation, Guide to Working with Non-federally Recognized Tribes in the Section 106 Process (Feb. 2018), www.achp.gov/sites/default/files/whitepapers/2018-06/

Other evidence of the growing awareness of the wide variety of perspectives on archaeological sites has occurred through rulemaking initiatives such as the Advisory Council on Historic Preservation's Section 106 regulations. The National Park Service has also taken significant steps to assert the importance of sites that used by present-day cultures to sustain their identities. In 1991 the NPS adopted Bulletin 38, a policy that gave federal agencies implementing the NHPA the basis to identify a Traditional Cultural Property, or TCP, as an eligible historic resource that might be affected by an undertaking for the purposes of Section 106.[17] The rationale for identifying TCPs as a resource type is to assure the survival of living communities. This is generally, but not exclusively Indian tribes, and the concept is tied to the protection of a place whether or not it contains physical evidence of the past.

D. PROFESSIONAL STANDARDS

The Register of Professional Archaeologists is a professional organization that sets educational standards for licensing archaeologists. This qualification is a standard condition when permitting requires archaeological work, including physical digging as well as monitoring of site construction. Accreditation in the field is critical for ensuring that material remains of the past are handled in a manner prescribed by law and accepted ethical practices. A license requires a graduate degree in the field and completion of a thesis on a specific topic.

GuidetoWorkingwithNon-FederallyRecognizedTribesintheSection106Process.pdf (last visited Feb. 15, 2026).

17. Patricia L. Parker and Thomas F. King, National Register Bulletin 38: Guidelines for Evaluating and Documenting Traditional Cultural Properties (1992), www.nps.gov/subjects/nationalregister/upload/NRB38-Completeweb.pdf (last visited Feb. 15, 2026) (stating traditional cultural significance is "derived from the role the property plays in a community's historically rooted beliefs, customs, and practices."); *see also* Paul R. Lusignan, *Traditional Cultural Places and the National Register*, George Wright Forum 37 (2009), available at www.georgewright.org/261lusignan.pdf (noting that TCPs are not a separate criterion but a method to "open up the range of property types that could be considered [for the National Register], affirming the potential eligibility of places that might have been previously overlooked by preservationists and/or the government in spite of their significance to contemporary peoples.").

The Department of the Interior also maintains a set of standards for "qualified" archaeologists to follow. The Secretary of the Interior's Qualification Standards for Archeologists require a graduate degree in archeology, anthropology, or a closely related field plus (1) at least one year of full-time professional experience or equivalent specialized training in archeological research, administration, or management; (2) at least four months of supervised field and analytic experience in general North American archeology; and (3) demonstrated ability to carry research to completion.[18]

In addition to these minimum qualifications, a professional in prehistoric archeology shall have at least one year of full-time professional experience at a supervisory level in the study of archeological resources of the prehistoric period. A professional in historic archeology shall have at least one year of full-time professional experience at a supervisory level in the study of archeological resources of the historic period.[19]

Registered archaeologists also have the option to join the Society of American Archaeologists, which requires adherence to a system of ethics. The most recent update of the SAA Principles of Archaeological Ethics was published in 2024.[20] These nine principles emphasize, among other things, the role of an archaeologist as a steward and educator, prohibitions on commercialization, and responsibility to recognize indigenous perspectives on archaeological resources.

E. BURIAL PROTECTION

The common law regarding the interment of human remains is unique to the United States yet informed by legal principles that existed in England and drew on other sources including principles of Greek and Roman law and Christian religious thought.[21] As early as 1829, the U.S. Supreme Court ruled

---

18. National Park Service, *Professional Qualifications Standards*, www.nps.gov/articles/sec-standards-prof-quals.htm (last visited Feb. 15, 2026).

19. *Id.*

20. Society for American Archaeology, *Principles of Archaeological Ethics*, https://saa.org/Member/SAAMember/Career-and-Practice/Principles-of-Archaeological-Ethics.aspx (last visited Feb. 15, 2026).

21. *See* Bethesda Afr. Cemetery Coal. v. Hous. Opportunities Comm'n, 322 A.3d 681, 690–91 (Md. 2024) (citation omitted).

that courts could be entrusted to protect the deceased and the feelings of the living, a role previously assigned to ecclesiastical courts during British rule.[22]

Federal legislation regarding burial grounds is largely limited to the treatment of the remains of Native American tribes encountered on federal land.[23] State law controls how burials might be treated. Typically, states criminalize intentional desecration of such sites, but they may provide a mechanism for disinterment or relocation in certain circumstances.[24]

Identification of burial sites and their associated history can be a challenge that can create confusion in how descendant communities are engaged and consulted. The National Register regulations indicate that cemeteries, absent special circumstances, do not have assumed eligibility to be a protected site.[25] For this reason, state GIS databases documenting eligible National Register resources for planning purposes may not be relied on to identify and flag issues in advance of project proposals. States increasingly need to operate outside the National Register framework to ensure consistent protection to burial locations.

The federal approach to limiting the extent of cemeteries eligible for the National Register may be based on a concern that it would lead to a preponderance of cemetery sites being considered for designation. Even if that rationale might be well founded, the decision to exclude these sacred spaces has had consequences for their protection. Inventories of cemeteries are rare, and many, particularly from poorer communities, have suffered erasure as they have not had the resources to erect permanent markers like headstones. For these reasons, the treatment of cemeteries as historic places varies considerably. In urban environments where the pressure to build on vacant land is significant, former burial grounds may not be included in local inventories

---

22. Beatty v. Kurtz, 27 U.S. 566, 584–85 (1829) (commenting on the court's jurisdiction to protect the sepulchres of the dead through the power of the injunction to "preserve the repose of the ashes of the dead, and the religious sensibilities of the living").

23. The Native American Graves Protection and Repatriation Act (NAGPRA), Pub. L. No. 101-601, 104 Stat. 3048 (1990) (codified as 25 U.S.C. § 3001–3013).

24. *See generally* Tanya Marsh & Daniel Gibson, Cemetery Law 363–64 (2015). In South Carolina, for instance, local governing bodies can authorize the removal of an abandoned cemetery if determined "necessary and expedient." S.C. Code Ann. § 27-43-40(1) (Westlaw through 2025 Act No. 94).

25. 36 C.F.R. § 60.4 (2025). The exception to this rule is when that cemetery "derives its primary significance from graves of persons of transcendent importance, from age, from distinctive design features, or from association with historic events."

of historic properties. Without more proactive survey work, this can lead to confusion and delays for both the regulators and applicants.[26]

In recent years there has been a growing awareness of how gravesites and burials are—and should be—treated as a cultural resource, whether or not on the National Register, as matter of human dignity.[27] Further, a seminal report for the American Anthropological Association in 2025 provides insight into practices around the world, concluding that the core goal is to obtain "informed consent" prior to the use of human remains, whether for research, relocation, or otherwise.[28]

F. FEDERAL LEGAL AUTHORITIES

Several seminal independent pieces of federal legislation afford protections for archaeological sites in addition to the compliance responsibilities federal agencies have under the NHPA, NEPA, and Section 4(f) of the Department of Transportation Act.

1. Antiquities Act

On June 8, 1906, President Theodore Roosevelt signed into law "An Act for the Preservation of American Antiquities."[29] The law was the culmination of nearly 25 years of congressional debate about the effective legislative

---

26. Several notable efforts in recent years have mapped burial sites outside the NRHP context and can provide a useful planning tool for local governments. For examples, *see* The Black Cemetery Network, available at https://blackcemeterynetwork.org/, or a local tool developed specifically in Charleston, South Carolina, that maps all cemetery sites: www.preservationsociety.org/programs-resources/mapping-charlestons-black-burial-grounds/.

27. Advisory Council on Historic Preservation, *Burial Sites, Human Remains, and Funerary Objects*, www.achp.gov/treatment-burial-sites (last visited Feb. 15, 2026) (stating as a core principle that "[d]isturbing or disinterring burial sites, human remains, or funerary objects, when not requested by descendants, associated Indian Tribes or NHOs, or required by applicable law or regulation, should not be pursued unless there are no other alternatives available and only after consultation with descendants or associated communities and fully considered avoidance of impact and preservation in place").

28. Sabrina C. Agarwal et al., The Commission for the Ethical Treatment of Human Remains American Anthropological Association (June 2024), available at www.americananthro.org/wp-content/uploads/tcethr-report-2024-06.pdf?_gl=1*15qtrf5*_ga*MTcw-Mjk2MzYzNS4xNzU0MzQyMTY5*_ga_NHV0Y97DC9*czE3NTQzNDIxNjgkbzEkZzEkd-DE3NTQzNDIzMjckajYwJGwwJGgw (last visited Feb. 15, 2026).

29. In 2014 Congress recodified the Antiquities Act at 54 U.S.C. §§ 320301–320303.

response to the widespread practice of looting archeological sites on federally owned public lands. This was a major issue in the desert Southwest and particularly the dramatically well-preserved sites associated with the Pueblo peoples associated with the Chacoan landscape. The cliff dwellings now contained in places like Mesa Verde National Park, well preserved in the xeric landscape, had suffered from commercial profiteering.

One of the primary focal points of the Antiquities Act was to give the federal government the authority to control archaeological investigations via a permit process.[30] Permits are strictly limited when the work is done for the benefit of educational institutions. All other excavations for private purposes (typically motivated by associated pecuniary rewards) are prohibited, and penalties are imposed for violations.[31]

In Section 2 of the Antiquities Act, Congress gave the president the unique authority to set aside national monuments on federal lands deserving of special conservation protections. Specifically, the president "in his discretion" may declare "historic landmarks, historic and prehistoric structures, and other objects of historic or scientific interest . . . situated upon [federal] lands."[32] The scope of the president's authority is wide; Congress only required that a monument be "confined to the smallest area compatible with the proper care and management of the objects to be protected."[33]

Since the time of its passage, every president has used the authority provided to them to create such designations by official proclamation. A majority of monuments have been created within the National Park System, though presidents also have the option to consider the National Forest System, National Wildlife Refuge System lands, and even waters under U.S. jurisdiction. At the time of this writing, 138 monuments have been designated through either proclamation or approval of special acts of Congress. The size of monuments varies considerably, and the proclamation text itself is an indispensable resource for understanding the basis of each president's decision.

---

30. 54 U.S.C.A. § 320302 (West, Westlaw through Pub. L. No. 119-59).

31. In *United States v. Smyer*, 596 F.2d 939 (10th Cir. 1979), the court upheld the Antiquities Act against a challenge that its terms were unconstitutionally vague when the government enforced penalties after defendants were found to have excavated an 800- to 900-year-old habitation site.

32. 54 U.S.C.A. § 320301(a) (West, Westlaw through Pub. L. No. 119-59.

33. *Id.* § 320301(b).

Courts have largely rejected efforts by local jurisdictions to invalidate designations out of a concern for resulting economic loss. In *Tulare County v. Bush*, the D.C. Court of Appeals rejected a California County's objection to the designation of Giant Sequoia National Monument.[34] The court found that Congress gave such broad authority to the executive branch in making designations that a proclamation need only identify the historic sites and objects warranting protection. In a subsequent case contesting the creation of the nearly 2-million-acre Grand Staircase–Escalante National Monument, the court similarly rejected the idea that a court will second-guess a president's judgment as to whether the site satisfies the "smallest area" requirement.[35]

In recent years, previous designations have become heavily politicized, raising legal questions concerning whether monument designations have a degree of permanence that cannot be undone.[36] The question remains an issue of first impression despite significant litigation resulting from President Trump's reduction of the 1.25-million-acre Bears Ears National Monument, which was established by President Obama in 2016. In his first term, President Trump reduced the size of the Monument by 85%. The Hopi Tribe and others sued, and that case remains stayed in the D.C. Circuit.[37] Subsequently, President Biden repealed President Trump's decision and Garfield County, Utah, which opposed the larger restored monument, sued. A decision is pending in the Tenth Circuit at the time of this publication.[38] In light of these challenges, history shows that Monument proclamations are most effective for creating legally assured protections when they serve as a basis

---

34. 306 F.3d 1138 (D.C. Cir. 2002).

35. Utah Ass'n of Cntys. v. Bush, 316 F. Supp. 2d 1172 (D. Utah 2004)

36. In the case of the Papahānaumokuākea Marine National Monument, President George W. Bush established initial protections in 2006 as a sacred and ancestral home of Native Hawaiians. The monument was subsequently enlarged fourfold by President Barack Obama in 2016 making it one of the world's largest protected areas, including strict limitations on commercial fishing. In 2025 President Donald Trump issued an executive order instructing the Department of Commerce to review all marine monuments and provide recommendations for opening them to commercial fishing in apparent contravention of the terms of the previous designations. E.O. 14276, Restoring American Seafood Competitiveness, April 17, 2025, Sec. 4(h).

37. Hopi Tribe v. Trump, No. 1:17-CV-02590 (TSC), 2024 WL 4880466 (D.D.C. Nov. 25, 2024).

38. Garfield Cnty. v. Biden, No. 4:22-CV-00059-DN-PK, 2023 WL 5180375 (D. Utah Aug. 11, 2023).

for subsequent legislation, as in the case of places like the Grand Canyon, which became a monument before its establishment as a National Park.

2. Historic Sites Act

In 1935 the U.S. Congress declared as a matter of "national policy" its intention to "preserve for public use historic sites, buildings, and objects of national significance for the inspiration and benefit of the people of the United States."[39] The Historic Sites Act laid essential groundwork for subsequent policy-implementing legislation like the National Historic Preservation Act of 1966.[40]

While the Historic Sites Act contained an ambitious declaration of policy, it functioned primarily to honor aspects of U.S. history with no action-forcing requirements that could serve as a legal basis to save them. It also allowed for wide subjectivity in defining national significance but lacked any substantive criteria for consistent decision-making.

Yet its provisions are instructive for understanding how subsequent preservation legislation worked to fill in the gaps. Congress authorized the Secretary of the Interior to recognize and study historic landmarks of national significance. This directive resulted in the National Historic Landmarks program, which recognizes sites, buildings, and objects with exceptional value as commemorating or illustrating the history of the United States.

The first list was announced in 1960 and included archeological sites. NHLs have been acknowledged in the NHPA as deserving protections exceeding those for properties in the National Register database.[41] The National Register program, a creature of NHPA, expanded the possibility of recognition by including properties of state and local importance.

The Historic Sites Act confirmed Congress's intent that the Interior Department be an active participant in the survey of historic resources and investigate and research sites throughout the nation, not only resources on federal land. The NHPA subsequently gave further definition to the Secretary's

39. 54 U.S.C.A. § 320101 (West, Westlaw through Pub. L. No. 119-59).

40. Hist. Green Springs, Inc. v. Bergland, 497 F. Supp. 839, 847 (E.D. Va. 1980) (stating that "[a] review of the legislative history of the 1935 Act and the 1966 Act reveals that the latter was necessitated by the narrow scope of the 1935 Act").

41. *See* 54 U.S.C.A. § 306107 (West, Westlaw through Pub. L. No. 119-59).

role. Among these are providing a role for state governments in determining the significance of a site, the authority to issue criteria, maintenance of a grant program, and establishing a "Keeper" of the National Register to make final determinations of the significance of a site in the event of dispute. The Historic Sites Act also envisioned the federal government's role in the acquisition of property through "gift, purchase or otherwise," a clause that has been interpreted to allow for the acquisition of sites through eminent domain.[42]

In 1960 Congress passed a subsequent law known as the Archaeological and Historic Preservation Act, also known as the Reservoir Salvage Act.[43] This law, enacted pursuant to the policies stated in the Historic Sites Act, imposed certain requirements for the preservation of materials slated to be lost as a result of major new dams permitted by the Army Corps of Engineers and Bureau of Reclamation. By placing these requirements on federal agencies involved in dam construction, it was an important recognition of the limits of previous laws and is notable for compelling federal agency action.

In 1974 Congress expanded the salvage requirements to all federal agencies, beyond dam construction. The so-called Moss-Bennett Act requires all federal agencies, including grant and loan agencies, to preserve archaeological objects that would otherwise be lost as a result of their activities.[44] The law also allows for agencies to transfer 1% of their construction funds to the Secretary of the Interior for this purpose.[45]

3. Archaeological Resources Protection Act

The scope of the Antiquities Act is limited to lands owned or controlled by the federal government. One of its central original provisions was to establish criminal penalties for illegal looting of sites. But in 1974 the Ninth Circuit Court of Appeals held the term "object of antiquity" ambiguous and this portion of the law unconstitutional.[46]

---

42. Barnidge v. United States, 101 F.2d 295 (8th Cir. 1939).

43. Pub. L. No. 86-523, 74 Stat. 220 (June 27, 1960).

44. Pub. L. No. 93-291.

45. The amended Act was formerly codified at 16 U.S.C. § 469 *et seq.*, but it was amended, repealed, and replaced in part by Pub. L. No. 113-287, 128 Stat. 3094 (Dec. 19, 2014) and is now codified at 54 U.S.C. § 312502 *et seq.*

46. United States v. Diaz, 499 F.2d 113 (9th Cir. 1974).

In response to the *Diaz* case, Congress took action in 1979 by passing new legislation to protect endangered archaeological sites. The Archaeological Resources Protection Act (ARPA)[47] establishes a permit system for archaeological excavations that gives federal agencies that manage federal lands (typically the Forest Service, Park Service, and Bureau of Land Management) the discretion to allow excavation work. One of the key factors agencies use in determining whether to award or condition a permit is the potential for harm to sites. Consultation with Indian tribes is required before any permit is issued under the explicit terms of ARPA.

While a major focus of ARPA is to regulate federal and Indian lands, one notable exception applies much more broadly to restrain sales of archaeological resources, regardless of where discovered. The Act states:

> no person may sell, purchase, exchange, transport, receive, or offer to sell, purchase, or exchange, in interstate or foreign commerce, any archaeological resource excavated, removed, sold, purchased, exchanged, transported, or received in violation of any provision, rule, regulation, ordinance, or permit in effect under State or local law.[48]

In the case of an individual criminally prosecuted under ARPA for taking and selling resources discovered on private land, the Seventh Circuit has made clear that ARPA was, indeed, intended to regulate more than just objects found on federal or tribal lands.[49]

Notably, the regulations set up a bright-line rule defining an archeological site as at least 100 years of age.[50] The regulations also have thorough definitions of the threshold for when the law applies. The federal land manager is instructed to consider any "material remains" that are "of archeological interest" subject to the law.[51] The rules contain a list of representative material as well as some notable exceptions such as coins, unless found in direct relationship with other archaeological material.[52]

---

47. 16 U.S.C.A. § 470aa–mm (West, Westlaw through Pub. L. No. 119-59).

48. 16 U.S.C.A § 470ee(c) (West, Westlaw through Pub. L. No. 119-59).

49. United States v. Gerber, 999 F.2d 1112 (7th Cir. 1993), *cert. denied*, 114 S. Ct. 878 (1994).

50. 36 C.F.R. § 296.3 (2025).

51. *Id.* § 296.3(a)(1), (2).

52. 36 C.F.R. § 296.3(a)(4)(ii) (2025).

Confidentiality of the location of sites is an important consideration under ARPA. Typically, state historic preservation offices maintain a sensitive database of sites that may be listed on or eligible for the National Register of Historic Places.[53] Note that additional provisions of state law may apply in addition to federal protections. Arizona, Utah, and Hawaii, for instance, have processes in place to ensure sensitive information about cultural sites is well protected.

4. Abandoned Shipwreck Act of 1987

The Abandoned Shipwreck Act (ASA) regulates the exploration of the estimated 50,000 abandoned shipwrecks in U.S. territorial waters.[54] The ASA asserts federal sovereignty over wreck sites and transfers title to the abandoned wrecks to the states in which they are located. States thereby have full management rights for shipwreck exploration and site control. Non-binding guidelines are issued by the National Park Service.[55]

G. MUNICIPAL REGULATION OF ARCHAEOLOGICAL RESOURCES

The discipline of historical archaeology emerged in the 1960s as a means to differentiate the study of prehistory, referring to the era of pre-Western contact in the Americas, from the study of early Western settlement. Several municipalities have adopted local ordinances to require certain investigations based on the emerging recognition that such resources had traditionally been undervalued and were threatened by modern development.

To balance the community interest in archaeological investigation with new development, the few localities that regulate in this field establish as much predictability as possible in advance. The three examples discussed

---

53. Section 304 of the NHPA also allows federal agencies to withhold information from the public in the event it would "impede the use of a traditional religious site." 54 U.S.C.A. § 307103(a)(3) (West, Westlaw through Pub. L. No. 119-59).

54. 43 U.S.C.A. §§ 2101–06 (West, Westlaw through Pub. L. No. 119-59); *see also* Russell G. Murphy, *The Abandoned Shipwreck Act of 1987 in the New Millennium: Incentives to High Tech Piracy?*, 8 OCEAN & COASTAL L.J. 167, 167 (2002).

55. 43 U.S.C.A. § 2104 (West, Westlaw through Pub. L. No. 119-59); *see also* 55 Fed. Reg. 50,116 (1990).

below are not an exhaustive list but reflect varying strategies affording protections. One of the strong commonalities of these approaches is that they rely on previous research to determine probabilities of discoveries within certain defined areas and tailor mandated action accordingly.

1. Alexandria, Virginia

The city of Alexandria has requirements for archaeological study as part of its permit process for preliminary or combined site plan or development approval within a certain zone defined on its Archaeological Resource Map.[56] If the site plan is required for ground-disturbing activity in a "potential resource area," then "reasonable archaeological evaluation reports and resource management plans" are required.[57]

The ordinance is administered by the director of Historic Alexandria, a governmental office that focuses on administering city-owned historic sites and properties. The director receives information about proposed ground-disturbing activities from an applicant necessary to make a preliminary assessment of the potential archaeological significance of any site plan area designated on the Archaeological Resources map.[58] The ordinance specifies six criteria to assist the director in making a "finding of archaeological significance."[59]

If the assessment contains a determination that the site "will have potential archaeological significance, and that the proposed development will have a substantial adverse impact on any known or potential archaeological resources," then the applicant is required to submit an archaeological evaluation report and a resource management plan as a supplement to the preliminary site plan application.[60] These reports must be prepared by "a qualified archaeologist or historian in conformity with professionally recognized standards for cultural resource management."[61]

---

56. Alexandria City Code § 11-411.

57. *Id.* § 11-411(A). While the Code allows certain projects to be exempt from site plan requirements in § 11-404, the exemption does not apply to land within archaeological resource areas required under § 11-403(D).

58. *Id.* § 11-411(D).

59. *Id.* § 11-411(E)(1)–(6). These include research value, rarity, public value, site integrity, presence of materials, and impact on resources.

60. *Id.* § 11-411(F)(2).

61. *Id.* § 11-411(G)(1).

The archaeological evaluation report must include:

- Detailed evaluation of the archaeological significance of the site plan area, including but not limited to reasonable measures for historic research, archaeological surveys, and test excavations.[62]
- Reasonable measures for the study and preservation of archaeological resources found within the site plan area, including but not limited to test and full-scale excavations, site construction monitoring, field recording, photography, laboratory analysis, conservation of organic and metal artifacts, curation of the collection (e.g., artifacts, notes, photographs), and preparation of reports.[63]

The plan "may" also include "reasonable measures for further archaeological study, restoration, reconstruction, disposition of recovered artifacts to an appropriate public or private collection or museum, and *in situ* preservation of archaeological resources found within the site plan area."[64]

The approval, disapproval, or approval with modifications or conditions of the archaeological evaluation report and resource management plan is made part of the overall site plan review process, thereby allowing for the utilization of procedures that have already been mandated and established.

Since the archaeological requirements are made part of the city's permitting process, there is no provision prescribing a penalty for the failure to follow the procedures, as any non-compliance will simply result in the denial of the applicant's permits.

2. St. Augustine, Florida

The city of St. Augustine establishes three distinct archaeological zones, tiered by significance, and 17 distinct subzones in its Code of Ordinances.[65] The ordinance is triggered when a major or minor disturbance requires a building, city right-of-way, or utility permit.[66] Any disturbance is subject to city review based on an archaeological review application though "major"

62. *Id.* § 11-411(G)(2).

63. *Id.* § 11-411(G)(3).

64. *Id.* § 11-411(G)(4).

65. St. Augustine City Code § 6-4.

66. *Id.* § 6-6(a).

disturbances, greater than 250 feet, are treated differently than "minor" disturbances.

Each of the three categories differs in the intensity of efforts required based on the extent of the disturbance. In Archaeological Zone I, for instance, major disturbances require intensive salvage archaeology while minor disturbances require only testing with the potential for salvage archaeology when recommended by the city archaeologist and approved by the city.[67] The ordinance imposes certain minimum and maximum delay periods, which can be extended upon agreement from city officials.

The city requires an archaeologist to manage the program, appointed by and working at the discretion of the city manager.[68] The archaeologist oversees permit applications, project cost proposals, recommendations, and requests, and conducts testing, salvage archaeology, and monitoring. They are responsible for preparing and submitting final reports on all projects and recording completed archaeological projects with the state. Additional proactive work is also a function of its scope, such as site surveys and educational programs.

The city also has a provision allowing for "analysis, cataloging, recording, and conservation" of all artifacts found on private property with written permission from the owner.[69] While objects recovered on private property belong to the property owner, the city urges donation of artifacts to the city for long-term storage, care, protection, and preservation.[70]

3. Scottsdale, Arizona

Scottsdale requires an archaeological survey or report to be prepared by a qualified archaeologist for all public or private development, unless the development falls into one of a number of exemptions.[71] This includes private single-family residences on a single-family lot or non-residential development with one acre or less of ground disturbing activity.[72]

After receiving the archaeological survey and report, and before any development or ground disturbance can occur, the city must review the

---

67. *Id.* § 6-6(b)(1), (4).

68. *Id.* § 6-11.

69. *Id.* § 6-8(b).

70. *Id.* § 6-9(a).

71. Scottsdale City Code § 46-130-137.

72. *Id.* § 46-132(1)(a)–(e).

survey and report and approve or disapprove the recommendation on the resource's significance.[73] The ordinance contains a set of considerations in making determinations of significance including its research potential and significance to the city's history or prehistory or the history of Native Americans.[74]

If it is determined that an effect will occur, the developer must obtain a certificate of approval. The applicant must present a mitigation plan prepared by a qualified archaeologist, subject to review by the city archaeologist and the historic preservation officer.[75] In deciding whether or not to accept such a mitigation plan, the city considers "methods to avoid, reduce, or mitigate effects on historic and cultural resources, such as a preservation easement, while taking into consideration the current needs of the property owner and reasonable methods for carrying out the recommended plan."[76] A certificate of approval is issued upon the implementation of the approved mitigation plan, and construction can proceed once all archaeological resources have been excavated and collected. Within one year of receiving the certificate of approval, a final report must be submitted that describes the collection and summarizes the findings.

73. *Id.* § 46-133(e).

74. *Id.* § 46-133(c)(1)–(9).

75. *Id.* § 46-133(f).

76. *Id.* § 46-133(f)(4)(b).

Conservation and Preservation Restrictions

9

Conservation and preservation restrictions are legally extremely similar. The only significant difference is in what they serve to do. Conservation restrictions protect landscapes with ecological value or aesthetic, historic, or archeological significance. On the other hand, preservation restrictions protect historic structures. In either case, owners agree to restraints that would be inconsistent with the underlying purpose in perpetuity and, in return, often receive back some other benefit such as favorable tax consequences.

A. UNIFORM CONSERVATION EASEMENT ACT

In 1981, the Uniform Conservation Easement Act (UCEA)[1] was created to help avoid glitches in state laws that either limited the reach of the protections or exposed them to

1. https://www.uniformlaws.org/committees/community-home/librarydocuments?communitykey=4297dc67-1a90-4e43-b704-7b277

invalidity. The drafters' purpose was very clearly to enhance the protections, not to limit them. The preface identifies its purpose:

> The Act enables durable restrictions and affirmative obligations to be attached to real property to protect natural and historic resources. Under the conditions spelled out in the Act, the restrictions and obligations are immune from certain common law impediments which might otherwise be raised. The Act maximizes the freedom of the creators of the transaction to impose restrictions on the use of land and improvements in order to protect them, and it allows a similar latitude to impose affirmative duties for the same purposes. In each instance, if the requirements of the Act are satisfied, the restrictions or affirmative duties are binding upon the successors and assigns of the original parties.

The Uniform Act is short: The entire act is only six sections (one of which is boilerplate).

The UCEA helped clean up snafus that the common law of states might present to conservation easements, but it also reduced the role of the watchful neighbor. One of the "cobwebs" that the UCEA swept away was the need for the holder of the easement to be contiguous with the preserved property, so-called appurtenant land. The drafters did not support a wholesale opening of permitted holders, though, and still required the holder to be a government or charitable organization. The committee voted against permitting private holders after considering the matter.[2] By requiring a charitable organization to hold private conservation easements, the drafters expected to benefit from whatever accountability provisions state laws otherwise placed on such organizations, given the longstanding faith of most Americans in charitable groups.[3]

---

c4a11bd&LibraryFolderKey=&DefaultView=&5a583082-7c67-452b-9777-e4bdf7e1c729=eyJsaWJyYXJ5ZW50cnkiOiI5N2VmOWFjZi00YmFmLTRiOGItODc2OS1lOTZkYjEzMDBmNzAifQ%3D%3D

2. The committee voted against permitting private holders after considering the matter. Proceedings in Comm. of the Whole, Uniform Conservation and Historic Preservation Agreements Act, 26 (Aug. 10, 1979) (statement of Bullivant).

3. Mary Ann King & Sally K. Fairfax, *Public Accountability and Conservation Easements: Learning from the Uniform Conservation Easement Act Debates*, 46 Nat. Resources J. 65, 92 (2006).

The UCEA does not require government review and approval of conservation easements. Requiring that approval might dissuade donors from taking part because of concerns about adding bureaucratic complexities.[4] Besides, since charitable holders would not likely indiscriminately take such easements, the system was viewed as having a built-in accountability. The limits imposed by federal, state, and local programs added to the accountability already.

Given the perpetual term of most conservation easements,[5] the UCEA needed to address who could not just enforce but modify and potentially terminate the easements. Section 3 identifies four categories: (1) the holder of the conservation easement and (2) the owner of the underlying fee land, but also (3) parties identified by the grantor and holder at the time of the conveyance and (4) a "person authorized by other law."

B. EASEMENTS

"All easements are just contracts."[6] That summary should put the minds of lawyers at ease that they can tackle the most common form of preservation instrument. While federal, state, and local laws protect historic resources in ways that no private agreement ever could, private agreements are the workhorses of preservation. The laws of each state vary widely on technical matters such as recording real estate documents, but the basics of easements should be familiar to most lawyers from Property Law in law school.

An easement is a private, legal interest granted by an owner to another party. Beyond that, the scope of the easement is wide open. Many lawyers might recall easements as grants of permission to enter the land of the grantors. In the classic example, an owner of land might convey an easement to a neighbor that allows the neighbor to cut across the owner's property either because the neighbor has no other way to reach his own ensiled property or just for convenience. In those cases, the right being conveyed is often one of access for the recipient of the easement.

4. UCEA preface.

5. The UCEA provides that "a conservation easement is unlimited in duration unless the instrument creating it otherwise provides." UCEA § 2(a).

6. Notes of comments of Brian Turner, president and CEO of the Pres. Soc'y of Charleston (Feb. 7, 2026) (on file with author).

But in preservation cases, easements are often *restrictions* on the *grantor*. An owner of a historic house might otherwise be free to paint it, cover it in vinyl siding, alter its details, or even demolish it. A preservation-minded owner, looking to safeguard her home against such changes by future owners, might voluntarily limit those rights by conveying an easement to a recipient that gives the recipient veto power over alterations. The fee simple title to the house can still be passed from owner to owner, but the right to approve alterations has been pulled from the bundle of ownership sticks and given to someone else.

The range of variants is vast. For example, easements can be donated or sold.[7] Many owners will grant easements free of charge out of a sentimental or civic-minded concern for a building (or perhaps for the tax benefits of making a gift of the easement). Others might sell an easement in the same way they would sell the fee simple title to the house itself. In addition, some easements known as term easements have specific lifespans and vanish after some period. Others run separately in perpetuity. And because preservation laws typically protect only the exterior of buildings, easements are a powerful tool to expand protections because they can just as easily be written to protect interiors as well.

Preservation easements most commonly exist to protect the exterior appearance of buildings. Exterior easements are sometimes called façade easements. They can specify unique features (e.g., the Mansard roof or a stained-glass window) or grant the entire building coverage.

An easement is a second layer of protection on top of other protections. It does not replace those other restraints. For example, in Charleston, South Carolina, the reach of the Board of Architectural Review is limited to changes that can be seen from the public right-of-way, meaning that the rear facades of some houses might be subject to unreviewed changes. If a house is protected by an easement that covers the entire exterior of the house, the holder of the easement—not the Board of Architectural Review—can prevent the changes. An easement holder can prevent changes to a structure even if the changes are also subject to BAR review. Indeed, the rights of the easement holder are not diminished even if the BAR actually approves the

7. Easements can even be created by operation of law, such as easements of necessity or by prescription. Because that subset of easements is not typically concerned with preservation, this chapter will disregard them.

changes. Because the easement operates in addition to other protections, both the BAR *and* the easement holder would have to sign off.

Technically, an easement can be given to almost any third party and can even be created at the time of sale and retained by the seller. However, if the grantor of the easement wants to ensure that the easement will not just exist but will be thoughtfully and vigorously enforced, the grantor should consider granting the easement to either some relevant governmental agency or a nonprofit organization whose mission focuses on preservation. In fact, because of the cost of possible litigation to enforce easements, some grantors actually have to *pay the recipients* to take them! Stewardship fees can be waived of course or set at a de minimis level, but often they can be thousands of dollars, either as a flat fee or a percentage of the value of the building. Because the fees pay for the costs of monitoring the properties and possibly fighting in court in perpetuity, the price is not typically going to be small.[8]

If a grantor plans to seek tax benefits from a charitable donation of an easement, the pool of recipients shrinks. For federal tax breaks to apply, the recipient organization must have (1) the preservation of historic places as a primary part of its mission and (2) the resources to monitor and enforce its easements. Often the easement holder is a local group that has the eyes in the community to stay on top of a property, but holders can be state or even national. A state's historic preservation office is often a good source for identifying qualified recipients.

C. VALUE OF CONSERVATION AND PRESERVATION RESTRICTIONS

Why would anyone handcuff himself and future owners? Wouldn't an easement diminish the value of the structure during resale? Apart from the personal interest that an owner might have in safeguarding a building—maybe

---

[8] The price of an easement to the owner can be included as part of the charitable gift. In *Dunlap v. Commissioner*, T.C.M. (RIA) 2012–126 (T.C. 2012), the taxpayer counted the price of an easement as part of the donation for preservation uses, but the IRS countered that the amount was paid only because of the taxpayer's self-interest in getting the tax credit. The court rejected that idea and noted that the donation was clearly designed to enable the preservation.

a generational family home or the recipient of years of sweat equity—some easements can provide financial benefits.

The common advice is that a building should be protected because of heartfelt concerns and not pocketbook issues because of the potential pitfalls in tax plans. The IRS openly warns that valuations of easements are subject to being challenged:

> In recognition of our need to preserve our heritage, Congress allowed an income tax deduction for owners of significant property who give up certain rights of ownership to preserve their land or buildings for future generations.
>
> The IRS has seen abuses of this tax provision that compromise the policy Congress intended to promote. We have seen taxpayers, often encouraged by promoters and armed with questionable appraisals, take inappropriately large deductions for easements. In some cases, taxpayers claim deductions when they are not entitled to any deduction at all (for example, when taxpayers fail to comply with the law and regulations governing deductions for contributions of conservation easements). Also, taxpayers have sometimes used or developed these properties in a manner inconsistent with section 501(c)(3). In other cases, the charity has allowed property owners to modify the easement or develop the land in a manner inconsistent with the easement's restrictions.
>
> Another problem arises in connection with historic easements, particularly façade easements. Here again, some taxpayers are taking improperly large deductions. They agree not to modify the façade of their historic house, and they give an easement to this effect to a charity. However, if the façade was already subject to restrictions under local zoning ordinances, the taxpayers may, in fact, be giving up nothing, or very little. A taxpayer cannot give up a right that he or she does not have.[9]

Remember that the granting of the easement and the ensuing tax benefits are independent. If an owner grants an expansive easement over his building in expectation of tax savings and the IRS successfully contests the

9. INTERNAL REVENUE SERVICE, *Conservation Easements*, www.irs.gov/charities-non-profits/conservation-easements (last visited Feb. 15, 2026).

valuation, the owner will be left with no financial benefit, but the easement will remain.

Easements protecting historic attributes of buildings have received favorable tax treatment since 1964, but following a series of articles about abuses in the *Washington Post* in 2004, Congress and the tax authorities became more skeptical.

Assuming that an owner wants to seek tax benefits, her lawyer will want to carefully study the requirements, starting with Section 170(h) of the tax code. This section defines what constitutes a "qualified conservation contribution" eligible for a deduction. To qualify, an easement must:

- Be a qualified real property interest, meaning that it exists in perpetuity.
- Be donated to a qualified organization.[10]
- Serve a recognized "conservation purpose." In other words, it preserves a "historically important land area or a certified historic structure." A "certified historic structure" is a building listed on the National Register of Historic Places or one located in a registered historic district and certified by the Secretary of the Interior as being of historic significance to the district.

Many owners will be motivated purely by the desire to preserve their properties to execute easements, but others will at least be prompted by the financial rewards, especially the tax consequences. The familiar metaphor of property is a bundle of sticks, and one of those sticks is the right to make changes to the property. When an owner donates an easement to a third party to safeguard the property's character, the owner has donated something of value and might be entitled to very large income tax deductions for charitable donations.

Notice that the value of the donation is not the only possible benefit to an owner. Even if the IRS does not accept any value for a charitable donation, the loss of the right to alter a building might tamp down the value of the building. In other words, a buyer would be less likely to pay top dollar for a house if the owner is not able to paint it or add to it. The reduction in the expected sales price might also cause the property to be valued lower. That reduction might, in turn, lead to lower state and local property taxes. The same reduced value might lower the inheritance taxes owed by heirs.

---

10. *See supra* Chapter 9, § B.

In all of these cases, the important question is: How much is that stick worth? Despite books of explanation devoted to the topic, "valuing preservation easements remains, most understandably, a complex and difficult undertaking that continues to challenge appraisers and the IRS."[11]

A taxpayer deducting the value of a donated facade conservation easement must first obtain a "qualified appraisal" of the partial interest donated.[12] The regulatory requirements of a qualified appraisal are many but generally require information about the property, the terms of the donation, the appraiser's identity and qualifications, and fair market value of the donation.

The IRS regulations name three valuation methods for the fair market value of the easement: the income approach, the market-data approach, and the replacement-cost-less-depreciation approach.[13]

One must remember that a preservation donation does not have to entirely surrender ownership of the land. Normally, those taking a charitable deduction for the donation of property must donate their complete interest in the property and not a part interest.[14] When an owner donates a fee simple ownership of a parcel, the owner gives up all control over the use and property. That is not necessary with preservation easements. The donation does need to be indefinite, but it can be just one stick from the bundle. An owner may retain various rights—most importantly, the right to occupy the land, to sell or mortgage it, and to make some changes to it—as long as the easement does not prohibit them.

The value of an easement compares the fair market value (FMV) before granting the easement and the FMV after the easement has been granted.

When a property is donated in fee simple, valuing a gift of property is normally a simple task, at least in theory, because there are easily accessible markets for such sales in a community. But when the gift is for just an easement, there are no markets for just those interests.[15] Instead, the value of the

---

11. Whitehouse Hotel Ltd. P'ship v. Comm'r, 615 F.3d 321, 329 (5th Cir. 2010).

12. *See* 26 U.S.C.A. § 170(f)(11)(C) (West, Westlaw through Pub. L. No. 119-59); Treas. Reg. § 1.170A-13(c)(2)(i)(A).

13. Treas. Reg. § 1.170A-13(c)(3)(ii)(J).

14. 26 U.S.C.A. § 170 (West, Westlaw through Pub. L. No. 119-59).

15. Hilborn v. Comm'r, 85 T.C. 677, 688 (1985) (observing that the before-and-after approach is approved by Congress and the IRS); S. Rep. No. 96–1007, at 14–15 (1980) ("[B]ecause markets generally are not well established for easements or similar restrictions . . . conservation easements are typically (but not necessarily) valued indirectly as the difference between the fair market value of the property involved before and after the grant of the easement.").

single stick from the bundle is typically assessed indirectly using the "before and after" valuation method.[16]

The burden falls on the taxpayer to prove the value of the donation.[17] Taxpayers who do not strictly comply with all the many requirements in the regulations risk having their donation disallowed and having to pay steep penalties to the IRS.[18]

Section 170 allows the federal tax deduction for federal charitable contributions. Deductions for a charitable contribution of a conservation easement are addressed in Regs. § 1.170A-14. The regulation provides:

> A qualified conservation contribution is the contribution of a qualified real property interest to a qualified organization exclusively for conservation purposes. To be eligible for a deduction under section 170(h) and this section, the conservation purpose must be protected in perpetuity.

Generally, for any contribution of property to be eligible as a charitable deduction, the taxpayer must obtain a "qualified appraisal" and retain other documentation related to the contribution.[19]

If an owner were to simply donate an entire building to a preservation group, say to use as its headquarters or to run as a museum house, then the valuation would be straightforward. For preservation easements, a taxpayer must look to Regs. § 1.170A-1(c)(2), which define FMV as "the price at which the property would change hands between a willing buyer and a willing seller, neither being under any compulsion to buy or sell and both having reasonable knowledge of relevant facts."

---

16. Nicoladis v. Comm'r, 55 T.C.M. (CCH) 624, 1988 WL 34501 (1988) ("When faced with [the valuation of facade easements] before[,] we have acknowledged, with approval, that the 'before and after approach' is the most feasible method of valuing such a donation.").

17. Hintz v. Comm'r, 712 F.2d 281, 284 (7th Cir. 1983) ("As a general matter, a deduction from income for tax purposes may be taken only when support for it can be found in the language of a statute, appurtenant regulations, or legislative history. . . . In every case, it is the taxpayer who bears the burden of showing that he or she is entitled to a particular deduction.").

18. Bruzewicz v. United States, 604 F. Supp. 2d 1197, 1209 (N.D. Ill. 2009).

19. *See* Regs. § 1.170(f)(11)(E)(i).

As with all other valuations of real estate, the best source to value fee simple interests are the recent sales of comparable properties. The best valuation for real property is the most recent sales price when sold reasonably close to a valuation date (Ambassador Apartments, 50 T.C. 236, 243–44 (1968)). Where possible, in the case of preservation easements, this valuation method should serve as the best "before" value of the land. But, no market exists for the sale of easements.

The "before-and-after method," as the name suggests, subtracts the value of a building encumbered with an easement from the value of the same building without one. The before-and-after approach requires an appraisal of the property immediately before the granting of the easement and an appraisal immediately after the easement is granted. The difference is the value of the conservation easement and the basis for the tax deduction. Regs. § 1.170A-14(h)(3)(i) explain that, in the absence of a direct comparable-sales method for determining value, the next best method that should be employed is the before-and-after approach.

The before-and-after approach is ideally based on comparables in the same way that comparables work in ordinary real estate listings. An appraiser looks for pairs of properties with one having an easement and one not having an easement. In practice, finding precisely identical properties is impossible, so tweaks have to be made to account for the innumerable differences that might swing the prices one way or the other.[20] Differences might explains deductions in comparables (e.g., the absence of a garage or the footage on a street) as well as increases (e.g., the fact that some comparables trended upward before and after easement because of the rising tide in the real estate market during the four to eight years between sales).[21]

While the easement itself might not have a ready market, there are possibly enough comparable properties with the same restrictions to do a comparison. In a dense area, there could easily be several buildings, all of which have similar restraints through easements. The resale value of those specific buildings could be used to determine an FMV for the remaining house or could at least justify an opinion about how much an easement limits the FMV (e.g., 20%).

If a preservation easement results in a net gain to the owner, then no charitable contribution deduction will be allowed. For example, if the value

---

20. Zarlengo v. Comm'r, No. 3701–10, 2014 WL 3907047 (Tax Ct. Aug. 11, 2014).

21. *Id.* at *19 n.17.

of the land increases due to the conservation easement, no deduction would be allowed. In *Browning*, 109 T.C. 303 (1997), the Tax Court applied the before-and-after method to determine the value of a conservation easement, emphasizing the importance of credible appraisals and market-based evidence in valuing conservation easements. For example, if limiting the development of one building into apartments with an interior easement not only safeguarded that building but led to an increase in the value of the donor's other building, then the benefit might override the value of the donation.

Ironically, the tax value of an easement might be *reduced* in precisely the areas where preservation is most *valued*. When pre-existing restraints already limit an owner's ability to make changes to a building, the easement limiting the owner in the same way is not granting anything of real value.[22] Agreeing not to replace the windows where a local ordinance already outlaws the replacement of windows is not an especially valuable donation. In some cases, the easement might not even serve the ends of preservation and be rejected for tax deductions entirely. For example, in *1982 E., LLC v. Commissioner*,[23] an owner claimed a $6.5 million deduction for the donation of a preservation easement and the donation of future development rights for a large townhouse built in 1894. Because of the townhouse's location, it was already covered by New York City's preservation laws that, among other things, limited the square footage and height of buildings on the parcel. There was no question but that the structure was a contributing historic building, but the Tax Court nevertheless disallowed the deduction since the easement did not preserve the historic structure: "Thus it is local law and the rules of the [Landmark Preservation Commission] that preserve the subject property and not the rights which [the donee of the easement] possessed under the deed of easement."

On the other hand, some easements do provide more protections than existing laws do. For example, in *Simmons v. Commissioner*,[24] the owner of two historic homes in Washington, D.C., sought a deduction for easements given to L'Enfant Trust, a corporation created to hold and enforce preservation easements. The easements most importantly required the permission of L'Enfant before making any alterations to the buildings; an exception for

---

22. Scheidelman v. Comm'r, 682 F.3d 189, 196 (2d Cir. 2012).

23. 101 T.C.M. (CCH) 1380 (T.C. 2011).

24. No. 18647–06, 2009 WL 2950610 (Tax Ct. Sep. 15, 2009), *aff'd*, 646 F.3d 6 (D.C. Cir. 2011).

repairs still required the work to be consistent with the historic aesthetic. Less significant obligations included the duty of the owner to install and keep polished a plaque commemorating L'Enfant's easement and to clear the houses.[25] The IRS argued that the easements did not require any change from the "before" and added no limits to what already was limited concerning the "after." The director of L'Enfant testified that L'Enfant restricted changes in paint color, which Washington, D.C.'s rules did not. And, she testified that existing rules were more forgiving about repairs. In addition, the donor claimed that the scrutiny of L'Enfant was itself worthy of valuation: "Petitioner contends that because the District of Columbia lacks funding to enforce its own rules and regulations and because L'Enfant continually monitors its easements, the L'Enfant easements increase petitioner's burdens even though the restrictions are similar." Although the Tax Court valued the donation at a point between the competing claims, the court agreed that stricter enforcement of even somewhat overlapping restrictions provided value. Just having to seek the approval of L'Enfant was itself something worth value.[26]

---

25. *Id.* at *2.

26. *Id.* at *11 ("Even if we were to accept respondent's contention that the easements did not impose any restrictions on petitioner over and above those imposed by the District of Columbia, the easements still added an additional level of approval before any changes could be made to the properties."); *see also Zarlengo*, 2014 WL 3907047 at *11 n.11 ("The [Landmark Preservation Commission] does not actively monitor properties subject to this standard. [It] instead relies on the local community to report violations. The Trust, on the other hand, actively monitors properties on which it owns a conservation easement through annual inspections. We find this difference to be significant.").

Preservation in Modern Development

10

This chapter discusses the interplay between historic preservation laws and modern land development in the United States. In recent decades, the United States has experienced an increase in urban development, economic expansion, and demographic shifts.[1] These forces have pressured cities and towns to accommodate new growth, infrastructure, and housing.[2] Amid this modern development increase is the

1. *See* Kim Parker et al., *Demographic and economic trends in urban, suburban and rural communities*, PEW RESEARCH CENTER, www.pewresearch.org/social-trends/2018/05/22/demographic-and-economic-trends-in-urban-suburban-and-rural-communities/ (May 22, 2018) (describing "growing racial and ethnic diversity, increasing immigration and rising numbers of older adults" as responsible for driving demographic changes while noting that urban development is driving movement away from rural populations seeking economic opportunity); U.S. CENSUS BUREAU, *Population Growth Reported Across Cities and Towns in All U.S. Regions*, www.census.gov/newsroom/press-releases/2025/vintage-2024-popest.html (last visited Feb. 15, 2026).

2. Allison Hanley, *Rethinking Zoning to Increase Affordable Housing*, J. OF HOUS. & COMM. DEV. (Dec. 22, 2024), available at www.nahro.org/journal_article/rethinking-zoning-to-increase-affordable-housing/ (last

perceived tension between the need for economic progress and the interest in preserving historic resources that exemplify cultural, architectural, and historical significance.[3] All the more important for modern law development, historic preservation laws serve as a safeguard against erasing the past and ensure that significant structures, sites, and districts are maintained for future generations.[4] This chapter aims to provide a comprehensive legal and policy analysis of historic preservation laws in the context of modern land development. It surveys the legal foundations, historical evolution, policy rationales, and contemporary challenges of preserving historic resources amidst growing urbanization and economic pressure; particular attention is paid to federal, state, and local frameworks; judicial interpretations; and case studies that show the interaction and friction between preservation and progress, as well as key court decisions and policy debates, highlighting the challenges—and opportunities—of integrating historic preservation ideals into modern land development.

A. HISTORICAL CONTEXT AND LEGAL FOUNDATIONS OF HISTORIC PRESERVATION

1. Origins of the Preservation Movement

The roots of the historic preservation movement in the United States can be traced to the mid-19th century, with early grassroots efforts such as the Mount Vernon Ladies' Association in 1853.[5] This organization, composed of private citizens, successfully preserved George Washington's Mount Vernon estate, setting a precedent for citizen-led preservation efforts.[6] Aside

---

visited Feb. 15, 2026) (noting the need for regulatory changes that allow "cities to adapt and grow in ways that align with the evolving needs of their communities").

3. *See* Advisory Council on Hist. Pres., *The National Historic Preservation Program at 50: Priorities and Recommendations for the Future* 5 (Mar. 2017) (underscoring the importance of recognizing the need for balance between traditional preservation and the "needs and values" of the community).

4. *See id.* at 8 ("Many citizens and elected officials grasp the value of preserving important historic places and documenting and telling their stories, especially when preservation is presented as a tool for creating thriving, culturally vibrant downtowns . . . or contributing to tourism[.]").

5. George Washington's Mount Vernon, *The Mount Vernon Ladies' Association*, www.mountvernon.org/preservation/mount-vernon-ladies-association (last visited Feb. 15, 2026).

6. George Washington's Mount Vernon, *The Birth of the Mount Vernon Ladies' Association*, www.mountvernon.org/preservation/mount-vernon-ladies-association/early-history/birth-of-the-mount-vernon-ladies-association (last visited Feb. 15, 2026) (noting that Mount

from the innovative efforts at Mount Vernon, the late 19th and early 20th centuries also witnessed a growing public awareness of the value of historic buildings,[7] spurred by the City Beautiful Movement and concerns over rapid industrialization and urbanization.[8]

The early preservation movement was fundamentally reactionary, responding to the visible loss of significant structures as American cities modernized. The Mount Vernon model demonstrated that private citizens could mobilize to save buildings of national importance, but this approach had inherent limitations. It required wealthy benefactors, widespread public interest in a particular site, and the absence of competing economic interests. Most threatened buildings lacked these advantages. As industrialization accelerated through the early 20th century, entire neighborhoods disappeared to make way for factories, rail yards, and commercial districts. The preservation movement remained largely focused on sites associated with great men and patriotic narratives, reflecting the values and blind spots of its predominantly White, upper-class advocates.

The Colonial Revival movement of the late 19th and early 20th centuries contributed significantly to preservation consciousness, though often in problematic ways. This movement romanticized pre-industrial America and sought to recreate or preserve colonial-era architecture and aesthetics. While it generated interest in protecting old buildings, it also promoted a narrow and selective vision of American history that centered White colonial experiences while marginalizing other narratives. The movement's legacy remains visible in the many restored colonial villages and historic house museums that often present sanitized versions of the past.

By the 1920s and 1930s, preservation efforts had expanded beyond individual house museums to encompass entire districts. Williamsburg,

---

Vernon Ladies' Association's founder, Ann Cunningham, specifically employed female citizens to assist in the preservation of George Washington's estate).

7. National Park Service, *The Historic American Buildings Survey During the New Deal Era: Documenting "A Complete Resume of the Builders' Art,"* www.nps.gov/crps/CRMJournal/Fall2003/article1.html (last visited Feb. 15, 2026) (outlining the establishment of the Historic American Buildings Survey in the early 1930s).

8. The New York Preservation Archive Project, *City Beautiful Movement*, www.nypap.org/preservation-history/city-beautiful-movement/ (last visited Feb. 15, 2026) ("The City Beautiful Movement emerged in response to the 1893 World's Columbian Exposition in Chicago. The fundamental idea expounded at the fair was that the city was no longer a symbol of economic development and industrialization, but could now be seen as enhancing the aesthetic environment of its many inhabitants.").

Virginia, underwent massive restoration beginning in 1926 with funding from John D. Rockefeller Jr., creating what became the nation's largest living history museum. Charleston, South Carolina, enacted the nation's first historic district ordinance in 1931, establishing a model for municipal preservation regulation that would be replicated across the country. These early efforts, while groundbreaking, often involved some historical reconstruction and selective interpretation that prioritized aesthetic appeal over historical accuracy.[9]

2. The National Historic Preservation Act (NHPA) of 1966

The cornerstone of federal historic preservation law is the National Historic Preservation Act (NHPA) of 1966.[10] Enacted in response to widespread destruction of historic resources during urban renewal projects,[11] the NHPA established a comprehensive national framework for preservation.[12] Key provisions include the creation of the National Register of Historic Places,[13] the designation of State Historic Preservation Officers (SHPOs),[14] and the Section 106 review process,[15] which requires federal agencies to consider the effects of their undertakings on historic properties.[16] Over time, the NHPA has been amended to strengthen its provisions and broaden the scope of resources eligible for protection.[17]

---

9. *See generally* Stephanie Yuhl, A Golden Haze of Memory: The Making of Historic Charleston (2005).

10. National Park Service, *National Historic Preservation Act of 1966*, www.nps.gov/subjects/archeology/national-historic-preservation-act.htm (last visited Feb. 15, 2026).

11. *See id.* ("By the mid-1960s, federally-funded infrastructure and urban renewal projects had resulted in the rapid destruction of places significant in the nation's history. Congress recognized that the federal government's historic preservation program was inadequate to ensure that future generations could appreciate and enjoy the rich heritage of the nation. NHPA was enacted in recognition that historic places were being lost or altered, and that preservation was in the public's interest.").

12. *Id.*

13. *Id.*

14. *Id.*

15. *Id.*

16. *Id.* ("NHPA . . . recognized that increased knowledge and better administration of historic resources would improve the planning and execution of Federal undertakings[.]").

17. *Id.*

The passage of the NHPA represented a watershed moment in American preservation policy. The Act emerged from a confluence of factors: the devastating losses of urban renewal programs, growing environmental consciousness, and Lady Bird Johnson's beautification campaigns. The demolition of New York's Pennsylvania Station in 1963 served as a galvanizing event, demonstrating that even monumental buildings of recognized significance could be destroyed in the absence of legal protections. The public outcry that followed revealed widespread support for preservation that transcended traditional preservationist circles.

The NHPA's Section 106 review process constitutes its most significant regulatory mechanism. This provision requires federal agencies to consider the effects of their undertakings on properties listed in or eligible for the National Register. The review process involves consultation with SHPOs, Tribal Historic Preservation Officers, and other interested parties to identify historic properties, assess adverse effects, and explore alternatives or mitigation measures. Importantly, Section 106 is a procedural requirement, not a substantive one. Federal agencies must consider effects on historic properties, but they are not prohibited from proceeding with projects that cause harm.

The National Register itself serves multiple functions within the preservation framework. Properties listed in the Register receive recognition of their historical significance and become subject to Section 106 review for federal undertakings. Register listing also makes properties eligible for certain preservation grants and tax incentives. However, listing does not impose restrictions on private property owners acting independently, a feature that reflects American property rights traditions but also limits the Register's protective capacity. Many significant properties have been demolished despite National Register listing because demolition was accomplished by private owners without federal involvement.

3. Other Federal Preservation Frameworks

Several other federal statutes complement the NHPA; for example, the Antiquities Act of 1906 empowers the president to designate national monuments on federal land to protect historic and scientific features.[18] Also, the

---

18. National Park Service, *Antiquities Act of 1906*, www.nps.gov/subjects/archeology/antiquities-act.htm (last visited Feb. 15, 2026) (defining a key aspect of the Antiquities Act as providing the president with the power "to establish national monuments").

National Environmental Policy Act (NEPA) mandates environmental assessments that include consideration of cultural resources.[19] And, Section 4(f) of the Department of Transportation Act prohibits the use of land from a historic site unless there is no feasible and prudent alternative.[20]

The intersection of various federal preservation statutes creates a complex regulatory landscape when federal agency action is required in any given project. While the NHPA provides the primary framework for identifying and considering effects on historic resources, other statutes offer additional layers of protection or review. NEPA's requirement for environmental impact statements has proven particularly valuable for preservation, as cultural resources must be analyzed alongside natural resources. This integration reflects a broader understanding of historic properties as components of the human environment deserving protection from federal actions.

Section 4(f) of the Transportation Act has generated significant litigation and shaped preservation outcomes in the context of highway and transit projects. This provision establishes a presumption against using historic sites for transportation projects and requires thorough examination of alternatives. Courts have interpreted Section 4(f) to require a genuine analysis of alternatives rather than a pro forma review, and have enjoined projects where agencies failed to adequately consider preservation concerns. The statute has proven particularly important for protecting parks and historic sites in urban areas threatened by highway expansion.

The Antiquities Act was designed to protect historic structures and landscapes as well as natural landmarks and archaeological sites. Presidential designations under the Act can swiftly establish protection for threatened resources, though such designations have sometimes proven controversial when they affect land use in communities that oppose federal intervention. The Act's breadth and the president's discretionary authority under it have made it both a powerful preservation tool and a source of political contention.

4. The Secretary of the Interior's Standards

A critical but often overlooked component of the federal preservation framework is the Secretary of the Interior's Standards for the Treatment of

---

19. National Preservation Institute, *What Are "Cultural Resources"?*, www.npi.org/what-are-cultural-resources (last visited Feb. 15, 2026) ("A good NEPA analysis should consider impacts on [cultural resources] and address the requirements [of preservation law].").

20. 49 U.S.C.A. § 303(c)(1) (West, Westlaw through Pub. L. No. 119-59).

Historic Properties. These Standards, first issued in 1977 and subsequently revised, provide detailed guidance for four treatment approaches: preservation, rehabilitation, restoration, and reconstruction. The Standards articulate principles for respecting historic materials, character, and integrity while allowing for appropriate contemporary interventions. Projects seeking federal tax credits or other benefits must comply with the Standards, making them a significant influence on preservation practice nationwide.

The Standards reflect a philosophy that balances historical authenticity with practical considerations. The Standards for Rehabilitation, the most commonly applied treatment, acknowledge that historic buildings must evolve to remain economically viable. They permit alterations and additions that are compatible with historic character while distinguishing new work from old. This approach has enabled countless preservation projects that might otherwise have been economically infeasible. The Standards have also influenced state and local preservation guidelines, creating relative consistency in preservation practice across jurisdictions.

B. STATE AND LOCAL HISTORIC PRESERVATION LAWS

1. State-Level Laws and Agencies

States play a vital role in implementing and expanding preservation efforts. Many states have enacted "enabling statutes" that authorize establishing historic preservation programs,[21] commissions,[22] and tax incentives.[23] These laws vary significantly in scope and administration,[24] reflecting local

---

21. *See, e.g.*, S.C. Code Ann. § 60-12-10 (Westlaw through 2025 Act No. 94); California Code Public Resources—PRC Division 5—Parks and Monuments—Chapter 1—State Parks and Monuments; New York State Historic Preservation Act of 1980 (Chapter 354 of the Laws of 1980); Fla. Stat. Ann. §§ 267.011 to -.22 (West, Westlaw through July 1, 2025, of the 2025 first regular session).

22. National Alliance of Preservation Commissions, *See Who We Are*, www.napcommissions.org/who-we-are (last visited Feb. 15, 2026) (illustrating the existence of a national network for municipal preservation commissions that began after a series of NHPA amendments).

23. *See, e.g.*, S.C. Code Ann. § 12-6-3535 (Westlaw through 2025 Act No. 94); Cal. Code Regs. tit. 14, § 4859.01 (Westlaw through 1/30/26 Register 2026, No. 5).

24. *See* Terry Adams & Sarah Leser, *Historic Preservation Reviews in Other States* (Nov. 28, 2023), https://prdext2.cga.ct.gov/2023/rpt/pdf/2023-R-0296.pdf (last visited Feb. 15, 2026)

priorities and resources.[25] Some states maintain comprehensive databases of historic resources and offer grants and loans for preservation projects.[26]

State preservation programs vary dramatically in their scope, funding, and effectiveness. Some states have developed robust programs with substantial staffing, comprehensive surveys of historic resources, and generous grant programs. Others maintain minimal programs with limited capacity to support preservation activities. These disparities reflect differing political priorities, budget constraints, and cultural attitudes toward preservation. States with strong preservation traditions, such as South Carolina and Massachusetts, have invested heavily in preservation infrastructure and tend to enforce more stringent protections. States experiencing rapid growth and development often struggle to balance preservation interests against demands for new construction and economic development.[27]

State environmental policy acts, enacted in many states as counterparts to NEPA, provide an additional layer of review for state-funded or state-approved projects affecting historic resources. These state-level environmental reviews can be more protective than federal reviews, particularly in states with strong environmental or preservation constituencies. California's Environmental Quality Act, for example, requires detailed analysis of impacts on historical resources and imposes substantive obligations to avoid or mitigate significant impacts where feasible. Such provisions give preservation interests meaningful leverage in the development review process, though they also contribute to concerns about regulatory burdens and project delays.

(Massachusetts state law requires private developers and SHPOs to work together to mitigate adverse effects on historic sites from new development); *but see id.* (Rhode Island state law mandates developers follow SHPO recommendations unless "compelling reasons not to" are provided).

25. *Id.*

26. SHAARD, *Welcome to SHAARD*, https://secure.in.gov/apps/dnr/shaard/welcome.html (last visited Feb. 15, 2026) ("The Indiana State Historic Architectural and Archaeological Research Database (SHAARD) allows users to search cultural resource information on known historic and archaeological resources throughout Indiana."); NEVADA HUMANITIES, *Nevada Humanities Grants to Nevada Nonprofit Organizations*, www.nevadahumanities.org/grants (last visited Feb. 15, 2026) ("Nevada Humanities creates and supports public programs statewide that articulate the Nevada experience . . . disseminate local culture and heritage . . . [through] annual matching project grants[.]").

27. For example, SB 423 in California requires ministerial review for affordable housing projects thus limiting the local protections. *See* www.sfheritage.org/advocacy/more-than-one-battle-after-another-building-a-movement-for-preservation/.

2. Local Ordinances and Commissions

At the municipal level, local governments wield significant authority over land use and historic preservation.[28] Through zoning ordinances, localities can establish historic districts and designate landmarks.[29] Historic preservation commissions are typically tasked with reviewing changes to designated properties through a Certificate of Appropriateness (COA) process.[30] These local mechanisms are essential in regulating alterations, demolitions, and new construction within historic areas.

The COA process represents the most direct regulatory control over historic properties in most jurisdictions. Property owners seeking to make exterior alterations, additions, or new construction in designated districts or with respect to individual landmarks must obtain approval from the local preservation commission. These commissions, typically composed of architects, historians, property owners, and interested citizens, evaluate proposed changes against established design guidelines. The process can be straightforward for minor alterations but becomes contentious when property owners seek substantial changes or demolitions. Tensions arise when commissions deny requests that property owners consider reasonable, leading to complaints about regulatory overreach and interference with property rights.

Design guidelines adopted by local preservation commissions vary in their specificity and restrictiveness. Some guidelines provide broad principles allowing substantial flexibility in design approaches, while others prescribe detailed requirements for materials, colors, architectural features, and

---

28. *See* S.C. Code Ann. § 6-29-870 (Westlaw through 2025 Act No. 94) (allowing for the appointment of a review board in connection with local ordinances specifically providing for preservation); *Local Governments*, South Carolina Department of Archives and History, https://scdah.sc.gov/historic-preservation/programs/local-governments (last visited June 24, 2025) ("The legal power to protect historic properties rests primarily with local governments, not state or federal governments[;] . . . the decisions and actions of local governments and individuals often decide the fate of the irreplaceable historic and prehistoric properties[.]")

29. *See* S.C. Code Ann. § 6-29-340 (Westlaw through 2025 Act No. 94) (describing the authority of local planning commissions as encompassing the ability to "place and maintain necessary monuments"); New Jersey Register of Historic Places Act, www.nj.gov/dep/hpo/2protection/njrevproc.pdf.

30. Preservation North Carolina, *Certificate of Appropriateness*, www.presnc.org/certificate-appropriateness/ (last visited Feb. 15, 2026) ("When an owner of a local historic landmark or a resident within a historic district wants to make changes to the exterior of his or her property, a COA is needed from the historic preservation commission in addition to other permits that may apply.").

proportions. More prescriptive guidelines reduce uncertainty and provide clear direction but can stifle creativity and impose excessive costs. Finding the right balance remains an ongoing challenge for communities. Guidelines must be specific enough to provide meaningful direction and ensure consistency, but flexible enough to accommodate diverse properties and evolving circumstances.

The question of new construction in historic districts presents particularly thorny issues. Most preservation ordinances permit new buildings in historic districts but require that new construction be compatible with the district's character. However, defining compatibility is a unique challenge with different perspectives Some argue that new buildings should clearly differentiate themselves as contemporary additions, while others advocate for replicating traditional forms and materials. Economic considerations also influence these debates, as contemporary construction methods and materials often differ substantially from historical practices, making strict adherence to traditional forms expensive or impractical.

3. Home Rule and Preemption Issues

The balance between local autonomy and state oversight presents legal and policy challenges. Although home rule municipalities enjoy broad powers to enact preservation ordinances,[31] conflicts can arise when state or federal interests intervene.[32] Courts have generally upheld the authority of local governments to enforce preservation laws,[33] provided they are not preempted by state or federal statutes.[34]

Preemption disputes frequently arise when state legislatures enact laws limiting local regulatory authority. In recent years, several states have passed legislation restricting local governments' ability to regulate specific aspects of

31. Mary-Michael Robertson, *Navigating the Tension Between Preservation and Development Pressure: Cities' Imperative to Save Independent Music Landmarks While Simultaneously Providing for Growth*, 211 VANDERBILT J. OF ENT. & TECH. Law (2023) ("[C]ities can use their power to enact zoning ordinances and create historic preservation district.").

32. *See id.* ("'Home rule' states, on the hand, grant broad legislative authorities to cities to act on any local issues no preempted or foreclosed by state legislature.").

33. *See id.* at 216–17 (describing the authority of cities in home rule states to establish preservation ordinances so long as those ordinances are consistent with the guardrails established by a state legislature).

34. *Id.*

land use or development. These statutes sometimes conflict with preservation ordinances, forcing courts to determine whether state law supersedes local preservation authority. Property rights advocates have increasingly pushed for state-level limitations on local preservation regulations, arguing that local commissions impose excessive burdens and reduce property values. Preservationists counter that local governments, being closest to the affected properties and communities, are best positioned to make preservation decisions.

The relationship between local preservation ordinances and state building codes illustrates another dimension of the home rule challenge. Building codes generally establish minimum standards for construction, safety, and accessibility. Applying these codes to historic buildings can be problematic, as strict compliance sometimes requires alterations that compromise historic character or prove economically prohibitive. Many states have adopted alternative compliance mechanisms or exceptions for historic buildings, recognizing that inflexible code enforcement can effectively prevent preservation.[35] However, these accommodations must be balanced against legitimate safety and accessibility concerns, creating ongoing tension between preservation goals and building regulation.[36]

C. PRESERVATION TOOLS AND INCENTIVES

1. Historic Tax Credits (Federal and State)

One of the most effective tools for promoting historic preservation is the federal Historic Rehabilitation Tax Credit (HTC) program.[37] Administered by the National Park Service and the Internal Revenue Service,[38] the HTC offers a 20% credit for the certified rehabilitation of income-producing historic structures.[39] Many states have enacted complementary tax credit

---

35. *E.g.*, California Historic Building Code; *see* https://ohp.parks.ca.gov/?page_id=21410.

36. Note there is also the International Existing Building Code (IEBC), which states can adopt; *see* https://codes.iccsafe.org/content/IEBC2021P2.

37. *See* 26 U.S.C.A. § 47 (West, Westlaw through Pub. L. No. 119-59).

38. National Park Service, *Tax Incentives for Preserving Historic Properties*, www.nps.gov/subjects/taxincentives/index.htm (last visited Feb. 15, 2026) ("The National Park Service, through its Technical Preservation Services division, and the Internal Revenue Service administer the [Tax Incentive Program] in partnership with State Historic Preservation Offices.").

39. 26 U.S.C.A. § 47(a)(2) (West, Westlaw through Pub. L. No. 119-59).

programs,[40] creating financial incentives for developers to undertake preservation projects.[41]

The federal HTC program has catalyzed billions of dollars in private investment in historic buildings since its inception. The 20% credit applies to qualified rehabilitation expenditures, making substantial renovation projects financially attractive that might otherwise be infeasible. To qualify, properties must be listed in the National Register or located in registered historic districts, and rehabilitation work must meet the Secretary of the Interior's Standards. The requirement that properties be income-producing limits the credit to commercial, industrial, and rental residential properties, excluding owner-occupied residences except in certain circumstances.

The Tax Cuts and Jobs Act of 2017 modified the federal HTC program, requiring developers to claim the credit over five years rather than in a single year. This change reduced the immediate cash flow benefit of the credit and diminished its attractiveness for some projects. The modification generated substantial controversy within the preservation community, with advocates arguing that weakening the credit would reduce rehabilitation activity and lead to more demolitions. Early data suggests some decrease in credit utilization following the change, though the program remains a significant driver of preservation investment.

State historic tax credit programs complement the federal credit and have proven particularly valuable in states with strong preservation priorities. Some states offer credits exceeding 20%, and many allow credits to be transferred or sold, creating flexibility for developers who cannot fully utilize the credits directly. Studies of state tax credit programs consistently demonstrate positive economic impacts, with preservation projects generating construction jobs, increasing property values, and stimulating commercial activity in historic districts. However, these programs represent forgone tax revenue, and budget-conscious legislatures sometimes view them skeptically, particularly during fiscal downturns.

---

40. National Trust for Historic Preservation, *State Historic Tax Credits*, https://savingplaces.org/state-historic-tax-credits (last visited Feb. 15, 2026) ("For more than 30 years, the National Trust has supported the enactment of 39 state historic tax credits, and today, the organization continues to work with partners to increase this number. These credits attract private investment to reuse historic properties, many of which would otherwise likely be demolished.").

41. *Id.*

2. Easements and Covenants

Preservation easements are legal agreements that permanently restrict the use or alteration of historic properties to protect their character.[42] These easements are often held by nonprofit organizations,[43] and can also provide tax benefits to property owners.[44] Covenants, often imposed as conditions of grant funding,[45] serve similar purposes and seek to ensure long-term compliance with preservation standards.[46]

The use of preservation easements has grown substantially in recent decades as preservationists recognize the need for permanent protections extending beyond the current property owner. An easement essentially divides the property rights bundle, separating the right to alter the property's historic character from other ownership rights. The easement holder, typically a nonprofit preservation organization or governmental entity, monitors the property and enforces the easement's terms. Property owners donating easements may claim federal income tax deductions for the value of the donated interest, providing financial incentive for participation.

Easement enforcement presents ongoing challenges for organizations holding large numbers of easements. Effective monitoring requires regular property inspections, documentation of conditions, and prompt response to violations. Organizations must maintain sufficient resources to fulfill these obligations indefinitely, creating significant long-term financial commitments. Some easement disputes have resulted in litigation when property

---

42. National Park Service, *Easements to Protect Historic Properties: A Useful Historic Preservation Tool with Potential Tax Benefits*, www.nps.gov/orgs/1739/upload/brochure-easements-historic-properties.pdf (2010) (last visited Feb. 15, 2026) ("Under the terms of a typical preservation easement, a property owner places restrictions on the development of, or changes to, the property and transfers these restrictions to a qualified organization whose mission includes environmental protection, land conservation, open space preservation, or historic preservation.").

43. Jonathan Stark-Sachs et al., *Conflicts in Stewardship: A Survey of Historic Preservation Easement Practice*, available at https://docs.rwu.edu/cgi/viewcontent.cgi?article=1019&context=hp_theses (using nonprofit organizations holding conservation easements as a model cohort for a survey of preservation practices).

44. *See* 26 U.S.C.A. § 170(h) (West, Westlaw through Pub. L. No. 119-59).

45. National Park Service, *Easements to Protect Historic Properties: A Useful Historic Preservation Tool with Potential Tax Benefits*, www.nps.gov/orgs/1739/upload/brochure-easements-historic-properties.pdf (2010) ("Preservation easements in some states may also be called preservation 'restrictions,' 'covenants,' or 'equitable servitudes.'").

46. *Id.*

owners sought to make changes prohibited by easement terms, or when organizations claimed inadequate maintenance constituted easement violations. Courts have generally upheld easements and required compliance, but litigation remains costly and time consuming for all parties.

3. Grants and Technical Assistance

Numerous federal and state programs provide financial and technical support for preservation activities.[47] The Historic Preservation Fund (HPF), administered by the National Park Service, allocates funds to SHPOs and Tribal Historic Preservation Offices (THPOs).[48] The Advisory Council on Historic Preservation (ACHP) offers guidance and training to support compliance with Section 106 and related requirements.[49]

The Historic Preservation Fund derives its funding from outer continental shelf oil and gas lease revenues, a funding mechanism that has provided relative stability but also subjects the program to political debates about offshore energy development.[50] HPF funds support state preservation offices, subgrants to local governments and organizations, and various specialized programs. However, annual appropriations consistently fall below the amounts authorized by statute, limiting the program's reach. Preservationists have long advocated for full funding of the HPF, arguing that the modest amounts involved represent a tiny fraction of federal spending but generate substantial public benefits.[51]

Technical assistance programs complement financial incentives by providing expertise to property owners, local governments, and preservation organizations. The National Park Service's Technical Preservation Services

---

47. Natural Resources Conservation Service, *Conservation Stewardship Program*, www.nrcs.usda.gov/programs-initiatives/csp-conservation-stewardship-program (last visited Feb. 15, 2026) (federal program providing technical and financial assistance to solve agricultural issues and promote "higher stewardship levels").

48. National Park Service, *The Historic Preservation Fund*, www.nps.gov/subjects/historicpreservationfund/about.htm (last visited Feb. 15, 2026) ("The HPF is implemented through partnerships with State Historic Preservation Offices (SHPOs) [and] Trial Historic Preservation Offices (THPOs).").

49. Advisory Council on Historic Preservation, *Training and Education Overview*, www.achp.gov/training (last visited Feb. 15, 2026).

50. *See* https://revenuedata.onrr.gov/how-revenue-works/hpf/.

51. *See* https://savingplaces.org/grassroots-advocacy.

division produces guidance documents, case studies, and preservation briefs covering specific technical issues. State preservation offices similarly provide technical assistance tailored to local conditions and building types. This support proves particularly valuable for smaller communities and less sophisticated property owners who lack access to preservation architects and consultants. Free or low-cost technical assistance helps ensure that preservation work meets appropriate standards and avoids common mistakes that compromise historic character.

D. CONSTITUTIONAL AND LEGAL CHALLENGES

1. Takings Clause Jurisprudence

Historic preservation laws have occasionally been challenged under the takings clause of the Fifth Amendment.[52] In *Penn Central Transportation Co. v. New York City*,[53] the Supreme Court upheld New York's landmark law,[54] ruling that it did not constitute a regulatory taking because it did not deprive the owner of its distinct, investment-backed expectations.[55] Courts have generally upheld preservation laws,[56] applying a fact-specific analysis to determine whether a taking has occurred.[57]

The *Penn Central* decision established the analytical framework that continues to govern regulatory takings challenges to preservation laws. The Court articulated a three-factor inquiry examining (1) the economic impact of the regulation on the property owner, (2) the extent to which the regulation interferes with distinct investment-backed expectations, and (3) the character of the governmental action. This multi-factor test eschews bright-line rules in favor of case-by-case adjudication, creating uncertainty but also flexibility.

---

52. Penn Cent. Transp. Co. v. City of N.Y., 438 U.S. 104 (1978); *see also* Lucas v. S.C. Coastal Council, 505 U.S. 1003 (1992) (examining a takings claim based on the effects of South Carolina's beach conservation legislation on a littoral property).

53. 438 U.S. 104 (1978).

54. *Id.* at 138.

55. *Id.*

56. *But see Lucas*, 505 U.S. at 1031–32 (holding that South Carolina must do more to show that the state did not effectuate a taking when regulating beachfront property).

57. Braden's Folly, LLC v. City of Folly Beach, 886 S.E.2d 674 (S.C. 2023) (finding that no taking occurred when applying the fact-intensive *Penn Central* after a South Carolina property owner contested a merger ordinance enacted to better preserve coastal land).

In *Penn Central*, the Court emphasized that the landmark designation left Grand Central Terminal capable of profitable use, that the owners could continue operating the terminal as they had for decades, and that transferable development rights provided some compensation for lost air rights.

Subsequent takings jurisprudence has complicated the *Penn Central* framework without overturning it. The Court's decision in *Lucas v. South Carolina Coastal Council* established a categorical rule that regulations denying all economically beneficial use of property constitute per se takings requiring compensation, subject to a background principles exception. This rule potentially applies to preservation regulations that prevent all development of a property, though few preservation restrictions are so comprehensive. More commonly, preservation regulations limit what can be done with property while leaving multiple viable uses, situating most cases firmly within *Penn Central*'s balancing framework. Nonetheless, many municipal preservation ordinances contain relief in cases of sincere economic hardship that might otherwise trigger a claim under the *Lucas* standard.

Lower courts have applied *Penn Central* to uphold most preservation regulations challenged as takings. Courts emphasize that property owners have no right to maximize profit or to develop property to its highest and best use. Preservation restrictions that reduce property value, sometimes substantially, have been upheld as valid exercises of the police power that do not require compensation. These outcomes remain fact specific and difficult to predict ex ante.

2. Due Process and Equal Protection Issues

Preservation ordinances have also faced challenges on procedural and substantive due process grounds.[58] Plaintiffs have argued that ordinances are unconstitutionally vague or arbitrarily enforced.[59] Although courts have

58. Conner v. City of Seattle, 223 P.3d 1201 (Wash. Ct. App. 2009) (arguing a substantive due process violation stemming from a monument ordinance imposing view restrictions); People *ex rel.* Klaeren v. Village of Lisle, 737 N.E.2d 1099, 1113 (Ill. Ct. App. 2000) (involving a court in Illinois overturning zoning decisions on procedural grounds when a local government failed to provide cross-examination opportunity); Jackson William Beck, *What Gives You the Right? Procedural Due Process and Historic Preservation Ordinance Administration*, Master of Historic Preservation Thesis, https://getd.libs.uga.edu/pdfs/beck_jackson_w_201905_mhp.pdf (outlining the procedural hurdles inherent in preservation ordinances).

59. *See* S. of Second Assocs. v. Georgetown, 580 P.2d 807 (Colo. 1978) (en banc) (finding a historic preservation ordinance "void for vagueness" because "a property owner cannot

required clear standards and fair procedures,[60] they have universally upheld preservation laws that provide adequate notice and opportunity to be heard.[61] Equal protection claims, particularly those alleging discriminatory enforcement, have met with limited success.[62]

Vagueness challenges to preservation ordinances typically focus on the standards applied by preservation commissions in evaluating proposed changes. Plaintiffs argue that terms like "appropriate," "compatible," or "harmonious" are insufficiently definite to guide property owners or constrain discretion. Courts evaluating these challenges examine whether ordinances provide adequate guidance for understanding what is prohibited or required, and whether they establish sufficiently objective criteria to prevent arbitrary enforcement. Most preservation ordinances survive vagueness challenges, particularly when accompanied by detailed design guidelines that flesh out general standards. However, ordinances relying exclusively on highly subjective aesthetic judgments without concrete guidance have been invalidated.

Procedural due process claims challenge the fairness of the procedures used to designate historic properties or evaluate applications for certificates of appropriateness. These claims succeed when preservation commissions deny property owners adequate notice of proceedings, fail to provide meaningful opportunities to present evidence and arguments, or render decisions without articulating reasons. Courts require that preservation commissions follow their own procedural rules, consider relevant evidence presented by property owners, and base decisions on the record developed. However, courts generally defer to preservation commission expertise and do not second-guess substantive determinations if procedures were followed.

---

reasonably ascertain which architectural designs would entitle him to a certificate of appropriateness"); *see also* Kruse v. Town of Castle Rock, 192 P.3d 591 (Colo. App. 2008) (ruling that an ordinance was both sufficiently clear on its face *and* as applied to the claimant).

60. *S. of Second Assocs.*, 580 P.2d at 811; *Conner*, 223 P.3d 1201 (finding that a preservation ordinance imposing building restrictions was not impermissibly vague because it outlined a clear process for "ascertaining the requirements for an acceptable project").

61. *Conner*, 223 P.3d 1201.

62. *See* Nevel v. Village of Schaumburg, 297 F.3d 673 (7th Cir. 2002) (finding no equal protections violation when an owner of a historic home was denied construction approvals that were granted to non-historic homes); *but see* Yick Wo v. Hopkins, 118 U.S. 356 (1886) (a landmark Supreme Court decision finding discriminatory intent based upon racial classifications was unconstitutional when an Asian laundromat owner was denied building use approvals that were granted to White citizens).

3. First Amendment and Religious Properties

Applying preservation laws to religious properties has raised First Amendment concerns.[63] The Religious Land Use and Institutionalized Persons Act (RLUIPA) restricts government regulation that substantially burdens religious exercise.[64] Courts have generally upheld preservation laws as neutral and generally applicable but have required accommodations in cases of substantial burden to religious properties.[65]

RLUIPA has significantly altered the legal landscape for religious properties within historic districts. The statute prohibits governments from imposing or implementing land-use regulations that substantially burden religious exercise unless the government demonstrates that the burden furthers a compelling governmental interest through the least restrictive means. This standard is considerably more stringent than the rational basis review typically applied to preservation regulations. Religious institutions have successfully invoked RLUIPA to obtain exemptions from preservation restrictions on alterations, additions, and demolitions that would otherwise be prohibited.

The application of preservation laws to religious properties involves competing interests of substantial weight. Preservationists argue that religious buildings often represent communities' most significant architectural landmarks and deserve protection equal to secular structures. Religious institutions counter that governmental restrictions on their ability to modify properties interfere with religious freedom and their ability to serve congregations' evolving needs. Finding appropriate balance requires case-by-case analysis. Courts have required preservation commissions to consider alternatives that accommodate religious needs while preserving historic character, and have invalidated restrictions that prevented institutions from carrying out core religious functions.

---

63. *See* Mintz v. Roman Catholic Bishop, 424 F. Supp. 2d 309 (D. Mass. 2006) (ruling that a church was exempt from certain preservation zoning requirements because the building subject to the restrictions was used for religious exercise); Living Water Church of God v. Charter Twp. of Meridian, 384 F. Supp. 2d 1123 (W.D. Mich. 2005) (finding a RLUIPA violation when a church was denied a building permit because the new construction would be too large given the surrounding neighborhood).

64. *Religious Land Use and Institutionalized Persons Act*, Civil Rights Division Department of Justice, www.justice.gov/crt/religious-land-use-and-institutionalized-persons-act (last visited June 24, 2025).

65. *See Mintz*, 424 F. Supp. 2d 309; *but see* Episcopal Student Found. v. City of Ann Arbor, 341 F. Supp. 2d 691 (E.D. Mich. 2004) (ruling that denial of a permit to a church was permissible where it did not impose any substantial burden on the exercise of religion).

E. TENSIONS BETWEEN DEVELOPMENT AND PRESERVATION

1. Urban Growth and Gentrification

Historic preservation can both mitigate and exacerbate the impacts of urban development. Although preservation helps maintain neighborhood character and prevent displacement,[66] it can also contribute to rising property values and gentrification.[67] Policymakers must navigate these dynamics carefully to ensure that historic preservation laws serve the public interest without excluding marginalized communities.[68]

The relationship between preservation and gentrification proves complex and context dependent. In some neighborhoods, preservation activism has emerged from existing residents seeking to maintain community character and resist displacement pressures from development. In these cases, preservation serves as a tool for community empowerment and resistance to market forces threatening to transform neighborhoods. However, in other contexts, preservation contributes to gentrification by restricting housing supply, increasing property values, and attracting affluent residents drawn to historic character. Historic designation can signal neighborhood desirability and accelerate demographic change.

Research on preservation's gentrification effects yields mixed findings. Preservation efforts could be viewed as a contributor to displacement, particularly in cities with tight housing markets. By restricting alterations to existing buildings and limiting new construction in historic districts, preservation regulations can constrain housing supply and drive up prices. On the other hand, preservation could be viewed as stabilizing neighborhoods and providing affordable housing opportunities by maintaining existing housing stock rather than replacing it with high-end development. The divergent findings reflect varying local conditions and the interaction of preservation with other market and policy forces.

---

66. *See* Bruce C. Mitchell, et al., *Displaced by Design: Fifty Years of Gentrification and Black Cultural Displacement in US Cities*, https://ncrc.org/displaced-by-design/ (May 2025) (outlining the trend of gentrification and displacement in American neighborhoods while noting the "superficial commemoration of [some] neighborhood's Black history" as an incommensurate price as compared to the negative impact on demographics) (last visited Feb. 15, 2026).

67. *Id.*

68. *Mitchell, supra* note 66; Providence Preservation Society, *The Plan* (Nov. 2021), https://ppsri.org/wp-content/uploads/2021/11/2021_strategic_plan_final.pdf (last visited Feb. 15, 2026).

Addressing preservation's equity implications requires intentional policy design. Some jurisdictions have adopted programs providing financial and technical assistance to low-income property owners in historic districts, helping them maintain properties that might otherwise fall into disrepair. Others have created hardship provisions allowing property owners to demonstrate that preservation requirements impose unreasonable financial burdens. More broadly, communities are recognizing the need to expand preservation beyond elite historic districts to encompass neighborhoods reflecting diverse histories and communities. Preservation that celebrates only affluent histories while ignoring working-class and minority communities exacerbates inequality.

2. Economic Development and Adaptive Reuse

Adaptive reuse—the process of repurposing old buildings for new uses—is a growing trend that bridges the gap between historic preservation and modern land development.[69] Successful adaptive reuse projects demonstrate that historic preservation can be economically viable and environmentally sustainable.[70] Cities like Portland, Oregon, and Denver, Colorado, have pioneered policies that facilitate adaptive reuse through incentives and flexible codes.[71]

Adaptive reuse has emerged as preservation's most compelling economic argument. Converting obsolete industrial buildings into housing, offices, or mixed-use developments demonstrates that preservation need not mean stagnation. High-profile successes like the Ponce City Market in Atlanta and Chelsea Market in New York showcase adaptive reuse's potential to create vibrant, economically productive spaces while retaining historic

---

69. Project Management Institute Phoenix, *Adaptive Reuse: Bridging the Gap Between Historical Preservation and Modern Architectural Practices*, https://pmiphx.org/presidents-corner/adaptive-reuse-bridging-the-gap-between-historical-preservation-and-modern-architectural-practices (last visited Feb. 15, 2026) ("Adaptive reuse is taking an existing building and transforming it for a new purpose while preserving its historical and architectural features.").

70. *Id.* (establishing that "sustainable design" is a paramount consideration when planning adaptive reuse projects, "aligning with broader goals of ecological responsibility" while allowing a historic structure to "serve contemporary needs").

71. Portland Zoning Code § 33.445.400 (Portland adaptive reuse incentives); *Adaptive Reuse Program Strategy Paper for the City and County of Denver, CO*, www.denvergov.org/files/assets/public/v/1/city-council/documents/d4/denver_adaptivereusestrategyreport_oct2020.pdf (Oct. 2020) (providing a comprehensive overview of Denver's adaptive reuse pilot program and implementation strategies).

character. These projects often command premium rents and attract creative industries drawn to authentic, distinctive environments. The economic success of adaptive reuse projects helps counter arguments that preservation constitutes regulatory burden impeding development.

Facilitating adaptive reuse requires regulatory flexibility. Traditional use restrictions embedded in historic district regulations can impede adaptive reuse by prohibiting contemporary uses in buildings designed for obsolete purposes. Progressive jurisdictions have reformed zoning to allow diverse uses in historic buildings and have created pathways for obtaining variances or special permits when necessary. Building code flexibility similarly proves crucial, as retrofitting historic buildings to current code standards can be prohibitively expensive if no accommodation is made for historic fabric. Alternative compliance mechanisms allowing equivalent safety through different means have proven essential for viable adaptive reuse.

The environmental benefits of adaptive reuse strengthen preservation's contemporary relevance. Buildings represent massive investments of energy and materials embedded in their construction. Demolishing functioning buildings and constructing replacements generate substantial waste and consume significant energy, even when new construction is highly efficient.[72] Preserving and adapting existing buildings avoids these environmental costs while maintaining embodied energy. Building reuse, even with extensive renovations, typically results in better environmental outcomes than demolition and new construction over time periods of several decades.

3. Case Studies

Several landmark cases and municipal examples illustrate the interaction between preservation and development. Demolishing New York's original Penn Station in 1963 spurred the modern historic preservation movement, leading to Grand Central Terminal's designation as a protected landmark and to *Penn Central*.[73] Charleston, South Carolina, exemplifies strong local preservation policies that balance tourism and livability.[74] San Francisco's

---

72. For example, the Carbon Avoided Retrofit Estimator Tool (CARE Tool) is a calculator used to compare the total carbon impacts of renovating an existing building versus replacing it with a new one; *see* www.caretool.org/.

73. Penn Cent. Transp. Co. v. City of N.Y., 438 U.S. 104 (1978).

74. *Livability & Tourism*, www.charleston-sc.gov/1380/Livability-Tourism (last visited June 24, 2025) (outlining the Charleston, SC, Departments of Livability and Tourism).

preservation efforts have been tested by pressure from the tech sector and housing demand, prompting innovative zoning and planning responses.[75]

The Penn Station demolition represents preservation's most iconic failure and galvanizing event. The station's destruction, despite its recognized architectural magnificence and cultural significance, demonstrated that even monumental buildings could be lost without legal protections. The public outcry that followed reflected growing preservation consciousness and generated political will for stronger preservation laws. The New York landmarks law enacted in response became a model for municipal preservation ordinances nationwide. The contrast between Penn Station's fate and Grand Central Terminal's preservation, validated by the Supreme Court in *Penn Central*, illustrates how legal frameworks can alter preservation outcomes.

Charleston's preservation program demonstrates how comprehensive local regulations can maintain historic character while accommodating growth. The city's Board of Architectural Review, established in 1931, represents the nation's oldest continuing preservation commission. Charleston's approach emphasizes contextual design in new construction, requiring new buildings to respect the scale, proportions, and materials of historic structures. The city has successfully maintained its historic character while developing tourism infrastructure and accommodating residential growth. However, Charleston also illustrates preservation's tensions, as historic district regulations have created substantial demands for tourism and second homes that have been challenging to manage. This has resulted in the perception that preservation is the cause of housing affordability challenges and pressures for difficult histories to be sanitized.

San Francisco's preservation battles reveal the pressures facing cities experiencing rapid economic growth. The city's extensive preservation regulations protect thousands of historic buildings and numerous historic districts. These protections have become increasingly controversial as housing costs have soared, and development interests argue that preservation limits necessary housing construction. The city has struggled to balance preservation of neighborhood character against demands for housing production. Recent policy changes have attempted to thread this needle by allowing

---

75. San Francisco Planning, *San Francisco Family Zoning Plan*, https://sfplanning.org/sf-family-zoning-plan#faqs (publicizing upcoming zoning changes in San Francisco designed to create new and additional affordable housing previously prohibited under zoning regulations in response to urban development) (last visited Feb. 15, 2026).

increased density in some areas while maintaining protections in others, though satisfying all constituencies remains impossible.[76]

F. EMERGING ISSUES AND FUTURE DIRECTIONS

1. Climate Change and Resilience Planning

Climate change poses significant threats to historic resources, particularly in coastal and flood-prone areas. Preservationists are increasingly involved in resilience planning,[77] advocating for strategies that protect historic assets from sea-level rise,[78] extreme weather,[79] and other climate impacts.[80] Integration of preservation into environmental policy is a growing area of focus.[81]

Coastal historic resources face existential threats from sea level rise and intensifying storms. Communities like Charleston, Annapolis, and New Orleans confront difficult questions about how to protect historic properties from flooding while maintaining historic character. Traditional flood mitigation strategies often conflict with preservation principles. Raising structures above flood levels, installing flood walls, and applying waterproof coatings all alter historic appearance and fabric. Preservationists are developing new approaches that provide flood protection while minimizing impacts on historic character, but many interventions remain costly and imperfect.[82]

---

76. *See* www.sfexaminer.com/news/the-city/major-policy-shift-law-approved-to-allow-denser-housing-across-s-f/article_d8b13424–4f3e-11ed-81b6–8342d95e8e6d.html.

77. Advisory Council on Historic Preservation, *Climate Resilience & Sustainability*, www.achp.gov/initiatives/sustainability-climate-resilience (last visited Feb. 15, 2025).

78. *Braden's Folly, LLC*, 886 S.E.2d 674 (finding that no taking occurred when applying the fact-intensive *Penn Central* after a South Carolina property owner contested a merger ordinance enacted to better preserve coastal land).

79. *Id.*; City of Long Branch v. Jui Yung Liu, 4 A.3d 542 (N.J. 2010) (examining coastal management efforts meant to preserve New Jersey shoreline from erosion).

80. Severance v. Patterson, 370 S.W.3d 705 (Tex. 2012) (examining coastal management efforts meant to preserve Texas Gulf Coast shoreline following intense bouts of erosion after a hurricane).

81. Advisory Council on Historic Preservation, *Climate Resilience & Sustainability*, www.achp.gov/initiatives/sustainability-climate-resilience (last visited Feb. 15, 2026) (discussing the importance of integrating environmental concerns into preservation efforts).

82. *See* Charleston, S.C., *Process for Elevation Projects*, www.charleston-sc.gov/2333/Elevating-Your-Structure (last visited Feb. 15, 2026) (discussing elevated building guidelines and process in Charleston, S.C.).

The tension between climate resilience and historic preservation extends beyond coastal areas. Wildfire threats in the western United States have prompted requirements for fire-resistant materials and vegetation management that may conflict with preservation standards. Extreme heat and changing precipitation patterns affect historic materials and accelerate deterioration. Adapting historic buildings to climate change involves both protecting them from climate impacts and improving their energy efficiency to reduce greenhouse gas emissions. These objectives sometimes conflict, as aggressive energy retrofits can compromise historic windows, walls, and roofs.

2. Equity and Inclusive Preservation

A new generation of preservationists is working to expand the scope of protected sites to include places significant to marginalized communities, such as First Nations,[83] African American,[84] and LGBTQ+ histories.[85] Inclusive preservation requires changes in policy, funding priorities, and community engagement practices.[86]

Historic preservation has traditionally focused on properties associated with elite histories and conventional architectural significance. This narrow focus has resulted in the protection of disproportionately White, wealthy, and male-associated places while neglecting sites significant to marginalized communities. African American churches, Native American cultural landscapes, LGBTQ+ gathering places, and working-class neighborhoods have been systematically undervalued and underprotected. Correcting this imbalance requires confronting preservation's historical biases and actively working to identify and protect diverse historic resources.

---

83. Claudia Sobrevila, The Role of Indigenous Peoples in Biodiversity Conservation *xii (May 2008), available at https://documents1.worldbank.org/curated/en/995271468177530126/pdf/443000WP0BOX321onservation01PUBLIC1.pdf (identifying the key areas for improvement in terms of historic preservation for early populations of "traditional indigenous territories," particularly by expanding "beyond national parks").

84. Di Gao et al., Preserving African American Places: Growing Preservation's Potential as a Path for Equity (October 2020), available at https://cdn.savingplaces.org/2023/08/10/13/57/18/226/AACHAF_EquityStudyReport_lo-res.pdf (highlighting the benefit that historic preservation provides to diversity and equity-focused initiatives).

85. Donna Graves and Gail Dubrow, *Taking Intersectionality Seriously*, 41 The Public Historian (May 2019) (identifying the need for improved coverage of LGBTQ history in the field of preservation).

86. *Id.*; Gao, *supra* note 84; National trust for Historic Preservation, *Goal 6: An Engaged Public*, https://savingplaces.org/goal-engaged-public (last visited Feb. 15, 2026) (defining civic engagement as a core goal of future preservation efforts).

The National Park Service's initiatives to identify and protect underrepresented histories represent important steps toward inclusive preservation. The African American Cultural Heritage Action Fund, for example, provides grants and technical assistance for preservation of sites associated with African American history. Similar efforts focus on Latino heritage, women's history, and LGBTQ+ history. These programs acknowledge that traditional preservation practice has failed to adequately document and protect diverse histories and seek to expand the preservation canon. However, funding for these initiatives remains limited relative to need, and many significant sites have been lost.

Community engagement constitutes a crucial component of inclusive preservation. Preservation decisions historically have been made by unrepresentative commissions and organizations dominated by White, affluent members. Inclusive preservation requires authentic community participation, centering the voices of people whose histories are at stake. This means not merely consulting communities about preservation decisions but involving them throughout the process, from identification and evaluation of significant sites to stewardship and interpretation. Some preservationists resist sharing authority with communities they view as lacking expertise, but meaningful inclusion requires accepting that communities themselves are experts on their own histories.

The challenge of preserving difficult histories remains contentious. How should preservation address sites associated with oppression, violence, and injustice? Confederate monuments and plantation landscapes exemplify these challenges. On the one hand, should these sites be preserved to provide opportunities for critical interpretation and education about historical injustices? On the other hand, does preserving such sites honor perpetrators and cause ongoing harm to marginalized communities? There are no easy answers, but preservation practice increasingly recognizes that simply preserving buildings and monuments without grappling with their complex meanings and impacts serves no one well. Interpretation matters as much as preservation.

3. "Smart Growth" and Sustainability

Preservation and "smart growth" share common goals, including compact development, walkability, and environmental stewardship.[87] Historic buildings

87. U.S. Environmental Protection Agency, *About Smart Growth*, www.epa.gov/smartgrowth/about-smart-growth (last visited Feb. 15, 2026) ("Smart growth is an overall approach of development and conservation strategies that can help protect our health and

are inherently sustainable due to their embodied energy and durable materials.[88] Policymakers are increasingly recognizing the interplay between historic preservation and sustainability in comprehensive planning.

The convergence of preservation and sustainability agendas represents one of preservation's most promising contemporary developments. Smart growth principles emphasizing compact, walkable development align naturally with preservation's focus on existing building stock and traditional neighborhood patterns. Historic commercial districts typically exhibit the mixed-use, pedestrian-oriented development that smart growth seeks to promote. Preserving these districts maintains infrastructure that supports sustainable transportation and reduces automobile dependence.

Historic buildings' environmental advantages extend beyond location and form. The materials used in traditional construction often prove more durable than contemporary alternatives. Old-growth timber, solid masonry, and traditional plasters can last centuries with appropriate maintenance, whereas contemporary construction often requires replacement after several decades. The embodied energy in existing buildings represents a substantial environmental asset that demolition squanders. Life-cycle assessments have demonstrated that building reuse, even accounting for energy inefficiencies in older structures, typically produces better environmental outcomes than demolition and new construction over time horizons of 20 to 50 years.

Energy efficiency improvements in historic buildings require careful balancing of preservation and sustainability goals. Aggressive efficiency retrofits involving replacement of historic windows, application of exterior insulation, or installation of contemporary mechanical systems can compromise historic character and materials. However, more modest interventions—improving attic and basement insulation, weatherstripping, upgrading lighting and appliances—can significantly reduce energy consumption while respecting historic fabric. Preservation and energy efficiency need not conflict when approached thoughtfully, though finding optimal solutions requires expertise in both disciplines.

---

natural environment and make our communities more attractive, economically stronger and resilient to climate change.").

88. Project Management Institute Phoenix, *Adaptive Reuse: Bridging the Gap Between Historical Preservation and Modern Architectural Practices*, https://pmiphx.org/presidents-corner/adaptive-reuse-bridging-the-gap-between-historical-preservation-and-modern-architectural-practices (last visited Feb. 15, 2026).

4. Technology and Digital Documentation

Technological advances are transforming preservation practice in ways that would have been unimaginable a generation ago. High-resolution photographic documentation, 3D laser scanning, and building information modeling create detailed records of historic properties that serve multiple purposes. These technologies enable accurate recording of existing conditions, facilitate planning for rehabilitation work, and provide permanent documentation in case properties are damaged or destroyed. Some preservationists advocate for comprehensive digital documentation of all significant historic resources as a form of insurance against loss.

Digital technologies also democratize access to preservation information and expand preservation's audience. Online databases of historic properties, virtual tours, and digital archives make preservation accessible to people who cannot physically visit sites. Social media platforms enable preservation organizations to reach new constituencies and mobilize support for threatened properties. However, digital engagement cannot replace the embodied experience of historic places, and preservationists must ensure that technology enhances rather than replacing direct engagement with historic resources.

The use of modern materials and methods in preservation work generates ongoing debate. Contemporary building science sometimes suggests interventions that conflict with traditional preservation approaches. For example, vapor barriers and air sealing recommended for energy efficiency can trap moisture in historic walls designed to breathe, causing deterioration. Similarly, modern waterproofing compounds may protect building materials in the short term but compromise long-term durability. Preservationists are developing updated guidance that integrates traditional building practices with modern building science, recognizing that historic buildings function differently than contemporary construction.

5. Preservation and Tourism

Tourism represents both an opportunity and a challenge for historic preservation. Tourist revenue provides economic justification for preservation investment and funds property maintenance. However, tourism can also damage historic resources through overuse and inappropriate development. Venice, Machu Picchu, and other heavily visited historic sites illustrate how tourism success can threaten the very resources that attract visitors.

Managing tourism to support rather than undermine preservation requires careful planning and regulation.

Overtourism has become a pressing concern in many historic cities. When visitor numbers overwhelm local infrastructure and degrade quality of life for residents, preservation's relationship with tourism becomes problematic. Historic neighborhoods transformed into tourist zones lose authenticity and residential character. Local businesses serving community needs are displaced by tourist-oriented shops and restaurants. Finding sustainable approaches to heritage tourism that benefit local communities and preserve authentic character remains an ongoing challenge. Some cities have implemented visitor caps, required reservations, or charged entrance fees to historic districts, though such measures prove controversial and difficult to enforce.

The interpretation and presentation of historic sites to tourists involve complex questions about authenticity, accuracy, and audience. Popular tourist sites often present simplified or romanticized narratives that obscure historical complexities. Challenging histories involving oppression, violence, or moral ambiguity may be sanitized to avoid discomforting visitors or generating controversy. Preservation professionals increasingly recognize the importance of honest, nuanced interpretation that acknowledges difficult histories while remaining accessible to diverse audiences. However, achieving this balance proves challenging when economic pressures favor easily consumable narratives over complicated truths.

G. PRESERVATION PRACTICE AND PROFESSIONAL STANDARDS

The professionalization of preservation practice has advanced significantly since the field's early days. Graduate programs in historic preservation, now offered by dozens of universities, provide specialized training in preservation history, theory, practice, and policy. Professional organizations like the National Trust for Historic Preservation and the Association for Preservation Technology offer continuing education, conferences, and publications that advance preservation knowledge. Board certification programs in historic preservation architecture and conservation provide credential mechanisms recognizing specialized expertise.

Despite these advances, preservation remains an inherently interdisciplinary field that resists complete professionalization. Effective preservation practice requires knowledge spanning architecture, history, law, materials science, and crafts. No single professional background provides all necessary expertise, making collaboration among professionals with different specializations essential. Architects, historians, archaeologists, preservation planners, craftspeople, and lawyers all contribute specialized knowledge to preservation projects. However, coordination among these diverse professionals can be challenging, and jurisdictional disputes sometimes arise over who is qualified to make particular preservation decisions.

The preservation trades—masonry, carpentry, plastering, and others—face significant workforce challenges. Traditional craft skills required for preservation work are increasingly scarce as older craftspeople retire, and fewer young people enter the trades. Training programs in traditional building trades have difficulty competing with other career paths that often offer better compensation and working conditions. Without skilled craftspeople capable of performing traditional preservation work, even well-funded preservation projects may produce poor results. Preservationists are working to expand training opportunities and improve compensation and working conditions in the preservation trades, but progress remains slow.

H. INTERNATIONAL PERSPECTIVES AND COMPARATIVE APPROACHES

American preservation law developed within a distinctive property rights tradition that shapes its character and limitations. Comparing American approaches with those of other countries illuminates alternative models and their trade-offs. European preservation systems typically involve more comprehensive protections and greater restrictions on private property rights. In many European countries, designated historic buildings cannot be demolished regardless of ownership, and alterations require governmental approval. These stronger protections reflect different cultural values and legal traditions that accept greater governmental authority over private property.

The UNESCO World Heritage Convention represents the most significant international preservation framework. World Heritage designation confers international recognition and can provide access to technical and financial assistance, but it also imposes obligations on signatory nations to protect designated sites. The United States has ratified the Convention and has numerous World Heritage sites, though the legal effect of designation remains limited. World Heritage designation does not create enforceable restrictions on private property owners and provides no funding for protection or maintenance. The designation's primary effect is symbolic, raising awareness and creating reputational incentives for protection.

Developing countries face distinctive preservation challenges that differ from those in wealthy nations. Limited financial resources, rapid urbanization, weak regulatory enforcement, and competing development priorities often relegate preservation to low priority. International preservation organizations have worked to support preservation in developing countries through technical assistance, training programs, and funding. However, these efforts must respect local priorities and avoid imposing Western preservation values and approaches that may be inappropriate in different cultural contexts. The tension between protecting irreplaceable cultural heritage and accommodating urgent development needs has no easy resolution.

I. LEGAL MECHANISMS AND ENFORCEMENT

Preservation law enforcement mechanisms vary considerably across jurisdictions and prove crucial to preservation effectiveness. Strong preservation regulations mean little without effective enforcement. Many preservation ordinances authorize fines for violations, injunctive relief to halt prohibited work, and requirements to restore properties to their previous condition. However, enforcement requires resources for monitoring, investigation, and prosecution that many preservation programs lack. Property owners sometimes demolish buildings illegally, calculating that fines will cost less than seeking permission that would likely be denied. This "demolition by neglect" problem—where property owners allow buildings to deteriorate to justify demolition—presents another enforcement challenge.

Stop-work orders and temporary restraining orders provide crucial tools for halting illegal demolition or alteration before irreparable damage occurs. Preservation commissions or local governments can seek emergency judicial relief when threatened historic properties face imminent harm. Courts generally grant such relief when petitioners demonstrate likelihood of success on the merits and irreparable harm absent intervention. However, obtaining emergency relief requires rapid action, and preservation organizations may lack the resources or awareness to respond quickly enough.

Criminal sanctions remain rare in preservation law but are occasionally imposed for egregious violations. Some jurisdictions classify unauthorized demolition of designated landmarks as criminal offenses punishable by fines or imprisonment. Criminal prosecution sends a strong message about preservation violations' seriousness but requires prosecutorial resources and willingness to pursue what are often viewed as low-priority offenses. Civil penalties and property-based sanctions prove more common and practical enforcement mechanisms.

In sum, historic preservation laws play a crucial role in maintaining the nation's architectural and cultural heritage. As development pressures intensify, the challenge lies in crafting policies that balance the need for growth with the obligation to protect historic property. Meeting the challenge requires collaboration among planners, developers, preservationists, and communities, using all the available legal tools, policies, and financial incentives, to protect history while accommodating modern land development.

Historic Preservation Laws and Tax Incentives

11

The preservation of historic buildings in the United States represents a unique convergence of cultural stewardship, economic development, and tax policy. Since the Tax Reform Act of 1976, the federal government has recognized that private property owners need financial incentives to undertake the often-expensive work of rehabilitating historic structures rather than demolishing them for more profitable new construction. What emerged is one of the most successful public-private partnerships in American historic preservation: the federal Historic Tax Credit (HTC) program, codified primarily in Section 47 of the Internal Revenue Code.

One of the most prominent methods by which the federal government promotes historic preservation is through subsidies embedded in tax policy. By drafting specific tax provisions that incentivize historic preservation, the federal government clearly signals its objectives. Title 26 of the U.S. Code provides two primary mechanisms for promoting historic preservation through the tax code. The code employs a two-pronged approach: tax credits encourage property owners to maintain historic property, while historic preservation easements help prevent such property from being demolished or altered in a way inconsistent with best preservation practice.

This chapter examines the tax benefits available to owners of historic preservation property, focusing on both federal incentives and selected state-level programs that complement or enhance federal benefits. Understanding these tax benefits requires grappling with complex questions about property qualification, permissible rehabilitation work, credit calculation, and the interaction between multiple tax incentive programs.

The economic impact of these programs has been substantial. Since its inception, the federal HTC has leveraged more than $235 billion in private investment toward rehabilitating historic buildings, creating jobs, and revitalizing communities nationwide.[1] Yet despite this success, the program remains poorly understood outside specialist circles, and recent years have seen legislative proposals both to expand and to curtail these benefits.

A. THE FEDERAL FRAMEWORK

1. Section 47: The Historic Preservation Tax Credit

The first provision, 26 U.S.C. § 47, allows owners of certain qualified real property to obtain valuable tax credits based upon expenses incurred when maintaining such property. The general goal is to incentivize owners to spend money on the upkeep of historic property rather than tear it down for different, more profitable investment or development purposes. Additionally, because certain historic property legally cannot be torn down, the tax credits provide an incentive that makes such property less likely to sit unmaintained and makes such property far more liquid by increasing its value.

2. Section 170(h): Historic Preservation Easements

The second provision, 26 U.S.C. § 170(h), allows for charitable contributions of "Historic Preservation Easements," essentially the owner's right to develop the property into something else later, functioning akin to a conservation easement. These easements are perpetual by definition, affording the

1. *See* https://savingplaces.org/historic-tax-credits.

property owner taxable deductions based upon the value of the property right donated, in exchange for an express limitation on the owner's ability to alter or develop historic property.

In essence, the purpose of tax incentives for historic preservation is to encourage private sector investment in the rehabilitation and reuse of historic buildings, thereby achieving a range of economic, social, and cultural goals. These tax incentives transform the preservation of historic properties from an often prohibitive cost into an attractive investment opportunity with broad public benefits.

B. SECTION 47 QUALIFICATION REQUIREMENTS

1. Legislative History and Policy Rationale

The federal government's use of tax incentives to encourage historic preservation evolved considerably before reaching its current form. The 1976 Tax Reform Act first introduced preferential tax treatment for certified historic structures, initially offering accelerated depreciation. The Economic Recovery Tax Act of 1981 expanded these benefits, creating a three-tiered system of investment tax credits.

The Tax Reform Act of 1986 significantly restructured these incentives, eliminating the tiered system and establishing the 20% credit for certified historic structures that remains in effect today (with modifications). This consolidation reflected a policy judgment that tax benefits should be targeted specifically at buildings with recognized historical significance rather than merely old buildings.

The policy rationale is multifaceted. First, these credits address a market failure: rehabilitation costs frequently exceed demolition and new construction costs. Second, they serve broader community development goals by encouraging investment in older urban cores and rural town centers. Third, they promote environmental sustainability through adaptive reuse of existing building stock. Finally, they preserve tangible connections to American history and culture.

2. Certified Historic Structure Requirement

Working with the IRS tax code is a nuanced, particularized endeavor and should always be done with the guidance of a certified tax professional. The building must qualify as a "certified historic structure" under Section 47(c)(3). Formal listing on the National Register of Historic Places is required, either individually or as a contributing resource in a district. In practice, the historic evaluation required to list the property (if it is not already listed) is referred to as "Part 1" of a historic tax credit application.[2]

> (3) Certified historic structure defined.
>
> (A) In general. The term "certified historic structure" means any building (and its structural components) which
>
> (i) is listed in the National Register, or
>
> (ii) is located in a registered historic district and is certified by the Secretary of the Interior to the Secretary as being of historic significance to the district.
>
> (B) Registered historic district. The term "registered historic district" means
>
> (i) any district listed in the National Register, and
>
> (ii) any district
>
> (I) which is designated under a statute of the appropriate State or local government, if such statute is certified by the Secretary of the Interior to the Secretary as containing criteria which will substantially achieve the purpose of preserving and rehabilitating buildings of historic significance to the district, and
>
> (II) which is certified by the Secretary of the Interior to the Secretary as meeting substantially all of the requirements for the listing of districts in the National Register.

This definition encompasses more than just buildings listed in the National Register, also including buildings located in a registered historic district. Yet, individual listing is a much more practical approach since building owners may not want to entertain the complexity of a full district-level historic evaluation. Section 47(3)(B) allows for a more case-specific, locally oriented approach than would otherwise be included, enabling communities to designate their own historic districts that can qualify for federal tax benefits if they meet the certification requirements.

---

2. *See* www.nps.gov/subjects/taxincentives/historic-preservation-certification-application.html.

3. Substantial Rehabilitation Test

Section 47(c)(1) requires that rehabilitations be "substantial," defined with mathematical precision:

(1)

(B) Substantially rehabilitated defined.

(i) In general. For purposes of subparagraph (A)(i), a building shall be treated as having been substantially rehabilitated only if the qualified rehabilitation expenditures during the 24-month period selected by the taxpayer (at the time and in the manner prescribed by regulation) and ending with or within the taxable year exceed the greater of

(I) the adjusted basis of such building (and its structural components), or

(II) $5,000.

In other words, only Qualified Rehabilitation Expenses, or QREs, are eligible. These costs must be accounted for separately than other project-based work. The adjusted basis of the building (and its structural components) shall be determined as of the beginning of the first day of such 24-month period, or of the holding period of the building, whichever is later. For purposes of the preceding sentence, the determination of the beginning of the holding period shall be made without regard to any reconstruction by the taxpayer in connection with the rehabilitation.

(ii) Special rule for phased rehabilitation. In the case of any rehabilitation which may reasonably be expected to be completed in phases set forth in architectural plans and specifications completed before the rehabilitation begins, clause (i) shall be applied by substituting "60-month period" for "24-month period."

(iii) Lessees. The Secretary shall prescribe by regulation rules for applying this subparagraph to lessees.

(C) Reconstruction. Rehabilitation includes reconstruction.

The adjusted basis calculation excludes land value, creating a favorable situation for taxpayers, particularly in urban areas where land may constitute a significant portion of total property value. For example, if a developer purchases a historic building for $1 million, with $300,000 allocated to land and $700,000 to the building, and the building has depreciated to an adjusted basis of $400,000 when rehabilitation begins, the taxpayer must spend more than $400,000 on qualified rehabilitation expenditures. If successful, they receive a 20% credit on all qualified expenditures, not merely those exceeding the threshold.

4. Qualified Rehabilitation Expenditures

Section 47(c)(2) defines what expenditures qualify for the credit:

> (2) Qualified rehabilitation expenditure defined.
>
> (A) In general. The term "qualified rehabilitation expenditure" means any amount properly chargeable to capital account
>
> (i) for property for which depreciation is allowable under section 168 and which is
>
> (I) nonresidential real property,
>
> (II) residential rental property,
>
> (III) real property which has a class life of more than 12.5 years, or
>
> (IV) an addition or improvement to property described in subclause (I), (II), or (III), and
>
> (ii) in connection with the rehabilitation of a qualified rehabilitated building.

Note the distinction between nonresidential real property and residential rental property. The credit does not apply to rehabilitation efforts made on one's own personal residence unless an exception applies. However, if a historic home is rented out, it would qualify as residential rental property, potentially qualifying for the tax credit.

The statute specifically excludes certain expenditures:

> (B) Certain expenditures not included. The term "qualified rehabilitation expenditure" does not include—
>
> (i) Straight line depreciation must be used. Any expenditure with respect to which the taxpayer does not use the straight line method over a recovery period determined under subsection (c) or (g) of section 168. The preceding sentence shall not apply to any expenditure to the extent the alternative depreciation system of section 168(g) applies to such expenditure by reason of subparagraph (B) or (C) of section 168(g)(1).

(ii) Cost of acquisition. The cost of acquiring any building or interest therein.
(iii) Enlargements. Any expenditure attributable to the enlargement of an existing building.
(iv) Certified historic structure. Any expenditure attributable to the rehabilitation of a qualified rehabilitated building unless the rehabilitation is a certified rehabilitation (within the meaning of subparagraph (C)).
(v) Tax-exempt use property.

(I) In general. Any expenditure in connection with the rehabilitation of a building which is allocable to the portion of such property which is (or may reasonably be expected to be) tax-exempt use property (within the meaning of section 168(h), except that "50 percent" shall be substituted for "35 percent" in paragraph (1)(B)(iii) thereof).
(II) Clause not to apply for purposes of paragraph (1)(C). This clause shall not apply for purposes of determining under paragraph (1)(C) whether a building has been substantially rehabilitated.

(vi) Expenditures of lessee. Any expenditure of a lessee of a building if, on the date the rehabilitation is completed, the remaining term of the lease (determined without regard to any renewal periods) is less than the recovery period determined under section 168(c).

5. Certified Rehabilitation

The rehabilitation work itself must meet preservation standards:

(C) Certified rehabilitation. For purposes of subparagraph (B), the term "certified rehabilitation" means any rehabilitation of a certified historic structure which the Secretary of the Interior has certified to the Secretary as being consistent with the historic character of such property or the district in which such property is located.
(D) Nonresidential real property; residential rental property; class life. For purposes of subparagraph (A), the terms "nonresidential real property," "residential rental property," and "class

life" have the respective meanings given such terms by section 168.

The National Park Service and SHPO have an important role in approving a rehabilitation plan in advance of work taking place, known as a Part 2 application. This certification requirement ensures that rehabilitations are not merely expensive but also appropriate from a preservation standpoint. The National Park Service has published detailed standards for rehabilitation work in the Secretary of the Interior's Standards for Rehabilitation, which provide flexible guidelines that balance preservation goals with practical realities.

6. Progress Expenditures

Section 47(d) addresses when credits may be claimed:

(d) Progress expenditures.

(1) In general. In the case of any building to which this subsection applies, except as provided in paragraph (3)—

(A) if such building is self-rehabilitated property, any qualified rehabilitation expenditure with respect to such building shall be taken into account for the taxable year for which such expenditure is properly chargeable to capital account with respect to such building, and

(B) if such building is not self-rehabilitated property, any qualified rehabilitation expenditure with respect to such building shall be taken into account for the taxable year in which paid.

The actual applicability of the tax credit varies based on the taxable year in which it is charged. Instead of waiting until the building is placed in service, if Section 47(d) applies, the taxpayer can claim credits year-by-year as expenditures are made or properly capitalized. Subsection (d)(1) creates two tracks depending on whether the building is "self-rehabilitated property."

(2) Properties to which subsection applies.

(A) In general. This subsection shall apply to any building which is being rehabilitated by or for the taxpayer if

(i) the normal rehabilitation period for such building is 2 years or more, and

(ii) it is reasonable to expect that such building will be a qualified rehabilitated building in the hands of the taxpayer when it is placed in service.

Clauses (i) and (ii) shall be applied on the basis of facts known as of the close of the taxable year of the taxpayer in which the rehabilitation begins (or, if later, at the close of the first taxable year to which an election under this subsection applies).

(B) Normal rehabilitation period. For purposes of subparagraph (A), the term "normal rehabilitation period" means the period reasonably expected to be required for the rehabilitation of the building

(i) beginning with the date on which physical work on the rehabilitation begins (or, if later, the first day of the first taxable year to which an election under this subsection applies), and

(ii) ending on the date on which it is expected that the property will be available for placing in service.

(4) Self-rehabilitated building. For purposes of this subsection, the term "self-rehabilitated building" means any building if it is reasonable to believe that more than half of the qualified rehabilitation expenditures for such building will be made directly by the taxpayer.

(5) Election. This subsection shall apply to any taxpayer only if such taxpayer has made an election under this paragraph. Such an election shall apply to the taxable year for which made and all subsequent taxable years. Such an election, once made, may be revoked only with the consent of the Secretary.

C. CREDIT CALCULATION AND LIMITATIONS

1. Basis Adjustment and Depreciation

Claiming the HTC affects tax treatment in two important ways. First, Section 47(d)(6) requires that the basis of the building be reduced by the full amount of the credit claimed. If a taxpayer spends $1 million on qualified rehabilitation expenditures and claims a $200,000 credit, the taxpayer's basis in the building for depreciation purposes is reduced by $200,000. This basis reduction diminishes future depreciation deductions, effectively spreading the benefit of the credit over time and preventing a double benefit.

Second, the taxpayer continues to depreciate the building using the modified accelerated cost recovery system (MACRS) applicable to nonresidential or residential rental real property. For nonresidential property, this means straight-line depreciation over 39 years; for residential rental property, it's straight-line depreciation over 27.5 years.

2. General Business Credit Limitations

The HTC is subject to the general business credit limitations of Section 38, which means it can only offset tax liability to a limited extent in any given year. Section 38(c) provides that the general business credit cannot exceed the taxpayer's net income tax over the greater of (1) the tentative minimum tax or (2) 25% of net regular tax liability above $25,000.

Section 39 provides for a one-year carryback and a 20-year carryforward of unused general business credits, giving taxpayers substantial time to utilize the credit.

3. Passive Activity Rules

More significantly, the HTC is subject to the passive activity loss rules of Section 469, which generally prevent passive losses and credits from offsetting non-passive income. For most individual taxpayers, rental real estate activities are passive activities. Section 469(d)(2) provides that passive activity credits can only offset tax liability attributable to passive activity income, not tax liability from other sources.

This creates a substantial barrier for individual investors who lack other passive income. The rise of specialized tax credit syndication structures allows individual taxpayers to sell their HTC-generating investments to corporations or other entities that can more readily use the credits.

4. Recapture Provisions

Sections 47(a)(5) and (b) contain recapture provisions that claw back the benefit of the credit if the taxpayer disposes of the property or ceases to use it in a qualifying manner within five years after the property is placed in service. The recapture percentage is 100% in year one, declining by 20 percentage points each subsequent year, so that no recapture applies after five full years.

These provisions ensure that taxpayers who receive the credit maintain the property in qualifying use for a meaningful period. They also create risk for taxpayers and complicate exit planning.

D. SECTION 170(H): HISTORIC PRESERVATION EASEMENTS

Although Section 170 is a comprehensive statute, only Section 170(h) applies specifically to Historic Structures. Historic Preservation Easements function as a type of servitude in favor of the state, forever preventing the property owner from developing their property in a way that would alter its historic character.[3] This marks an important departure from the rehabilitation-focused tax credits, which incentivize beneficial use of historic property; Section 170(h) aims to foreclose future development.

> (h) Qualified conservation contribution.—
>
> (1) In general.—For purposes of subsection (f)(3)(B)(iii), the term "qualified conservation contribution" means a contribution—
>
> (A) of a qualified real property interest,
>
> (B) to a qualified organization,
>
> (C) exclusively for conservation purposes.
>
> (2) Qualified real property interest.—For purposes of this subsection, the term "qualified real property interest" means any of the following interests in real property:
>
> (A) the entire interest of the donor other than a qualified mineral interest,
>
> (B) a remainder interest, and
>
> (C) a restriction (granted in perpetuity) on the use which may be made of the real property.
>
> (3) Qualified organization.—For purposes of paragraph (1), the term "qualified organization" means an organization which—
>
> (A) is described in clause (v) or (vi) of subsection (b)(1)(A), or
>
> (B) is described in section 501(c)(3) and—
>
> (i) meets the requirements of section 509(a)(2), or
>
> (ii) meets the requirements of section 509(a)(3) and is controlled by an organization described in subparagraph (A) or in clause (i) of this subparagraph.

---

3. Consider Kissling v. Commissioner, (T.C. Memo. 2020–153) Dkt. No. 19857 (July 16, 2015) at https://brieflytaxing.com/kissling-v-commissioner-t-c-memo-2020–153/, standing for the defense of there being a rationale for a deduction even when a local preservation ordinance covers the same protections. The U.S. Tax Court ruled that a New York couple did not owe 40% penalties on facade easements, despite the IRS challenging the valuation. The court found the actual value was only 15% less than claimed, failing to meet the "gross valuation misstatement" threshold.

(4) Conservation purpose defined.—

(A) In general.—For purposes of this subsection, the term "conservation purpose" means—

(i) the preservation of land areas for outdoor recreation by, or the education of, the general public,

(ii) the protection of a relatively natural habitat of fish, wildlife, or plants, or similar ecosystem,

(iii) the preservation of open space (including farmland and forest land) where such preservation is—

(I) for the scenic enjoyment of the general public, or

(II) pursuant to a clearly delineated Federal, State, or local governmental conservation policy, and will yield a significant public benefit, or

(iv) the preservation of an historically important land area or a certified historic structure.

(B) Special rules with respect to buildings in registered historic districts.—In the case of any contribution of a qualified real property interest which is a restriction with respect to the exterior of a building described in subparagraph (C)(ii), such contribution shall not be considered to be exclusively for conservation purposes unless—

(i) such interest—

(I) includes a restriction which preserves the entire exterior of the building (including the front, sides, rear, and height of the building), and

(II) prohibits any change in the exterior of the building which is inconsistent with the historical character of such exterior,

(ii) the donor and donee enter into a written agreement certifying, under penalty of perjury, that the donee—

(I) is a qualified organization (as defined in paragraph (3)) with a purpose of environmental protection, land conservation, open space preservation, or historic preservation, and

(II) has the resources to manage and enforce the restriction and a commitment to do so, and

(iii) in the case of any contribution made in a taxable year beginning after the date of the enactment of this subparagraph, the taxpayer includes with the taxpayer's return for the taxable year of the contribution—

(I) a qualified appraisal (within the meaning of subsection (f)(11)(E)) of the qualified property interest,

(II) photographs of the entire exterior of the building, and

(III) a description of all restrictions on the development of the building.

(C) Certified historic structure.—For purposes of subparagraph (A)(iv), the term "certified historic structure" means—

(i) any building, structure, or land area which is listed in the National Register, or

(ii) any building which is located in a registered historic district (as defined in section 47(c)(3)(B)) and is certified by the Secretary of the Interior to the Secretary as being of historic significance to the district.

A building, structure, or land area satisfies the preceding sentence if it satisfies such sentence either at the time of the transfer or on the due date (including extensions) for filing the transferor's return under this chapter for the taxable year in which the transfer is made.

(5) Exclusively for conservation purposes.—For purposes of this subsection—

(A) Conservation purpose must be protected.—A contribution shall not be treated as exclusively for conservation purposes unless the conservation purpose is protected in perpetuity.

(B) No surface mining permitted.—

(i) In general. Except as provided in clause (ii), in the case of a contribution of any interest where there is a retention of a qualified mineral interest, subparagraph (A) shall not be treated as met if at any time there may be extraction or removal of minerals by any surface mining method.

(ii) Special rule. With respect to any contribution of property in which the ownership of the surface estate and mineral interests has been and remains separated, subparagraph (A) shall be treated as met if the probability of surface mining occurring on such property is so remote as to be negligible.

(6) Qualified mineral interest.—For purposes of this subsection, the term "qualified mineral interest" means—

(A) subsurface oil, gas, or other minerals, and

(B) the right to access to such minerals.

1. Limitations on Pass-Through Entities

Tax code abuse has forced the IRS to adjust provisions to combat investment structures that exploited available credits, such as through limits on Syndicated Conservation Easements. Notably, however, Historic Preservation Services was exempted from this change, demonstrating ongoing commitment to promoting historic preservation.

(7) Limitation on deduction for qualified conservation contributions made by pass-through entities.—

(A) In general.—A contribution by a partnership (whether directly or as a distributive share of a contribution of another partnership) shall not be treated as a qualified conservation contribution for purposes of this section if the amount of such contribution exceeds 2.5 times the sum of each partner's relevant basis in such partnership.

(B) Relevant basis.—For purposes of this paragraph—

(i) In general. The term "relevant basis" means, with respect to any partner, the portion of such partner's modified basis in the partnership which is allocable (under rules similar to the rules of section 755) to the portion of the real property with respect to which the contribution described in subparagraph (A) is made.

(ii) Modified basis. The term "modified basis" means, with respect to any partner, such partner's adjusted basis in the partnership as determined—

(I) immediately before the contribution described in subparagraph (A),

(II) without regard to section 752, and

(III) by the partnership after taking into account the adjustments described in subclauses (I) and (II) and such other adjustments as the Secretary may provide.

(C) Exception for contributions outside 3-year holding period.—Subparagraph (A) shall not apply to any contribution which is made at least 3 years after the latest of—

(i) the last date on which the partnership that made such contribution acquired any portion of the real property with respect to which such contribution is made,

(ii) the last date on which any partner in the partnership that made such contribution acquired any interest in such partnership, and

(iii) if the interest in the partnership that made such contribution is held through 1 or more partnerships—

(I) the last date on which any such partnership acquired any interest in any other such partnership, and

(II) the last date on which any partner in any such partnership acquired any interest in such partnership.

(D) Exception for family partnerships.—

(i) In general. Subparagraph (A) shall not apply with respect to any contribution made by any partnership if substantially all of the partnership interests in such partnership are held, directly or indirectly, by an individual and members of the family of such individual.

(ii) Members of the family. For purposes of this subparagraph, the term "members of the family" means, with respect to any individual—

(I) the spouse of such individual, and

(II) any individual who bears a relationship to such individual which is described in subparagraphs (A) through (G) of section 152(d)(2).

(E) Exception for contributions to preserve certified historic structures.—Subparagraph (A) shall not apply to any qualified conservation contribution the conservation purpose of which is the preservation of any building which is a certified historic structure (as defined in paragraph (4)(C)).

(F) Application to other pass-through entities. Except as may be otherwise provided by the Secretary, the rules of this paragraph shall apply to S corporations and other pass-through entities in the same manner as such rules apply to partnerships.

(G) Regulations.—The Secretary shall prescribe such regulations or other guidance as may be necessary or appropriate to carry out the purposes of this paragraph, including regulations or other guidance—

(i) to require reporting, including reporting related to tiered partnerships and the modified basis of partners, and
(ii) to prevent the avoidance of the purposes of this paragraph.

E. STATE HISTORIC TAX CREDIT PROGRAMS

While the federal HTC provides the foundation for preservation tax incentives nationwide, many states have enacted their own programs. These vary widely in structure, generosity, and qualification requirements. Some closely mirror the federal program, while others operate independently.

1. Missouri: A Generous Complementary Program

Missouri offers one of the nation's most generous state programs. Under Missouri Revised Statutes § 253.545 to 253.559, the state provides a 25% tax credit for qualified rehabilitation expenditures on eligible historic structures, available statewide for both commercial and residential properties.

Missouri requires that buildings be listed on the National Register, either individually or as contributing buildings within a National Register district, ensuring coordination between state and federal incentives. The rehabilitation work must meet the Secretary of the Interior's Standards and be certified by the Missouri State Historic Preservation Office.

For income-producing properties, the 25% credit applies to the lesser of the qualified rehabilitation expenditures or $500,000 per eligible property. For owner-occupied residential properties, the program offers a 25% credit on the first $50,000 of qualified expenditures, providing up to $12,500 in state tax credits. This residential component is particularly significant because owner-occupied residences are excluded from the federal HTC.

Missouri's credits are transferable, creating a secondary market where credits typically sell at 85–90 cents on the dollar. The program has leveraged billions in private investment, transforming downtowns across the state.

2. Georgia: Tiered Credits and Rural Preferences

Georgia takes a different approach with tiered credits designed to incentivize rehabilitation in smaller communities. Under O.C.G.A. § 48-7-29.8, taxpayers can receive state income tax credits equal to 25% of qualified rehabilitation expenditures for properties in "less developed census tracts" and 20% for properties in other areas.

Georgia requires certification by the Georgia State Historic Preservation Office, with work meeting the Secretary of the Interior's Standards. The program requires qualified expenditures to exceed $5000 for residential properties or $10,000 for income-producing properties—much lower thresholds than the federal test.

Georgia's credits are transferable but with limitations. The original taxpayer must hold the credit for one year before transferring, and the transferee can only use the credit to offset up to 50% of their Georgia income tax liability in any given year, with unused credits carrying forward for up to ten years.

Georgia also offers property tax benefits. Under the preferential assessment program, counties may offer property tax freezes for eight and a half years, during which the property is assessed at its pre-rehabilitation value.

3. New York: Enhanced Credits for Distressed Areas

New York's Historic Tax Credit (Tax Law Section 606(oo)) provides a base credit of 20% of qualified expenditures, mirroring the federal rate. However, New York provides enhanced credits: 30% for projects in economically distressed census tracts, and an additional 5% for projects including affordable housing components, bringing the total potential state credit to 35%.

New York imposes a substantial rehabilitation test requiring qualified expenditures to exceed $5000 or the adjusted basis, whichever is greater. The program is available for both income-producing and owner-occupied residential properties, though residential properties are subject to a $50,000 cap on qualified expenditures.

The credits are not directly transferable but can be claimed by partners in a partnership or LLC members that undertake the rehabilitation, creating opportunities for tax credit equity financing.

F. TAX CREDIT SYNDICATION AND FINANCING STRUCTURES

The value of historic tax credits is only fully realized if taxpayers can use them to offset tax liability. For many developers, particularly smaller entities or pass-through entities, generating sufficient tax liability to absorb large credits is challenging. This gave rise to sophisticated financing structures.

1. Partnership Syndication Structures

The most common structure is the partnership syndication, or "tax credit equity financing." A developer who undertakes a historic rehabilitation forms a partnership with an investor who has substantial tax liability. The investor contributes capital to the partnership in exchange for a significant allocation of partnership income, losses, and credits, including the HTCs.

An investor might contribute capital equal to 80%–85% of the expected value of the tax credits. For example, if a project will generate $1 million in federal HTCs, an investor might contribute $850,000 to the partnership for the right to claim those credits. This provides the developer with upfront capital while giving the investor a tax benefit with a built-in discount.

These structures must comply with partnership tax rules, particularly the substantial economic effect requirements of Treasury Regulation § 1.704–1(b). The partnership agreement must allocate items in a manner that respects the economic arrangement between parties.

2. Layering with Other Incentives

The Tax Cuts and Jobs Act of 2017 created Qualified Opportunity Zones (QOZs), designated census tracts in economically distressed areas. Many historic buildings eligible for HTCs are located in QOZs, creating opportunities to layer tax benefits. An investor can invest capital gains in a Qualified Opportunity Fund that invests in a historic rehabilitation project, receiving both HTC benefits and QOZ benefits.

Another potential layering involves combining HTCs with New Markets Tax Credits (NMTCs), which provide tax credits for investments in low-income communities under Section 45D. When successfully combined, HTCs and NMTCs can provide extraordinary levels of tax benefits, potentially covering 50% or more of project costs.

G. RECENT LEGISLATIVE CHANGES AND POLICY DEBATES

1. The Tax Cuts and Jobs Act of 2017

The Tax Cuts and Jobs Act significantly modified the federal HTC, changing it from a credit claimed entirely in the year the rehabilitated property was placed in service to one claimed ratably over five years. This change reduced the present value of the credit by requiring taxpayers to wait longer to receive the full benefit.

The five-year spread interacts awkwardly with the passive activity rules. A taxpayer who generates credits ratably over five years must have passive income in each of those years to use the credits as they become available.

2. Critiques and Counterarguments

Critics argue that the credit is inefficient from a fiscal perspective, providing windfalls to taxpayers who would have undertaken rehabilitations even without the credit. They contend that the credit disproportionately benefits wealthy investors and corporations rather than the communities where rehabilitated buildings are located.

Some preservationists argue the credit has inadvertently encouraged a formulaic approach that prioritizes financial returns over thoughtful preservation. Economists question whether tax credits are the most effective tool compared to alternatives like direct grants or low-interest loans.

Supporters counter that the program has demonstrably advanced preservation goals while generating broader economic and community development benefits. The federal HTC has leveraged tens of billions of dollars in private investment, creating jobs and revitalizing communities. Buildings that might have been demolished have been rehabilitated and returned to productive use.

3. State Program Evolution

State HTC programs continue to evolve in response to fiscal pressures, preservation needs, and political dynamics. Some states have expanded their programs in recent years, recognizing the economic development benefits and relatively modest net costs. Others have constrained programs through annual caps, reduced credit percentages, or stricter qualification requirements in response to budget pressures.

Several states have recently enacted new HTC programs or reinstated programs that had lapsed. Oklahoma, for example, reinstated its state HTC in 2020 after allowing a prior program to expire. The new Oklahoma program provides a 20% credit for qualified rehabilitation expenditures on properties listed in the National Register, with enhanced credits available for projects in smaller communities.

Other states have experimented with program designs that target specific policy goals beyond preservation. Some programs provide enhanced credits for rehabilitations that include affordable housing components, reflecting concerns about housing affordability. Others enhance credits for projects in rural areas or economically distressed urban neighborhoods, using preservation incentives as economic development tools.

H. PRACTICAL CONSIDERATIONS AND COMMON PITFALLS

Claiming historic preservation tax credits requires careful planning, extensive documentation, and patience with bureaucratic processes. Practitioners advising clients on these matters should be aware of common pitfalls and practical challenges.

1. Timing and Documentation

The timing of expenditures is critical for satisfying the substantial rehabilitation test. Taxpayers must ensure that qualifying expenditures fall within the 24-month (or 60-month for phased rehabilitations) measuring period. This requires careful project management and accounting. Expenditures incurred too early may not count toward the test, while delays that push expenditures beyond the measuring period can jeopardize qualification.

Documentation requirements are extensive. The NPS requires detailed applications with architectural plans, specifications, photographs (before, during, and after rehabilitation), and written descriptions of all work. Many failed applications result from inadequate documentation rather than substantive problems with the proposed work. Hiring experienced historic preservation consultants and architects familiar with the HTC application process is often money well spent.

Taxpayers should obtain NPS certification before incurring significant rehabilitation costs. While the statute allows expenditures incurred in anticipation of certification to qualify if the taxpayer demonstrates a reasonable expectation of certification, this creates risk. If certification is ultimately denied, those expenditures do not generate credits, potentially rendering a project financially unviable.

2. Common Design Issues

Certain types of rehabilitation work frequently generate disputes with the NPS. Rooftop additions often encounter resistance if they are visible from public streets or if they require alterations to significant historic features. Similarly, proposals to remove interior features—walls, decorative elements, historic finishes—may be rejected if those features contribute to the building's historic character, even if removal would make the space more marketable.

The Secretary of the Interior's Standards require that new work be compatible with the historic character of the building but distinguishable from historic fabric. This can create design challenges: new work should not replicate historic features so closely that it creates a false sense of historical development, but it also should not clash with the building's architectural style. Finding this balance requires skill and experience.

Energy efficiency improvements present another common challenge. While the NPS recognizes that energy efficiency is important for economic viability and environmental sustainability, some energy-related work can damage historic character. Replacing historic windows with modern units typically encounters resistance, though interior storm windows and weatherstripping often receive approval. Installing exterior insulation can obscure decorative brickwork or architectural details. Taxpayers should consult with preservation professionals early in the design process to identify approaches that achieve energy goals while maintaining historic integrity.

Consider a practical example: Developer owns Hotel A, a historic property registered in the National Register. Hotel A has an adjusted basis of $500,000. Over the following 24 months, Developer spends $600,000 on qualified rehabilitation. Because $600,000 exceeds $500,000, the substantial rehabilitation test is met, and Developer qualifies for a credit of $120,000 (20% of $600,000). However, if the rehabilitation involves converting the Victorian-style architecture to Mid-Century Modern design, the NPS would likely deny certification because the work is inconsistent with the building's historic character as described in the National Register.

Alternatively, if Hotel A is not individually listed in the National Register but is located in the "Old District" of Town A, a designated registered historic district, it could still qualify under Section 47(c)(3)(B). The rehabilitation must then be consistent with the historic character of the district rather than just the individual building.

3. Dealing with Uncertainty and Risk

The HTC program involves inherent uncertainties that create risk for taxpayers. The NPS can deny certification, modify project plans, or withdraw preliminary approvals if subsequent review reveals concerns. Market conditions can change during the lengthy rehabilitation process, affecting project economics. Tax law changes can alter the value of credits or the availability of complementary incentives.

Sophisticated developers mitigate these risks through several strategies. Obtaining conceptual approval from the SHPO and NPS before closing on a property reduces the risk of discovering that desired rehabilitation approaches will not be approved. Building contingencies into project budgets accounts for the possibility of unexpected costs arising from preservation requirements. Structuring financing with flexibility to adjust to changing conditions—such as revolving credit facilities rather than fixed construction loans—provides breathing room if timelines extend.

Insurance products have also emerged to address HTC risks. Some insurers offer policies that protect against denial of credits due to technical non-compliance with program requirements, providing a backstop if documentation errors or procedural missteps threaten credit availability. While these policies add to project costs, they can make financing easier to obtain by reducing lender concerns about credit risk.

I. STRATEGIC PLANNING AND COMBINED BENEFITS

1. Federal and State Credit Interaction

The combined value of federal and state credits can be substantial. In states with generous programs, taxpayers may receive combined credits exceeding 40% of qualified rehabilitation expenditures. For example, a project in Missouri qualifying for both the 20% federal credit (spread over five years) and the 25% state credit (claimed immediately in Missouri) receives 45% of costs back through tax credits, though the present value is somewhat lower due to the five-year federal spread.

However, calculating combined credit value requires attention to interactions between programs. Most significantly, state tax credits are generally includible in federal taxable income under the tax benefit rule, particularly if the state credits reduce state tax liability that was previously deducted on the federal return. This means that receiving a $100,000 state tax credit might increase federal taxable income by a similar amount, creating federal tax liability that partially offsets the state credit benefit.

Additionally, the basis reduction required by Section 47(d)(6) applies to the federal credit but not necessarily to state credits, depending on state law. Some states require their own basis adjustments for state credit purposes, while others do not. These variations affect depreciation deductions and gain calculations on subsequent sale, requiring careful modeling to determine true after-tax economics.

2. Residential Property Considerations

A unique situation arises with residential properties. Consider a Developer who owns House A, a historic property registered in the National Register or located in a designated historic district. If Developer plans to live in this home as a primary residence, it would be excluded from the federal tax credit as residential real property under Section 47(c)(2)(B). However, if House A were to be rented out to local college students, the building would qualify as residential rental property, potentially qualifying for both federal and state tax credits.

This distinction creates planning opportunities. A developer might acquire a historic residence, rehabilitate it as a rental property to qualify for credits, and maintain it as a rental for the required five-year period to avoid recapture. After the recapture period expires, the developer could convert the property to personal use without triggering credit recapture.

In states like Missouri that offer residential credits for owner-occupied properties, homeowners can receive state benefits even without federal credits. This makes historic home rehabilitation more financially feasible for individual homeowners who would otherwise be excluded from tax benefits entirely.

J. INTERNATIONAL COMPARATIVE PERSPECTIVES

While this chapter focuses on U.S. federal and state programs, examining international approaches to incentivizing historic preservation provides useful context for evaluating American policy choices.

1. European Approaches

Many European countries, with older building stocks and longer preservation traditions, take different approaches to incentivizing the rehabilitation of historic structures. The United Kingdom, for example, generally does not impose Value Added Tax (VAT) on approved alterations to listed buildings, creating a significant cost advantage for rehabilitation over new construction, which bears full VAT. This approach uses the tax system to incentivize preservation but does so through exemption rather than credit.

France provides income tax credits for certain heritage property restoration expenditures, though the French system is more restrictive than the American HTC, limiting benefits to properties of exceptional heritage value. France also uses direct grants administered through the Ministry of Culture to support preservation, reflecting a tradition of more centralized cultural policy.

Germany's approach emphasizes depreciation benefits rather than credits. Enhanced depreciation allowances for qualified rehabilitation of historic buildings allow taxpayers to recover costs more quickly, reducing the present value of their tax liability over time. While less dramatic than tax credits, enhanced depreciation is simpler to administer and less susceptible to valuation disputes.

2. Lessons for American Policy

International comparisons suggest several observations relevant to American policy. First, the United States relies more heavily on tax incentives and less on direct appropriations for preservation than most European countries. This reflects broader American preferences for operating cultural policy through the tax system rather than direct government spending.

Second, American programs are relatively generous in their credit percentages compared to international norms. The 20% federal credit plus potential state credits exceeding 25% compare favorably to incentives available in most other countries. This generosity has likely contributed to the programs' success in spurring private investment but also to their fiscal cost and vulnerability to budget-driven reforms.

Third, the American certification process, with its detailed substantive review of rehabilitation plans by preservation professionals, is more rigorous than some international approaches that rely more heavily on categorical eligibility or less intensive review. This rigor has benefits—ensuring quality preservation work—and costs—administrative burden and delay.

K. THE POLICY CASE FOR HISTORIC PRESERVATION TAX BENEFITS

The enduring success of historic preservation tax credits over nearly five decades suggests they have achieved a workable balance between public policy goals and private economic interests. The policy rationale supporting these programs is multifaceted and compelling.

1. Market Failure Correction

Left to pure market forces, historic buildings face systematic disadvantages. Rehabilitation often costs more than demolition and new construction, particularly when preservation standards require retention of historic materials and features. The tax credits help level this playing field by offsetting some rehabilitation costs, making preservation economically competitive with demolition and replacement.

This addresses a classic market failure: the private market systematically undervalues the public benefits of historic preservation. While individual property owners bear the full costs of preservation, the benefits—cultural continuity, community character, educational value—accrue to society broadly. Tax credits internalize some of these external benefits, aligning private incentives with public interests.

2. Economic Development and Job Creation

Historic rehabilitation projects generate substantial economic activity. Construction jobs, professional services (architects, engineers, consultants), and subsequent economic activity in rehabilitated buildings contribute to local and regional economies. Studies have consistently shown that rehabilitation projects generate more jobs per dollar spent than new construction, partly because rehabilitation is more labor-intensive and partly because rehabilitation dollars stay more local (less spent on materials shipped from distant locations).

The economic development benefits extend beyond immediate construction activity. Rehabilitated historic buildings often anchor downtown revitalization, attracting other investment and contributing to "placemaking" that draws residents, businesses, and tourists. Tax credit projects have been credited with catalyzing broader neighborhood transformations in communities across the country.

3. Environmental Sustainability

The environmental case for historic preservation has grown stronger as climate change concerns intensify. Rehabilitating existing buildings avoids the enormous environmental costs of demolition (waste generation, landfill burden) and new construction (material extraction, manufacturing, transportation). The embodied energy in existing buildings represents a substantial resource that is squandered when buildings are demolished.

Studies have shown that it can take decades for a new energy-efficient building to recover, through operational savings, the environmental cost of demolition and new construction compared to rehabilitating and upgrading an existing building. As society focuses more on reducing carbon emissions and resource consumption, the environmental argument for preservation becomes increasingly compelling.

4. Cultural and Educational Values

Beyond economic and environmental considerations, historic buildings provide tangible connections to our collective past. They serve educational functions, helping communities understand their history and development. They contribute to sense of place and community identity in ways that new construction rarely replicates.

These cultural values are difficult to quantify but nonetheless real and important. Tax credits provide a mechanism for society to express, through fiscal policy, that it values these cultural connections enough to subsidize their preservation. This represents a legitimate use of tax policy to advance social goals beyond revenue collection.

L. CONCLUSION

The tax benefits available to owners of historic preservation property represent a significant policy tool that has demonstrably advanced preservation goals while generating broader economic and community development benefits. The federal Historic Tax Credit, providing a 20% credit for qualified rehabilitation of certified historic structures, has leveraged tens of billions of dollars in private investment since its creation. State programs add substantially to these benefits in many jurisdictions, with states like Missouri, Georgia, New York, and Pennsylvania offering credits that can equal or exceed the federal benefit.

Yet these programs operate within complex legal and regulatory frameworks that require careful navigation. Qualification requirements concerning property certification, substantial rehabilitation tests, and work certification create opportunities for taxpayers to stumble. Credit limitations, passive activity rules, and basis adjustments affect the real economic value of the incentives. Recapture provisions create risks that extend for five years after property is placed in service. And the interaction between federal and state programs, while potentially multiplicative in terms of benefits, increases administrative burden and planning complexity.

For law students and practitioners, historic preservation tax credits offer an opportunity to work at the intersection of tax law, real estate, cultural policy, and community development. The field demands both technical precision in navigating Code sections and regulations and creative problem-solving in structuring transactions to maximize benefits while satisfying multiple constituencies. It requires understanding not just tax law but also the substantive preservation principles embodied in the Secretary of the Interior's Standards and the administrative processes of the National Park Service and state historic preservation offices.

The interplay between Section 47's rehabilitation tax credits and Section 170(h)'s preservation easements demonstrates the sophisticated two-pronged approach Congress has taken to historic preservation. The credits incentivize active rehabilitation and beneficial reuse, while the easements prevent inappropriate future development. Together, these provisions create a comprehensive framework for preserving America's architectural heritage through private sector action guided by public policy.

Looking forward, historic preservation tax credit programs face both opportunities and challenges. Growing recognition of the environmental benefits of building reuse may strengthen political support for these programs as climate change concerns intensify. The intersection with newer incentive programs like qualified opportunity zones creates possibilities for even more powerful interventions in distressed communities. The successful exemption of historic preservation easements from the syndicated conservation easement limitations demonstrates continued congressional commitment to these programs.

At the same time, fiscal pressures, critiques of tax expenditures generally, and concerns about gentrification and displacement may generate proposals to constrain or restructure the programs. The 2017 change to a five-year credit spread reduced the present value of the federal credit, illustrating how program economics can change with legislative amendments. Practitioners must stay attuned to these policy debates as they may affect long-term planning for rehabilitation projects.

The enduring success of historic preservation tax credits over nearly five decades suggests they have achieved a workable balance between public policy goals and private economic interests. Buildings that might have been demolished have been rehabilitated and returned to productive use.

Communities have been revitalized. Jobs have been created. And the nation's architectural heritage has been preserved for future generations. Whether these programs continue in their current form or evolve in response to changing priorities and constraints, they have already secured their place as one of the most effective public-private partnerships in American cultural policy.

For practitioners advising clients on historic rehabilitation projects, several lessons emerge clearly. First, tax benefits can be substantial—combined federal and state credits can cover 40% or more of qualified rehabilitation expenditures in generous jurisdictions. Second, realizing these benefits requires careful planning, rigorous attention to qualification requirements, and sophisticated structuring of ownership and financing. Third, the certification requirements, while adding administrative burden, ensure that rehabilitations meet preservation standards and protect the credits from challenge. Fourth, syndication structures and other financing mechanisms can help developers monetize credits even when they lack sufficient tax liability to use the credits directly.

The programs also illustrate broader lessons about tax policy design. They show that tax incentives can successfully shape private behavior to achieve public goals when the incentives are properly calibrated and administered. They demonstrate the value of coordination between federal and state programs, with state enhancements building on the federal foundation. They reveal tensions inherent in using the tax system for social policy—the complexity of qualification requirements, the distributional effects favoring sophisticated taxpayers, and the difficulty of measuring effectiveness and preventing abuse.

Ultimately, historic preservation tax credits succeed because they align private interests with public values. Developers and investors receive financial returns that justify the complexities and risks of rehabilitation projects. Communities benefit from revitalized buildings and neighborhoods. And society preserves tangible connections to its past for future generations. That combination of private profit and public benefit is what makes historic preservation tax credits both sound policy and effective law.

As we move forward, the challenge will be to maintain and enhance these programs while addressing legitimate concerns about their structure and effects. This may involve simplifying qualification requirements to reduce administrative burden, targeting benefits more precisely to areas of greatest need, ensuring that benefits flow to communities and not just investors, or exploring alternative delivery mechanisms that achieve preservation goals more efficiently.

Whatever changes may come, the fundamental insight underlying these programs remains valid: private property owners are more likely to preserve historic buildings when doing so makes financial sense. Tax policy provides a powerful tool for making preservation financially attractive, and the historic tax credit programs have proven that this tool, properly designed and administered, can achieve remarkable results. For the thousands of historic buildings that have been saved and rehabilitated, and for the communities that have been transformed by their restoration, these programs have made an indelible contribution to American life and culture.

Index